Praise for

Families Apart . . .

"WILL SHOW READERS THAT LIFE AFTER DIVORCE NEED NOT BE MARKED BY CONTINUING TRAUMA."
—*Publishers Weekly*

"REASSURING . . . She pulls anecdotes not only from interviews with 150 divorced parents and children, but also from her own experiences."   —*Fort Worth Star-Telegram*

"SENSIBLE, DOWN-TO-EARTH, EMINENTLY DOABLE STRATEGIES."
—Judith Wallerstein

"THIS POWERFUL BOOK is a wonderful blend of the author's own research and that of other experts. Rich in anecdotal information, it has the wisdom born of years of experience in co-parenting. If you are a divorced or never-married parent, give your kids a gift—let this book be your teacher."
—David L. Levy, Esq., President, Children's Rights Council

"WITH COMPELLING HONESTY, *Families Apart* details the steps that concerned, committed parents have to scale to nurture, discipline, and cherish their children." —Rene McDonald, former editor of *The Single Parent*, the journal of Parents Without Partners, Inc.

"A WELCOME AND IMPORTANT ADDITION to the literature on post-divorce family life . . . Easy to read, written with warmth, sensitivity and humor." —Miriam Galper Cohen, family therapist and author of *The Joint Custody Handbook* and *Long-Distance Parenting*

"EXCELLENT ADVICE TO PARENTS . . . WRITTEN FROM THE HEART. While reminding parents of their responsibility, Blau is never harsh or judgmental. She has been through it herself."
—Marla B. Isaacs, Ph.D., coauthor of *The Difficult Divorce*

Families Apart

Ten Keys
to Successful
Co-Parenting

Melinda Blau

A PERIGEE BOOK

A Perigee Book
Published by The Berkley Publishing Group
200 Madison Avenue
New York, NY 10016

G. P. Putnam's Sons edition: January 1994
First Perigee edition: January 1995
Perigee ISBN: 0-399-52150-X
Published simultaneously in Canada.

The Library of Congress has cataloged the G.P. Putnam's Sons edition as follows:

Blau, Melinda, date.
    Families apart : ten keys to successful co-parenting / Melinda Blau.
        p. cm.
    Includes index.
    ISBN 0-399-13895-1
    1. Parenting, Part-time—United States. 2. Divorced parents—United States.
    3. Child rearing—United States. 4 Children of divorced parents—
        United States. I. Title.
HQ755.8.B59   1994
306.87—dc20   93—5870 CIP

Printed in The United States of America
10   9   8   7   6   5   4   3   2   1

To My Family Apart

Mark,
who helped make it a reality

and

Jennifer and Jeremy,
who have always forgiven our limitations
and applauded our efforts;

and

To Other Families Apart,
who have added their stories to ours.

ACKNOWLEDGMENTS

Whenever I am asked why family dynamics are so compelling, I always say that I am drawn to the subject for the same reason most of the therapists I interview enter the mental-health profession: to help understand your own life. Writing *Families Apart* certainly accomplished that often difficult task.

I couldn't have attempted this book without a great deal of help—first and foremost from other parents and children; their ideas and experiences both validated and broadened my own views. I thank them all for their candor when answering my questions and for their enthusiasm for creating new models of postdivorce parenting.

Families Apart is also informed by the ideas of many gifted clinicians and researchers whom I've met along the way. They have extended themselves personally and shared their clinical experience and research findings. In many cases, they suggested co-parents I could contact. They include: Constance Ahrons, Deborah Anderson, Judith Bauersfeld, Anne Bernstein, Fredda Herz Brown, Sally Brush, Betty Carter, Phyllis Diamond, Christopher L. Hayes, Evan Imber-Black, Marla Isaacs, Neil Kalter, Joan Kelly, Gayle Kimball, Sari Kramer, Harriet Lerner, Marcia Lebowitz, Sandra Mann, Hugh McIsaac, Patricia Papernow, Kay Pasley, Judith Stern Peck, Isolina Ricci, Janine Roberts, Ron Taffel, Emily and John Visher, Judith Wallerstein, Michelle Weiner-Davis, Beverly Willis, and Bonnie Winter.

I am also grateful to those whose work I have come to know either through their research, their publications and/or brief phone interviews: Dawn Aikens, Donald Baucom, Cheryl Beuhler, Claire Berman, Betty Lou Bettner, Sanford Bravers, James Bray, Andrew Cherlin, Marilyn Coleman, Carolyn and Philip Cowan, Craig Everett, Roger Fisher, Frank R. Furstenberg, Jr., Lawrence H. Ganong, Richard Gardener, Paul Glick, John Gottman, Arlie Hochschild, Harville Hendrix, E. Mavis Hetherington, Florence Kaslow, Gay Kitson, Amy Lew, Deborah Luepnitz, Eleanor Maccoby, Sam Margulies, Elizabeth McGonagle, Bruce Miller, Robert Mnookin, Linda Seaver, Deborah Tannen, Edward Teyber, William Ury, Sandra Volgy, Dudley Weeks, Robert Weiss, and Lenore Weitzman.

Special thanks go to David L. Levy, cofounder and president of the Children's Rights Council, and Rene MacDonald, editor of *The Single Parent* (the magazine of Parents Without Partners), both of whom championed this project from its inception and helped me locate co-parents, and to John L. Bauserman at CRC, who combed the manuscript and supplied a wealth of research material. A number of fellow writers (some of whom are also mental-health professionals), drawn to this subject through their own experiences, also have been generous and encouraging, adding their ideas to my own: Miriam Galper Cohen, Patricia Greshner-Nedry, Sharon Hanna, Vicki Lansky, Marcella Sabo, Ciji Ware, Marilyn Webb, as well as filmmaker Josie Dean.

Writers cannot exist without insightful editors, and I am fortunate to have had several sensitive, intelligent women in my professional life who are not only willing to listen to my ideas but who are willing to share their own. Over the past few years, Stephanie von Hirschberg, at *New Woman,* inspired me to investigate healing after divorce, stepfamily reorganization, and anger, and Judith Groch at *American Health* suggested that I examine gender issues; in each case, those explorations enhanced my understanding of the complexities of co-parenting. In 1988, Deborah Harkins at *New York* urged me to write about our family's experiences in an article about family therapy called "In It Together." The following year, she helped me build a case for a book about co-parenting by assigning "Divorce Family Style." And, in 1990, Freddi Greenberg encouraged me to write "The New Family" column for *Child* (and Yanick Rice Lamb keeps me at it); writing the column has helped (and continues to help) me formulate many of my ideas about divorce and about families in general.

Four very special editors bear mention for their work on *Families Apart:* Marsha Melnick, officially my agent, is an editor at heart and always a friend; she believed in this book, encouraged me to write it, and helped me trust my own instincts along the way. Ellen Lefcourt, my Northampton editor, shared her wisdom and life experience; her (sometimes merciless!) honesty and perception enhanced the manuscript and helped me hone my craft. Laura Yorke, my editor at Putnam, has become an alter ego; she has an uncanny ability to cut right to the heart of the matter—the way I would If *I* were an editor! Our working together has been a constant amazement and a delight, made all the smoother by her assistant, Eileen Cope, editor of this paperback edition, who is knowledgeable, resourceful, and always helpful.

Finally, this book is about family, and it is family I must thank. I couldn't have written it without my family apart, Mark, Jennifer, and Jeremy, to whom this book is rightfully dedicated. We couldn't have done the hard work it takes without the ongoing support of our families: on Mark's side, his partner, Cay, and his family—Joe, Dorothy, Eileen and Bob, and Eric; and on mine, my father Julie, my sister Sandra and her brood—Stanley, Elliott and Eleanor, Jeffrey and Tracy, Heidi, Lewis, Skylar, Karen, and Mariah—and my brother Irwin, flanked by Judy, Jack and Bonnie, Debbie and Tom.

CONTENTS

— 1 —

BECOMING FAMILIES APART

How Our Family Apart and This Book Took Shape

Beginning the Rest of Our Lives

Ten years ago, I stood weak-kneed behind a table in a small, dusty courtroom in New York City, anxiously fingering a fifty-eight-page separation agreement—the blueprint for my new life. The judge's heavy wooden gavel punctuated the finality of our divorce, just as, seventeen years earlier, the sound of glass crunching beneath my new husband's foot had heralded the beginning of our marriage.

It's over, I thought to myself. *Now I can get on with my life—without him.* But in the following years, I was to realize that, though our ties as a couple were legally severed that day, we would always be a family. Jennifer and Jeremy, then thirteen and ten, would always be our children. And we would always be joined, if not in holy matrimony, by a union even more enduring.

During the endless ordeal of my legal divorce, I thought I'd never be able to look Mark in the eye or have a civil conversation with him. The idea of having to "share kids" with this man for the rest of my life was anathema.

We couldn't face each other. We were frightened and angry, guilty, and quick to point fingers. We fought about money, custody, who would get the neon clock. Everything assumed major importance then; I never dreamed that someday I'd actually forget what we had fought over.

For nine long months after making the decision to separate, we lived together, still sharing everything—the apartment, the car, the house on Fire Island. We even shared a king-sized bed for a few months—until the mattress began to shrink from the heat of our conflict. No longer able to tolerate sleeping with the enemy, I turned the den into a bedroom. Our lives finally began to diverge onto separate tracks. After an evening out, I'd venture into the DMZ zone, a hallway separating the bathroom from the (appropriately named) master bedroom, and get undressed inside our mutual closet, careful not to touch his clothing, not to arouse his suspicions if I took too long, not to provoke yet another argument.

Life was a fight waiting to happen. And no one felt the tension of that period more than our children. We shared them, too, on a schedule that seemed to boggle the minds of most adults. Mark "had them" every Thursday night, every other weekend, and alternate Mondays. We had decided early on that we would "do what's best for the kids." We weren't going to be the kind of divorced parents who demanded two school conferences or duplicate reports and phone calls. I certainly wasn't the kind of mother who would deny her kids their father. Mark would never abandon his children.

Still, it was hell. When it came to actually making an appearance together for the children—at school, a piano recital, or a doctor's appointment—we did it with clenched teeth. On a few rare occasions, one of us didn't show up—or wasn't invited. I remember friends scheduling our respective arrivals at their annual holiday party. I had the early shift, and Mark was penciled in for the last two hours. The kids came with him, since it was "his" Sunday. At school plays and birthday parties, we acted civilly but avoided eye contact. I have no idea what thoughts were going through Mark's head, but even as I was making small talk across a room, I wondered what legal maneuver he might launch next, and I noticed every new piece of clothing, every wrinkle, every wrong move or misstatement. The air around us was always thick with tension; other adults claimed it made them uncomfortable. I can't imagine how it made the kids feel.

Like a videotape on fast-forward, the events of those first two years are mostly flashes of images with no sound track. When the divorce was finalized, and he remarried, it was no better. In fact, it was worse, more complicated. Far too many chiefs—with the

Indians out of control. We needed help. Not the kind we'd been getting from family or friends and certainly not the kind we'd had from our lawyers. Mine, in fact, had maintained that I was "crazy" even to request that family therapy be mandated in the divorce papers, no less to think that Mark would participate. But somewhere through the divorce-induced insanity of our lives, we both knew the idea had merit. To my attorney's amazement, Mark agreed to pay for it.

Once the divorce was legally over and neither custody nor financial agreements could be compromised, we went into family therapy. It marked the first time in years that we cautiously allowed ourselves to be vulnerable in each other's presence and to listen—to each other and to our children. It's impossible to pinpoint exactly when the scales began to fall from our eyes, but we did eventually remove the armor—and got down to the business of being a new kind of family again—a family apart.

In It Together

Always the journalist, I vowed I'd write about it all someday when I was far enough away from the pain. I first touched on the subject when I wrote "In It Together," an article on family therapy that appeared in *New York* magazine in August of 1989. I hadn't actually intended to report my personal experience, but my editor, intrigued by the idea of ex-spouses going into therapy with their kids *after* the divorce, encouraged me to write about it. Ultimately, our story (thinly disguised) became the opening anecdote, used to show how the members of a reconfigured family could learn new ways of relating to one another.

Since our divorce, Mark and I have learned how to share birthdays, graduations, and school plays. We have come together in crises, both large and small. We've gone to parents' weekends, attended innumerable school conferences, and held powwows of our own over curfews, allowances, vacation plans, music lessons, homework schedules—the consistent minutiae of our past and present family life.

Some events have been real benchmarks in our progress:

jointly, we produced a gala reception in honor of our son's Bar Mitzvah. To celebrate our daughter's eighteenth birthday, we spent a "family" weekend in San Francisco, each bunking with the same-sex child. And in 1988, rather than figuring out who "had Thanksgiving" that year, I hosted dinner for both families, including new partners, grandparents, and various other members of our extended clans. The kids loved having everyone under one roof. We all knew that we had come a long way.

Ten years after our "official" divorce in 1983, fourteen since the separation, Mark and I have lived apart as long as we lived together. We lead very separate lives, but we also communicate on a fairly regular basis—mostly about our children. We talk about who the kids' friends are, whom they're dating, whether they're having safe sex. Together, we wonder and worry: Are they happy or depressed or angry? We ponder their futures, take pride in their accomplishments, shudder at their faults, and we realize that though they may not be growing up exactly as we had planned, in many ways, they are more than we ever could have dreamed of. Of course, neither of us can be truly objective.

We can only imagine what the children say about us. Always very close, they merged even more intensely in their parents' trauma. Today both in their early twenties, Jeremy and Jennifer are the best of friends. During the worst times, they each became an island of strength for the other, forming an alliance that helped stave off fears of abandonment and feelings of blame. They also became savvy manipulators, sometimes creating crises to force their parents together, always parlaying their knowledge of our differences to get what they wanted. During the best times, they cheered us on, thrilled by our increasing maturity and our decision to lay down our swords, get on with our individual lives, and still be there for them—as the responsible parents we were supposed to be.

'Til Death Do Us Part

As Mark and I found out, divorce ends a marriage—it does not end a family; we got divorced—our children didn't. Millions of parents find themselves coping with the same paradox. They quarrel, fall out of love, find other lovers, do mean things to each other, and go to court (not necessarily in that order). But no matter what happens between them, no matter how powerful the forces that wrench them apart, they will be forever bound by the major and minor milestones of their children's lives—in sickness and in health, 'til death do them part.

Sadly, in about half of all divorces, parents don't accept that reality. The lens of egocentric grief and pity limits their vision. They can't rise above their own adult agony to see their children's pain. Bitter legal battles rage on for years while parents seem unable to see the dire consequences: children become emotional yo-yos in the struggle, feeling torn between the two people they love and need most; and when the dust settles, they often lose one of their parents.

As many as 30 to 50 percent of all children of divorce pay this price. They become angry and troubled; they suffer from a vague, abiding sadness that colors their moods and diminishes their self-esteem; they carry these memories and feelings into their outside relationships, becoming adolescents and adults who don't trust and are afraid of commitment. In popular literature, much has been made of various "Adult Child" syndromes. Adult Children of Divorce, as it is fashionable these days to call them, are no different from any adults who grew up in families torn by conflict, in which children are often expected to take over adult roles and keep their own feelings under wraps.

Fortunately, the flip side is there, too: In *Growing Up with Divorce: Helping Your Child Avoid Immediate and Later Emotional Problems,* psychologist Neil Kalter, former director of the Center for the Child and Family at the University of Michigan at Ann Arbor, points out that 50 to 70 percent of children from divorced parents "do not appear to have long-lasting problems attributable to divorce." Although most parents in the aftermath of divorce suffer from temporary insanity, many of us manage to get past it, or, at least, to act as if we had—for the sake of our children. And then we get down to the business of being parents again, with the very person that we once thought we would (pardon the pun) "ex" out of our lives.

In many ways, co-parenting after divorce is a heroic feat. We overcome a smorgasbord of unpleasant feelings—anger, remorse, shame, rage, grief, embarrassment, guilt—and rise to a higher purpose, hunkering down to the vital task of raising our children. It is the least we can do for our kids. After all, *we* broke the contract. Our kids were *supposed* to have two parents—divorce or no divorce.

An Idea Whose Time Has Come

I could never have written this book a decade ago. For one thing, I had no perspective as a co-parent. Though my views may evolve further by the time I'm a co-grandparent, at this point my ex and I have built an amazingly strong, flexible—and workable—foundation for our family apart.

Reasons for this book go beyond the personal, however. Ten years ago, we also didn't know as much about divorce, and the idea of caring for a child in two households was unheard of. Constance Ahrons, Ph.D, a family therapist, professor of sociology and associate director of the Marriage and Family Therapy Program at the University of Southern California, points out that as recently as the early seventies, "divorce law was still based on the belief that divorce was immoral and threatened the institution of the family." Some of her fellow clinicians were among those who regarded a positive postdivorce relationship as "abnormal." Is it any wonder that so few divorcing parents even *considered* raising kids together? The ones who did were lonely pioneers, staking out unknown territory, often in the face of family and friends' disapproval.

But Ahrons was struck by the fact that neither she nor many of the divorcing couples she saw in her clinical practice necessarily acted the way the textbooks said they should. As the divorce rate began to climb in the mid-seventies, she became even more resolute in her belief that it was time to "normalize" divorce and to offer different kinds of postdivorce alternatives.

Around the same time, other groundbreaking researchers were similarly compelled by personal as well as professional experi-

ence. As they explored changes in families, they exhorted fellow
professionals to view divorced and remarried families, single-
parent families, and stepfamilies through a fresh lens—as no less
"normal" than nuclear families, just different—and to look at the
relationships that shape a family, not the structure.

The family therapists, psychologists, psychiatrists, sociologists,
lawyers, mediators, and other experts who have put marriage,
divorce, and remarriage under the microscope have had a major
impact on our understanding of complex family dynamics and
change. Analyzing the research and extrapolating from the kinds
of problems seen in clinical settings and in family courts, these
professionals can now educate parents about what not to do *and*
reinforce what they are doing right.

A spate of books about divorce and remarriage came out in the
late seventies and early eighties when Divorce Fever was at its
peak. However, only three dealt specifically with co-parenting:
Mom's House, Dad's House by Isolina Ricci, Ph.D., a family therapist and divorce mediator; *Co-Parenting: Sharing Your Child Equally*
by Miriam Galper Cohen, a family therapist; and *Sharing Parenthood After Divorce* by Ciji Ware, a journalist. They are excellent
books—I'd recommend them*—but they were published more
than ten years ago, when only 3 percent of parents opted for joint
custody (Cohen and Ware among the trailblazers), and there were
not as many co-parenting veterans to survey. Today, many of the
children of those early pioneers are, by now, in their teens and
twenties and can talk about what it has been like to live in a family
apart. And a number of longitudinal studies have since validated
what these brave new families found out: *Children fare best after
divorce when they are shielded from conflict and cared for by both parents.*

I have no doubt that co-parenting after divorce—a commitment to support and care for your children, regardless of the legal
designation—is an idea whose time has come. More and more
parents are acutely aware of the effects of divorce and of the
importance of *both* parents. It appears that many white- and

---

*Miriam Galper Cohen's book is out of print, but the original material was
updated for her 1991 book, *The Joint Custody Handbook* (see Resources, Appendix III).

blue-collar fathers—divorced or not—are taking an increasingly more active role in their children's lives. And although the number of parents who opt for joint physical custody lingers between 10 percent and 12 percent nationally (between 15 percent and 20 percent in California)*, legal statistics belie the trend.

Some observers suspect that the actual number of co-parents is higher, because some parents who have sole custody also work out shared parenting arrangements that ensure children's access to both parents. Notably, one of the most recent large-scale studies, the 1988 Stanford Custody Project spearheaded by lawyer Robert Mnookin, former director of the Stanford Center on Conflict and Negotiation, and psychologist Eleanor Maccoby, a professor emeritus at Stanford University, contradicts the findings of earlier studies that report high drop-out rates for fathers. "By contrast, we have found that, three and a half years after parental separation, there were very few children who had not seen their fathers within the past year, and most children in mother-residence families were visiting on a regular basis."

The Stanford Custody Project reflects a California population of couples divorcing in the eighties, as opposed to a 1981 national sample of couples divorcing a decade earlier who were polled by sociologist Frank R. Furstenberg, Jr., and his colleagues. Both samples have their biases, admit the researchers. Still, they believe that it's reasonable to assume that because of the steadily climbing divorce rate over the past several decades, "parents who divorce now include different kinds of people than the smaller groups who divorced at an earlier time—perhaps, specifically, more committed fathers." Maccoby and Mnookin suspect that the public is definitely more aware of "the continuing responsibilities of both parents following divorce" and also that (certainly in California) laws and attitudes have changed, helping to establish "pro-contact assumptions in the minds of divorcing parents . . ."

---

*Most states don't keep formal records of custody dispensation. These generally accepted statistics are derived from studies conducted in various states.

Although only a quarter of the Stanford sample qualified as "cooperative" (an almost equal percentage was "conflicted," most were "disengaged"), Maccoby and Mnookin stress that their study's most important message to parents is to strive for a cooperative co-parental relationship. "The fact that a significant number of parents after divorce are able to create and sustain cooperative co-parenting demonstrates that it is not an impossible task." If you can't cooperate, they add, then at least disengage, which avoids putting your kids in the middle. The findings indicate that many divorced couples, who practice "parallel parenting" become increasingly cooperative over time.

Practical considerations also favor the trend toward co-parenting. With two-thirds of all mothers in the workplace (67 percent of them full time), co-parenting is one way of coping with the demands of what sociologist Arlie Hochschild has labeled the "second shift"—the job of running a house and caring for children when we come home after work. To survive the daily grind, working parents have discovered that they *have* to share the burden. That's even more true for divorced families, in which there is only one parent per household and much less adult time and energy to go around. Mothers and fathers who co-parent provide buffers for each other when the going gets tough; most important, they give each other the precious gifts of time and solitude, and they give their children wonderful role models of parents who aren't locked into traditional roles.

Sally Brush, director of Beech Acres' Aring Institute in Cincinnati, Ohio, runs groups for divorced parents and children; she confirms and endorses the trend, especially fathers' involvement: "Men *are* doing more. And that's going to help women—and help the children."

There's another reason that the time is ripe for a closer look at co-parenting: We have to take a new look at divorce. Many who ponder sociological phenomena characterize the nineties as the "We Decade"—a time of going back to basics and embracing old-fashioned values. Not surprisingly, along with this retro sentiment, there's been an antidivorce backlash. After all, divorce has always signified the dissolution of "the family."

However, romanticizing marriage and the nuclear family is no better than abandoning all hope for families. Granted, the notion popularized in the seventies of divorce as a way of "doing your own thing" was harshly blasted by reality in the eighties when mothers discovered that they couldn't make ends meet, fathers realized they missed their children, and everyone found out that second marriages have an even greater chance of failing (60 percent) than first ones (50 percent). There are still no quick and easy answers to make relationships, or families, work. But bringing back hula hoops and poodle skirts won't transform us into the Cleavers or the Nelsons. No nostalgic trend—indeed, no major sociological shift—will make the American family today the same as the American family of generations past.

And make no mistake: Although the divorce rate has declined somewhat since 1987, divorce—and remarriage—are still very much on the horizon. Demographer Paul Glick predicts that of the couples who married in the eighties, 60 percent will ultimately divorce. About half of all marriages that take place every year are remarriages. The once "traditional" nuclear family—a first-time marriage in which Dad is breadwinner and Mom a full-time homemaker—has already been pushed from center stage, by single-parent and remarried families. And by the year 2000, an estimated 50 to 70 percent of all children born since 1980 will live in single-parent homes or stepfamilies by the time they're eighteen!

Adversarial divorce certainly doesn't fit the nineties' image of a "We" generation, but the idea of divorcing families transforming themselves into "families apart" does. That is not to advocate divorce. Surely, it would be a sorry state if all couples married with the *intent* to divorce. And, it would be infinitely better if so many marriages didn't actually end in divorce. But the fact is, many do; of them, 60 percent have children under eighteen.

Every year, the parents of over a million children must decide how their kids will be cared for after divorce. Rather than automatically assuming that those families will be shattered and the children forever lose one of their parents, it's time to change the way we think. As Constance Ahrons asked her colleagues at a 1990 gathering of family therapists, "Why do we still glorify the so-called 'intact family,' still continue to label divorced families as 'broken,' 'incomplete'?" Ahrons prefers "binuclear families," a nonpejorative term she coined in the late seventies to describe "a family which spans two households." In her ten-year Binuclear Family Study, one of this country's major longitudinal examinations of divorce, Ahrons found that about half of her sample were able to reorganize into healthy binuclear families.

Ahrons's findings dovetail with those of researcher and family therapist Judith Wallerstein. Although the media made headlines out of the fact that in her 1989 book, *Second Chances: Men, Women, and Children a Decade after Divorce,* Wallerstein reported that 54 percent of children are derailed, *46 percent of the children in her study were back on track.* They were able to attend to schoolwork, pursue their own interests, develop relationships with their peers, and have fun—because their parents did not involve them in their struggle and because one parent, if not both, continued to give them the nurturing they needed to develop.

Wallerstein, who sees thousands of divorced families every year at her Center for the Families in Transition, in Corte Madera, California, agrees that almost all parents can learn to work with each other on some level and, thus, ease their children's adjustment: "Of course I think it's possible to be cooperative co-parents. There's no point in studying divorce if you don't think you can *do* something about it." Wallerstein also laments that somehow people have gotten the idea that she is antidivorce. "I'm not saying people shouldn't get divorced. I'm saying, 'Let's do it better.' "

Divorce Family Style

In the fall of 1989, after my article about family therapy came out, I, too, believed that parents could be taught to do divorce better. Mark and I were in the process of learning how; and I knew other co-parenting couples who were learning, too. But when I first spoke to book editors about this project, I was amazed by their responses. "Her ex-husband must be a wimp!" declared one bitter (probably divorced) male editor at a major publishing house. "No one gets along with his ex-wife." People all around me were "recovering"—from drug and alcohol addiction, gambling, overeating, even incest. And yet the implication was that no one can really recover from divorce.

To prove the skeptics wrong, I interviewed sixteen other divorced couples in the tristate area (New York, New Jersey, and Connecticut) and then wrote "Divorce Family Style" for *New York*. I was touched, reassured, and struck by the common threads that ran through our stories, and I continued to be amazed when I later cast my net throughout other parts of the country to research this book. I relied largely on word of mouth to find other co-parents, as well as colleagues in national organizations, such as Parents Without Partners and the Children's Rights Council, who graciously ran ads for me. I also called family therapists, psychologists, divorce mediators, and conciliation court counselors for names of successful graduates. To my delight, when I explained the nature of this project, most people were eager to share their experiences or help me find parents who could.

For this book, I *deliberately* didn't deal with fathers (and some mothers) who willfully abandoned their kids (financially or emotionally) or parents who kidnap their children or falsely accuse the other parent of sexual abuse just to prevent him or her from getting close to their children. Sadly, they do exist—their stories are blazoned in the headlines and blared on the evening news. But theirs are situations that, more often than not, reflect severe psychological disturbances, issues that go beyond matters of marriage and divorce.

My mission has been to trumpet the accomplishments of parents who are doing it right: parents you're (unfortunately) less likely to see on TV talk shows. I believe that parents today crave a beacon of hope; they need to hear about other parents who have divorced but haven't abandoned their kids, torn them apart, or left them to swim alone in a sea of adult problems. Too many articles and books already have been written that publicize the dire effects of divorce and, in so doing, show how not to parent after divorce. Parents need to be shown *how*—to listen, to sacrifice, and to cooperate—so that their kids are less susceptible to the dangers of divorce. I hope that the pages that follow will serve this purpose.

The *Families Apart* Questionnaire

To test my initial premises about what it takes to co-parent, I devised a four-page questionnaire (see appendix I), designed to elicit attitudes about co-parenting and to pinpoint what issues, events, or situations were most commonly problematic and what factors changed the co-parenting relationship over the years. The questionnaire was disseminated to 84 co-parents, 51 mothers and 33 fathers, representing 60 families and 95 children. I then interviewed most of the survey respondents, some of their children, other co-parents, and other children of divorce as well.

In all, 112 adults and 34 children were interviewed.* The selected stories and quotes used throughout this book are drawn from the transcripts of more than half of the adults and all the children; often, the same families reappear in several chapters. I chose their stories because, in my opinion, they were the most quotable and universal—representative of the overall picture. However, whenever statistics are cited, they always reflect the 84 co-parents who responded to my survey.

To be sure, each family is unique, and all divorces have rhythms of their own. I focused on how the co-parents pulled off this tough business of forming a family apart. Some grasped the importance of co-parenting from the moment they made the decision to split up, or at least they knew that they would *try* to work toward a cooperative co-parenting arrangement; some didn't. Some had greater emotional resources, some had greater financial resources, and some were more graceful than others in establishing new family patterns that worked to the adults' and children's benefit. And although many co-parents live relatively

---

*With the exception of a few parents who are cited in their professional roles, all parents' and children's names have been changed.

close to each other, some households are several hundred miles, an entire country, or as much as an ocean apart.

Furthermore, each family's definition of "co-parenting" is different. Some parents refer to their arrangements as "shared parenting," while others, especially those who have made a successful adjustment to remarriage, say they have "parenting coalitions,"* consisting of as many as four parenting adults, two biological and two steps—a committee of adults who watch over the kids.

Legal labels often camouflage the actual co-parenting arrangement. Parents with joint custody, which means that legally each parent has equal responsibility and authority over the children, don't necessarily share equal *parenting* time. And in some sole-custody families, in which technically only one parent is the legal guardian, both parents might share the day-to-day responsibility for their kids' welfare, regardless of how their divorce papers read.

The details and infinite variety of their situations are as colorful and intricate as the families themselves. No matter what they call the arrangement, how they divide time, juggle responsibilities, dictate authority, or make joint decisions, every co-parent I interviewed expressed a common priority: *taking care of the children.*

My sample is certainly not representative of *all* divorced families. It was a self-selecting group of people who responded to the call for "co-parents," however each one defines the term. Nevertheless, it is interesting to note certain rather compelling statistics: In response to the statement "No matter what *I* think of my ex, I know it's important that he/she is in my child(ren)'s life," an overwhelming 85 percent marked "always." The rest, 15 percent, said "almost always."

The co-parents in my sample also acknowledged the importance of the long-term perspective when they responded to the statement "I believe that as long as we're both still alive, my ex and I will always be "kin"—connected through our children." Two-thirds answered "always" and 15 percent "almost always."

---

*The term was coined by Emily and John Visher, a psychologist and psychiatrist, who have written a number of seminal works on family reorganization (see p. 213).

The Real Experts

Listening to other parents, I realized that in many ways Mark and I were fortunate. We were able to set up two comfortable house-holds and, most important, to afford a professional referee. Several parents in my study had to struggle considerably harder to make ends meet. Many never consulted a marriage or divorce counselor, never had individual therapy, had never even read a self-help book on divorce. And yet they were able to rely on extended family or friends, tap resources in the community, join support groups, and use their own inner reserves of emotional strength to create and sustain their families apart.

Although one out of five parents credits "education regarding the effects of divorce on children" for positive changes in their postdivorce relationships and equal numbers have availed themselves of some type of postdivorce therapy, *we* are the experts when it comes to co-parenting on an everyday basis. The message in our stories is an important one: that co-parenting after divorce *is* possible. Collectively, we possess a wealth of concrete information that even the best therapist working alone can't give us. And we definitely offer a new perspective on what "family" can mean.

Even though a few of us have been at this for many long years, we are still trailblazers. Often, we feel as if we're reinventing the wheel, because . . . we are! In fact, just when we think things are going smoothly, something happens. "Fragile," "explosive," "trying," "nerve-racking," "difficult," "complicated," "busy," "scary," "amazing," "unpredictable"—these are just some of the words parents use to describe postdivorce relationships. And over time descriptions change.

Clearly, some co-parenting arrangements are more tenuous than others, but all need time to mature. I know I write differently about Mark's and my relationship now than I did just a few years ago. In my survey, only about 10 percent characterized their relationships as "friendly" or "very friendly" during the first year after divorce. The rest placed themselves on a continuum ranging from "extremely hostile" to "civil but cold," with most describing themselves as "moderately angry"! For many, it takes longer to work effectively as a team, although *all* my respondents considered their relationships to be at least "civil but cold" (12 percent), if not "friendly" (54 percent) or "very friendly" (8 percent) after five years.* Sadly, some co-parenting arrangements break down years later, most often when a new spouse enters the picture. Jealousy, competition, resentment about money and attention going to the "other household" are likely to disrupt a once smooth-running co-parenting situation.

In any case, life keeps happening, especially if you divorce when children are young. As kids get older, their social lives change, the paraphernalia they cart from house to house increases, and college tuition, which seemed so far in the future when you split up, begins to loom ominously close. One parent starts dating a person that the other one doesn't like; another parent is fired or offered a job out of town or in another country. Who takes up the slack when adults want to have a social life again, go back to school, advance a career? Or worse, what happens when someone gets sick, one spouse has emotional or financial trouble, or a child falters in school?

Co-parenting is not something you can simply figure out once. Many of the experts talk about the various developmental "stages" of divorce (see pp. 37–47), and about the tasks a person must accomplish in order to go on to the next. If you're floundering in the wake of separation, such guidelines can be useful.

However, stages by no means tell the whole story. A number of other variables influence postdivorce adjustment: how old you are, how old your kids are, your finances, your work situation, the state of your marriage before separation and the circumstances that led to the split, how close you are to your family and to friends, and, of course, your basic emotional health. The divorce process, complex and often convoluted, is not a linear event that can be boiled down into discrete phases. You don't fit a certain profile just because you happen to be at a particular point in time after your separation.

In fact, under the inordinate strain of divorce, it's not uncom-

*Some respondents had not yet been divorced five years or longer; these percentages are based on 61 parents.

mon to revert to a prior stage—and that might be only a week or two after you thought you had zoomed ahead to a new plateau! Luckily, the reverse is true, too. Just as you're about to throw in the towel—your kids are having problems, your ex is relentlessly cruel or inept, and you hate your lawyer—something jolts the system and things get better.

This book is about what it takes to become a "family apart." Rather than look at divorce chronologically and set out a series of goals you must accomplish in order to get through various stages of divorce, it focuses on what you need to know about co-parenting from the day you decide to separate. Children can't wait for you to feel better or heal. They need both of you right away.

Doing It Better

Thinking about Judith Wallerstein's rallying cry, "Let's do [divorce] better," I'm proud that Mark and I have. We certainly did it better than my parents, who got divorced after thirty-five years of marriage. Even though my sister and brother and I were married by then, we each felt like Solomon's baby, nearly torn between two parents who claimed to love us. Bitterness resounded up and down the generations, and family occasions were tainted by melodrama: Would Dad arrive with Shirley, his new wife, who was once my mother's best friend? Where would we seat them? No room seemed big enough to contain their collective animosity.

Mark and I also did it better than some friends. One charged back to court seven years after the breakup. Another kidnapped his son. And one of Jennifer's friends told us at Jennifer's graduation dinner, "I wish my parents could give me a party together. They can't even stand to be in the same room. At my graduation, I'm sure they'll sit on opposite sides of the auditorium . . . *if* they both come."

The people in this book have done it better, too. Many of them have seen their own parents, friends' parents, and their contemporaries battered by divorce. "I saw what their parents' divorce did to some of my friends in high school," explained the recently separated mother of a six-year-old. "I can't live with Don—but he's the father of that little girl, too. Sometimes I have to grit my teeth, but I'll be damned if I'm going to let my feelings get in the way of our kid's happiness."

It is apparent that these parents educated themselves and worked hard to provide what Marla Isaacs, author of *The Difficult Divorce,* calls "a mantle of protection" for their children. Among the parents I surveyed, a reassuring 83 percent said they "almost always" or "always" restrain themselves in front of the children; the remaining 17 percent said "usually." An even greater percentage indicated that they "don't ask the children to side with me against my ex." They also did it better in another important way: No one suggested that mothers inherently knew more or were inherently better equipped as parents. Some fathers were involved in child rearing before the divorce; an even higher percentage participated afterward.

Our children can feel the difference when we actively try to cooperate with our ex-spouses. One of the eighteen-year-olds I interviewed, whose parents divorced when he was nine, agreed— as do many children—that the most positive effect of his parents' divorce was that it stopped the arguing. "It was for the better," he insists. "I always watched the tension between them when they were married. After the divorce, when my father came to pick me up, I sensed how uncomfortable he was about walking into a house he had once lived in. But I knew in my mind that they were working at being friends—at least, they could have a conversation."

Our children will also *be* different as a result of our joint caring and our commitment to their welfare. Hugh McIsaac, former director of family court services in Los Angeles and a long-time advocate of shared parenting, recalls a panel in 1989, on which several pioneering California parents who first opted for joint custody in the late seventies were brought together, with their children, to share a decade's worth of experience. "When those parents started out, they felt as if they were sailing off the end of the world. They entered into shared parenting agreements with a great deal of trepidation and concern. Ten years later, the proof was in their kids. One of the teenage boys on the panel said, 'It's complicated but it's not confusing. This is all I've known, but I'm glad that my parents decided to have a good divorce—that I didn't have to lose either of them.' "

Over the years, McIsaac has "kept in touch" with many of the children whose families have used the L.A. Conciliation Court services, which provides counseling and education for divorcing families. "When parents are really able to put aside their anger and work together, their kids are terrific. Maybe what we're seeing is an emergence of a new kind of family system—it's not better or worse, it's just different." Of the kids, he says, "Years later, they're doing well socially and academically."

Neil Kalter agrees that in "well-handled divorces," children "become independent more quickly—they take responsibility for their lives, and as long as we're talking about age-appropriate responsibilities, that's a good thing." That children of divorce are often "more cautious" about relationships, in Kalter's view, is a plus. "They're more realistic about marriage, and that may be the best way to prevent divorce." Kalter observes that many of these kids want to wait until they're "close to thirty" before committing themselves—which would certainly give them more of an opportunity to forge a separate identity and therefore bring more strength to their marriages than many of their parents did.

"I think a more subtle effect," Kalter adds, "is that they learn that adults can make it independently. This is especially true of girls looking at their mothers."

The Ten Keys

There are no formulas, no "cookbook" solutions for successful co-parenting. However, after talking to countless researchers and clinicians who deal with divorced couples, as well as taking into account my own experience and that of parents and children I interviewed, particular themes persist in well-functioning families apart.

The ten "keys" identified below are *principles of sound parenting.* They can make the road a little smoother and, in fact, would be useful to remember in *any* family situation. After all, in a sense, all parents must be "co-parents." And all parents have challenges. In nondivorced homes, parents must juggle work schedules and child-rearing responsibilities. In nondivorced homes, parents struggle to find the best way to communicate—with one another and with their children. In nondivorced homes, parents, burdened by personal problems, are additionally pressed by rapid-fire changes in society. And in nondivorced homes, parents sometimes have conflicting opinions or parenting styles, and it takes effort for them to make decisions jointly. The difference is, in divorced homes, parents have to work harder. Those who co-parent successfully (although never perfectly) have certain elements in common which, in concert, seem to make shared parenting work.

Key #1: Heal yourself—so that you can get on with your own life, without leaning on your kids (chapter 2).

Key #2: Act maturely—whether or not you really *feel* it; you and your co-parent are the adults, with the responsibility to care for your kids and to act in their best interest (chapter 3).

Key #3: Listen to your children; understand their needs (chapter 4).

Key #4: Respect each other's competence as parents and love for the children (chapter 5).

Key #5: Divide parenting time—somehow, in some way, so that the children feel they still have two parents (chapter 6).

Key #6: Accept each other's differences—even though one of you is a health-food nut and the other eats Twinkies, one is laid-back and the other a disciplinarian, one's fanatically neat, the other is a slob (chapter 7)!

Key #7: Communicate about (and with) the children—directly, not *through* them (chapter 8).

Key #8: Step out of traditional gender roles. Mom learns how to fix a bike and knows what the "first down" is if her son's into football, and Dad can take his daughter shopping and talk with her about dates (chapter 9).

Key #9: Recognize and accept that change is inevitable and therefore can be anticipated (chapter 10).

Key #10: Know that co-parenting is forever; be prepared to handle holidays, birthdays, graduations, and other milestones in your children's lives with a minimum of stress and encourage your respective extended families to do the same (chapter 11).

The ten keys follow a logical rather than sequential order. It's not a matter of "mastering" one and then moving on to the next. Look at them as parts of a whole. Each key represents a cog in the co-parenting mechanism; and they all work together. Once the machine is running smoothly, some of the cogs will rarely need oiling or repair; others may require more vigilant maintenance work; and sometimes, when you least expect it, several cogs get stuck, and the machine may break down entirely.

If you're going through a divorce and need reassurance that it's possible to co-parent, if you've been divorced for a few years and need role models, or if you simply want to know how best to support a family member or close friend who is in the throes of this crisis, read on. This book is seasoned with ample sprinklings of advice from professionals in the field, but, more important, it gives voice to families apart who have kept their co-parenting machines working.

The mothers and fathers in this book have been co-parenting anywhere from one to sixteen years. We have faltered along the way, even failed at times. You can learn from our mistakes. And you can learn from our triumphs, for we have succeeded too—rarely as soon or as well as we would have liked, and, often, against great odds. We are all infinitely wiser in retrospect! The situations in this book may not fit yours exactly. There are no absolute rules, and there are certainly no pat answers—only stories about what various parents have tried. Take what feels right; adapt ideas to suit your needs. In our stories and in the feedback from our kids are at least a few valuable grains of insight and hope for all families apart.

— 2 —

GETTING THROUGH
THE FIRE

Key #1: Heal Yourself after Divorce

The Horrible-Smelling Drawer

A terrible stench emanated from an empty bathroom drawer in a house I rented. For a long time, whenever I had to retrieve something from that drawer, the odor overwhelmed me. Each time it happened, I let out a loud *"Yeeech!"* followed by *"Ugh, that smell!"* I was angry at the landlord, but because the rest of the house was close to perfect, I only fantasized about confronting her. What could she do about it, anyway? I sprayed the inside of the drawer with Lysol, sprinkled it with baby powder and baking soda, and left clumps of sweet-scented apple-cinnamon-spice potpourri to do the rest. Nothing worked. Eventually, I realized I would have to learn to live with the smell. I never learned to like it, but I stopped railing against it and finally learned to live with it.

Then one day, the smell was gone.

My divorce was like that drawer. Most of the foul memories have dimmed with age, becoming faint, almost imperceptible reminders of something that once had seemed noxious.

At the time, the battle seemed constant and endless—accusations, angry phone calls, appointments with lawyers who probably built summer homes on our misery. And the evidence gathering: a neighbor (whose motives remain suspect) spied on me through a telescope aimed at my living room, relaying to Mark tales of misconduct, while I tirelessly sought out sworn statements from "friends" who would attest to his cruelty and neglect.

Ten years later, it is clear that our actions were patently ridiculous and spiteful.

The images of my behavior that endure are some of the most embarrassing: the night Mark and I made up The List (of who gets what), and I ended up throwing a chair at him; the sunny Saturday in May when I showed up, a local policeman in tow, to oust his girlfriend and him from the beach house, insisting that it was "my turn"; the time I maliciously stole into the garage and loosened a critical wire from the engine of our car. I'm sure Mark has long since forgotten this last incident—his annoyance could not have lingered as long as my guilt. If not, as he reads this, he will understand why the car wouldn't start on that hot Friday in June when it was his weekend to use it. (Sorry, Mark!)

Not counting the ups and downs that led up to it, our divorce took five years out of our lives. It was almost four years from Decision Day—the day we set the process in motion—to the day the marriage was legally terminated in court and another six months before I moved out of the "marital apartment" and into my own. Even then, there was unfinished business. But like the smell diminishing in that bathroom drawer, one day I realized that things had become different—even a little better.

Parent, Heal Thyself

Divorce is not an event; it's a process. And if you're like most of the parents I interviewed, you'll need some help along the way. One thing is certain: There's no way around the divorce process, no shortcuts. As one of my interviewees remarked, "It's a fire you have to go through." The experts say that recovering from divorce can take as little as two years, an average of four or five, or as long as a lifetime if you're not willing to let go. The healing is usually gradual, as it was in my case.

To say that divorce is an especially demanding process is an understatement. In all cases, it is no less than a complete overhaul of your intimate relationships, your physical surroundings, your economic life, and your standing among friends, in the community, and in the world at large. Work feels more taxing than usual, the obligatory phone call to an aging parent engenders more resentment than usual, financial worries loom larger. Anything, from volunteer work to doing your taxes to arguing with the dry cleaner, threatens to pull you down. Coping becomes an end unto itself.

While you're busy soothing your wounds and tending to *your* needs, what about the kids? Divorce turns a child's world upside down, too. When parents give priority to their own emotional and social needs, the cruel irony is that this often translates into even greater stress for the children.

Even though you're still struggling, your children need you. Remember that the divorce was the grown-ups' idea. It's your job to help protect children from the adult conflicts and to keep the disruptions in their lives to a minimum. A tall order, no doubt, but *you* are the parent.

Clearly, you can't rush the emotional process, nor do you have to hide all your feelings from your children. In fact, it's a good lesson for them to see that adults can experience sadness or anger (within reason) and then recover. For example, when a child whose parent is crying says, "I'm sad about the divorce," it gives the child license to verbalize what she's feeling. If that child later sees the parent going about the business of the day, the message is that we can experience emotions and still get on with our lives. Besides, kids see through us, and it's better to learn how to be honest with them than to try to fool them (more about talking to kids in chapter 4).

On the other hand, you also owe it to your children to do whatever you can to shield them from the particularly ugly aspects of your divorce and from any of your emotions that will wound them. As Judith Wallerstein puts it, "It comes down to a moral choice. What's wrong with exercising a little restraint? You don't have to lie—but you also don't have to say to a kid, 'Your father's a jerk!' "

You owe it to your children to move yourself along and, at the same time, to safeguard their development. The rest of this chapter is about recognizing the process—and benefits—of healing, so that the children can regain a sense of equilibrium and support from both parents in their emerging family apart.

According to the Experts: The Stages

Back in 1967, psychologists Thomas Holmes and Richard Rahe had the good sense to put divorce and marital separation at the top of the list on their often-cited "Social Readjustment Scale," preceded only by the death of a spouse. Since then, the number of divorces has almost tripled, the phenomenon has warranted a lot of media coverage, and a number of researchers have observed that the trauma of divorce is second only to the death of a child. Talking to a group of her peers, family therapist and divorce researcher Sandra Volgy explains why: "It's a much more difficult experience for many people than the death of a spouse because it represents a continuing loss. The lost object is out there in the world but inaccessible to the person who has lost him or her."

We certainly know a great deal more than we used to, but the process itself hasn't gotten any easier. When *your* marriage is ending, it doesn't matter that every year over a million other couples are filing for divorce or that researchers have amassed truckloads of data on the subject. We still don't know how to make sense of the overwhelming feelings. "It is a very difficult loss for people to define—especially for children—but for adults as well," says Volgy, "because it represents a loss of dreams, of fantasies, of expectations for the future." Moreover, in divorce *one* emotion rarely predominates; rather, we experience a full range of feelings—from euphoria to despair (sometime, within the same hour!), and the feelings keep changing!

Although professional observers generally divide divorce into developmental stages—characterized by the peaks and valleys of various transitions that the family must go through—divorcing couples make it clear that the lines between the so-called stages are often painfully imprecise. One step forward may lead to a couple of steps back. And no two people experience divorce exactly the same way, not even two who are involved in the same divorce.

Still, a description of the stages and the tasks you must master to make each transition can help you recognize approximately where you are, and, no less important, validate your own sanity and stability in the midst of chaos. "Couples find it a great relief to understand that there is a process involved, that there is a continuum, and that they're not stuck in a quagmire of emotional intensity," explains Sandra Volgy, who often counsels couples going through a divorce.

Predivorce   The symptoms of a dying relationship never crop up overnight. Long before the words *separation* or *divorce* are uttered, the signs emerge. In the predivorce phase, the spouses are rarely in synch with one another. One partner feels that the marriage is "empty," and fantasizes a better life without the other one. The discontented partner is often "ripe" for an adventure, but she or he may not realize it—until something happens.

So it was with Patricia Davenport. After three children and six years of marriage, she recounts, "I met an old boyfriend that summer and became infatuated with him. Suddenly my marriage seemed all wrong. I was miserable. It seemed to me that if I could fall in love with someone else that easily, I was not with the right person."

Often, one partner senses the imbalance and tries to keep the boat from rocking too much. Explanations are demanded, arguments ensue, and, rather than stabilizing, the relationship continues to falter. The disequilibrium threatens to capsize the couple. One person often tries to deny the reality ("I never realized she was so unhappy"), bargain ("I know when I get this raise and we have less financial stress, our life together will improve"), or pile on the guilt ("How could you do this to our family?"), but the other spouse is resolute.

Patricia—the one who felt there was no turning back—admits, "I was thinking in very simplistic, black-and-white terms, but at the time I couldn't react any other way. Whenever I tried to argue myself out of the divorce, I came to the same bottom line: I never again wanted to make love to my husband."

Although one or both partners might be in denial at this stage, the children rarely are. It's no accident that Jeremy, our son, began having major problems in school during Mark's and my final year together. Or that seven months before we agreed to separate, our then ten-year-old daughter, Jennifer, gave me a handmade Mother's Day card assuring me that "things will get better when we move to the new house." It was like a bullet between the eyes.

Reviewing the predivorce stage can help you look at how you and your ex-spouse did battle during marriage, how you will react to each other during divorce and, most importantly, how you will fare as co-parents. Research bears out this important correlation: The Stanford Custody Project, which interviewed divorcing couples shortly after filing, six months later, eighteen months later, and then three years later, found significant evidence that early conflict is carried over into patterns of co-parenting.

However, you are only doomed to repeat history if you don't acknowledge it. By analyzing your predivorce relationship, you can start to troubleshoot early on and head off some of the heartache. For example, you and your ex-spouse probably didn't communicate well during marriage; discussions always deteriorated into arguments, because you interrupted each other, didn't know how to listen. You can bet that those old habits will become even worse in divorce. What is more, they'll make it more difficult for you to co-parent cooperatively and to form a healthy family apart—unless you do something to change those patterns of behavior as quickly and effectively as you can (see pp. 81–84 for some concrete suggestions about how).

The Decision   Typically, even in the face of one partner's intense efforts to save the relationship (or, sometimes, because of it), the other partner leaves. How bad must a marriage get before one person decides to call it quits? Analyzing data collected over a twelve-year period from 1974 to 1986, based on samples of upper-middle-class, middle-class, and working-class families in suburban Cleveland, sociologist Gay Kitson reports that 40 percent said that their relationships had deteriorated within the last three years. Over 90 percent mentioned a particular date when things began to go bad, such as "In 1968, I started to realize a lot of things."

Despite the notion that divorce is "easier" now than it was forty years ago, comparing her findings with a 1956 study, Kitson concludes, "There is some evidence that the decision period has been lengthening in recent years." Reasons for hesitancy include the partners' ages, length of the marriage, responsibility for children, and the need to make preparations for living on one's own.

Why the decision is made is a different issue—and the answer often depends on which spouse you ask. Of the couples in my survey, answers regarding who initiated the divorce usually matched, but their comments revealed different perceptions of the same situation.

Bill Paterson writes in his questionnaire, "Loretta fell in love with an engineer at her office." He also notes in passing that the couple had "less definitive problems preceding this that resulted in the divorce," but reading Loretta O'Brien's (his ex-wife's) questionnaire, it would appear that she was a lot more "definitive" about their problems: "I was married at nineteen. Over the years we grew apart. We were more like brother and sister than husband and wife—no fighting or problems. We got along fine, but one day I realized I was no longer 'in love' with my husband. When I requested a separation, I was already involved with someone else." Loretta explains that they tried counseling, but it was too late. Although Bill would have been content to maintain the status quo, she says, she "had given up and wanted something more."

In a developmental sense, because one partner is often more "ready" to leave than the other, the decision is usually unilateral. Judith Wallerstein says that in her study of sixty families, "only one couple decided to divorce by mutual agreement." She notes that 65 percent of the women and 35 percent of the men "actively sought to end the marriage in the face of opposition. Among my respondents, women also more frequently identified themselves as the initiator (39 percent) than did men (16 percent). A surprising 34 percent indicated that it was a "mutual decision" but when asked to explain, their explanations revealed that one of them had actually set the process in motion: "My wife wanted the separation, but I filed for divorce," or "When I found out my husband was having an affair, I went to a lawyer."

With some couples, a skillful therapist can help reconcile differences even after one partner leaves (literally or figuratively), but according to sociologist Robert Weiss, who has done extensive research on separation and divorce, for about half of the couples who split up, separation marks the point of no return. The feuding becomes so vitriolic that it's impossible for either party to de-escalate the war. Weiss, who has explored various types of loss over the last twenty years, suggests that the closer you get to a legal divorce—for example, if one spouse has already consulted a lawyer—the less likely your chances of reconciling.

This period of marital decline—immediately before and after Decision Day—is crucial for the children. Even if they remember little else, kids of all ages often have at least a vague sense of parents fighting. Wallerstein notes that there's "enormous variance" in what children retain. "A number of youngsters report a very troublesome amnesia—they can't remember anything before the age of twelve." Others remember a particular scene in vivid detail, often an episode of anger or violence. Several older children I interviewed also remarked that they "saw divorce coming," even if a parent had never told them about it.

Many children remember the day their father moved out. "My parents would get into a lot of fights and one day my dad left," recalls eleven-year-old Dawn Carver, who was four when her parents divorced. "Emotionally, I have no memories," claims Adam Hartman, eighteen; he was also four when his parents split up. "But I have a physical memory of my father moving out and my helping him move into an apartment."

Especially when one of the partners is taken by surprise, or when there is a substantial difference regarding the decision to divorce, it may be difficult for the parents to separate their needs from their children's. However, they must. Whatever the circumstances, this should be the time when parents realize the importance of co-parenting and start to discuss the logistics—with each other as well as with the kids (see the section in chapter 4 "Telling the Children").

For all their differences, Bill Paterson and Loretta O'Brien, like many of the couples in my sample, at least agreed about the children. Loretta notes, "Our main concern was for the children, and we vowed to always make sure they came first, that they would always have two actively involved parents, and that we would not 'use' them to get back at each other."

"I wanted to be successful in relationships," Bill comments. "My marriage failed, but I could make our divorce successful through open communication and friendship and minimize the effects on our children."

The Aftermath   If you felt the earth move when you first kissed, watch out for how you feel when you first separate—even if you're the one who actively pushed for it. This acute, or crisis, stage, which usually lasts from six months to a year or two after a couple splits up, is sometimes referred to as the "aftermath"— as in earthquakes and other natural disasters! Your private agony goes public. Accusations fly. Tempers flare wildly. Nothing is stable, and everything's up for grabs—property, finances, and, unfortunately in some cases, the children's welfare.

Some divorces seem to start out on an even keel, but none is immune to the ups and downs of this crisis stage. In one of several longitudinal studies on divorce, University of Virginia researcher E. Mavis Hetherington found that families are at their worst one year after divorce—worse than at just two months afterward. Divorcing spouses typically go through what Hetherington calls "emotional lability"—in layman's terms, feeling crazy. You switch from euphoria to depression, forgiveness to revenge, and from being convinced that the divorce is the best thing that could happen to feeling it's the worst mistake you've ever made.

Psychologist Neil Kalter says that in 70 to 90 percent of the cases he sees, both partners experience "acute stress"—a whirligig of agonizing and unpredictable emotions. Hetherington, who summarizes the findings of a number of studies, also notes that at this stage and particularly in the social arena, research indicates that "his" and "her" divorces are more similar than different. Both spouses tend to lead "disorganized and demanding" lives. Both are "more anxious, depressed, angry, rejected, and incompetent than still-married parents." And both seem to have problems getting back on track socially in the first year.

"I'm just not myself," is a common refrain. One woman says that in the first six months, she never knew when—or where— she would burst into tears. She remembers being in the supermarket, and when the clerk told her they were out of Charmin Free, she got hysterical. A man admits to following his soon-to-be ex-wife and her boyfriend and crouching in the bushes outside the man's garden apartment to get a better look.

Based on a review of the research, Hetherington concludes that men often enter a frenetic phase of dating—dabbling in a "sexual smorgasbord," if you will. Women, too, engage in a great deal of casual sex, but they report not liking it as much as the men. One would expect, however, that some degree of gender-blending over the last decade has minimized such differences. In their 1985 study of American couples, sociologists Philip Blumberg and Pepper Schwartz concluded that young women were more "liberated" about non-monogamy than the older women they polled. And while no comparison data exist, many observers suspect that the number of women conducting extramarital affairs has increased over the last decade; it's reasonable to assume that divorced women probably have become more sexually active as well. At the same time, the threat of AIDS will probably continue to make both genders more cautious.

No matter what women *or* men do to stave off the feelings, the number and kinds of new responsibilities, crucial decisions, and major events that appear in this phase are staggering: telling the children; letting family, friends, and members of the community know about the divorce; choosing a lawyer to guide you through the legal labyrinth. In short, you will be negotiating every aspect of your future life, from the division of property to co-parenting arrangements.

Some experts mark the end of the acute stage when one parent moves out, but that's not always the case. Mark didn't move out until his lawyer said it was okay, nine months after we decided to separate—a common divorce scenario, especially in pinched economic times. During that period, we had to at least come up with some tentative ground rules for "sharing" our joint possessions. Difficult though it may be to admit, initially we often acted as if *the kids* were part of that package. We were unfocused, inconsistent, and unstable. Arrangements often fell apart, and promises made to the kids and to each other were frequently broken. A change of plan, a change of mood, finding out a new piece of information about the other one—anything could set us off and running. Unfortunately, we didn't seek professional counseling at that point; we should have.

Looking back, I realize just how typical we were, and I can understand why Wallerstein calls this a time of "diminished parenting capacities." Hetherington agrees that in the first year after divorce, parents tend to be preoccupied, emotionally unstable, and exhausted. Binge eating, heavy drinking and drugging, and other self-destructive coping strategies add insult to injury; it's bad enough to have a parent who is distracted, but one who is debilitated can be downright toxic.

The acute stage is a terrible, uncertain time for children; they often fear that they'll be "divorced," too. Although the situation is one they had no part in creating, most kids feel that it must be their fault. They feel as though they're living with strangers whose behavior is weird and unpredictable. They are further threatened by the prospect of new schedules, new schools, new homes, new significant others. Many recount the sting of embarrassment and despair when teachers passed out permissions forms (with space for only one home, one parent's address) and announced, "Have your mothers and fathers sign this."

Children need parents' support to help them understand what's happening in their family and to face the world outside. That's why this is the best time for professional counseling—ideally, as a couple. Someone who has experience with divorced families can help you manage your new lives and make decisions in a more rational, less impulsive way. Both of you must face the hard emotional work of dealing with the losses—your marriage, your hopes for the future, the idealized image of what "family" meant to you. And the sooner you get help, the sooner your children's lives will be set on a somewhat more even keel.

The Transition   Fortunately, at some point in all the chaos of the aftermath, a transitional stage of divorce begins to emerge; some professionals also refer to it as the "realignment" phase. It can last anywhere from two to four years—more if there's a great deal of bitterness or if one partner is mired in self-pity. Neil Kalter calls this a "short-term" stage, but given the tasks one must accomplish, when you're in it, it can feel like a lifetime.

Emotions still run high, and the realities of the future are bearing down hard on the entire family. The couple now has or is well on the way to having a "document" in hand, a separation agreement that outlines the division of property, and a co-parenting plan. This makes life a little easier; at least concrete guidelines exist.

As in the first stage, economic difficulties are common among women, although by now many mothers have gone back to work, changed from part- to full-time employment, or they have gone back to school. Fathers have probably gotten a little more accustomed to hands-on day-to-day parenting, an especially taxing adjustment for those who had not taken much responsibility for the kids prior to the breakup. Feeling ill at ease in the new role, some dads are particularly sensitive when kids says things like "That's not how Mom makes our cereal" or when a child develops a rash and they don't know what to do.

In short, this is a time of regrouping—making major external changes, such as moving, switching schools, getting a different job, and redefining old relationships and venturing into new ones. So much of daily life seems unfamiliar and is therefore often overwhelming. It's not uncommon for physical ailments to further debilitate both parents and kids. Behavioral and school-related problems in children sometimes run parallel to social and job-related problems in adults—all of which put additional stress on the new family apart.

As the reality of the divorce sinks in, some parents experience such great pain during the periods of separation from their children that they try to blot out the loneliness in a frenzy of activity, unintentionally distancing themselves from their kids; they then find it hard to allow themselves to get close to them again. Other parents, feeling dislocated and lonely, cling to the children for support, inadvertently using them as surrogate spouses, divulging inappropriate information about their own lives and about the other parent. Both are dangerous traps; neither extreme results in healthy children.

As if all the outside changes weren't overpowering enough, there are monumental internal changes as well—a continued mourning of the picket-fence dream; seeing yourself as a single person and as a single parent; rediscovering parts of yourself that were unexpressed or squelched in the marriage; and, most important, taking responsibility for your part in the end of the marriage. Painful and wrenching as these moments may be, they ultimately lead you closer to a new life.

In the meantime, the children are undergoing similar adjustment. They, too, have to be allowed to verbalize their sadness and voice their fears, to deal with their (undeserved) guilt and to express their anger about what is happening in the family. Parents must gently shepherd children through this unfamiliar territory and assure them that, even though they no longer love each other, they will always love and protect their children.

Ironically, when the adults get down to the business of co-parenting and focus on children's needs, it actually makes this transition smoother. It gets you outside yourself, forces you to rise to a higher purpose and to see your ex—and yourself—from a less egocentric perspective. You're no longer a spouse, but you're still a parent—a damn good one if you get your priorities straight. Particularly for fathers, who often fear that they'll lose the kids, studies indicate that involvement with the children can help alleviate depression. "Perhaps the most important development for me was the eventual realization that my children see me as a good father," says Barry Hubert, whose wife of eleven years asked for the trial separation. They never got back together, but, over time, parenting his daughters helped Barry view himself in a more positive light.

Becoming a Family Apart   Although there are no hard-and-fast rules, getting to this final stage of family reorganization usually takes at least three years, if not longer. Finally, everything begins to settle in. One day you realize that an entire twenty-four hours has gone by and you haven't thought about your ex, you haven't had a secret fantasy of plotting revenge, you haven't ridden a roller coaster of emotions, and you haven't called a lawyer, an accountant, a real estate agent, or a therapist! Depending on who you are, your age, the length of your marriage, the age of your children, and other aspects of your life, "healing" will be marked by different events or circumstances. Some people remember a single moment. For one woman, it was when she finally balanced her checkbook; for a man, the evening the kids complimented his cooking. Whatever your marker, you'll feel "a renewed sense of stability," comments Judith Wallerstein.

Ideally, at this stage both of you have done your emotional homework and have begun to accept your role in the new family apart. If not, you'll see a constant resurgence of conflict, your children will be drawn into the middle, and you may continue to do battle in court. Not so incidentally, you will also see problems in your children. Young ones may regress, withdraw, or become aggressive; school-age children may exhibit learning difficulties or behavior problems; older kids may become defiant or abuse drugs and alcohol.

The smooth sailing of this final stage of divorce can also be upset by third-party complications—lovers left over from predivorce affairs or rebound relationships launched in the aftermath stage. Seventy-five percent of women and 80 percent of men remarry, about half of them within the first three years after separation. If sufficient healing hasn't taken place, a new marriage rarely leads to it. In fact, given the complications of dealing with exes and steps, new and old in-laws, remarriage can have just the opposite effect, initiating yet an additional complex phase of family readjustment (see chapter 10, "Going with the Flow").

Changing Your Perspective: Common Stumbling Blocks

Time itself may propel you, but healing isn't just a matter of waiting out the calendar, especially if you have kids. You need to be ready to console them.

Most parents admit that they had to work hard to change their perspective after divorce. It can be particularly difficult if you separate after a relatively short marriage, or when the children are very young. You may not have much shared time to look back on. Still, try to remember that, if nothing else, your children are the product of your marriage. *You* chose to have them.

When you can keep the *entire* marriage in perspective, not just the horrendous period immediately before and after the divorce, you've reached a major turning point. Steve Posner, whose wife ended their marriage in the mid-seventies to pursue her own dreams, says that after the initial shock, anger, and self-recrimination, "I came to the conclusion that in nine years of marriage Joyce and I had had lots of good times. And we had Brian. We grew apart. I had to accept that—and move on." No doubt, this kind of maturity takes work, but it's clearly a prerequisite to healing.

Start to change your perspective by becoming more aware of what you're feeling and how it might impede healing and retard the process of becoming a family apart. Don't beat yourself up, but do take an honest inventory of your feelings. Keep a journal or, if you have trouble writing, talk into a tape recorder. Reading it back to yourself or replaying the tape is not as important as expressing the feelings. In fact, most people don't reread their divorce diaries until many, many years later, if at all.

Before you write, go through a typical day in your mind, and try to assess your feelings. Do you recognize your own thought patterns in any of the following statements? If so, you may be inadvertently programming yourself to stay in certain self-defeating feelings (which appear in parentheses after each quote). If you're just beginning the divorce process, don't be surprised if you identify with more than one!

"This is all his/her fault." (BLAME)   Except in cases of extreme violence, substance abuse, or severe mental illness, divorce is never one-sided, although sometimes it doesn't appear that way at first. Take Fran Gordon, forty-seven, whose same-age husband left her after twenty-five years of marriage—for a twenty-three-year-old who happened to be one of her daughter's friends. Or, Betty Hudson, whose marriage ended when her husband of thirteen years told her he was a homosexual. On the surface, each case seems quite cut-and-dried—those women were "innocent victims." However, Fran today can admit that she had distanced herself emotionally and didn't really want to be more involved with her husband; and Betty knew there was "something wrong" with her marriage for years before it ended, but she was afraid of confrontation.

Many others who answered the *Families Apart* questionnaire acknowledged that although their partner was the one who spoke the words "I want a divorce," or "I'm involved with someone else," the "innocent" one also had eroded the relationship. As one man put it, "She cheated on me, but I soon realized I was just as unhappy in our marriage as she was. I just wasn't doing anything overt to change it one way or the other."

Acknowledging your part in the breakup helps set in motion the healing process. "I try to get them to the point of making the divorce mutual," explains Betty Carter, director of the Family Institute of Westchester, who often works with divorcing couples. "Even though there was a betrayal, I tell the partner, 'It wasn't working for you, either. You've overlooked something. You're so mad at him or her that you're missing something.' When the person gets that, it's a major turning point—it's empowering." It's also better for the children, because when parents stop playing blame games, they have time and energy for the kids.

Beware of friends who feed the blame monster inside you. It may feel great when someone agrees that it was "all her fault" or says, "I always thought he was a bastard." But, in the long run, those kind of (generally inaccurate) indictments don't aid your healing process. In contrast, an *objective* friend, who knew you and your ex before the divorce, can be a valuable ally. Ask the friend to give you an honest appraisal of what you were like before and during your marriage. Your image of yourself and your perception of the marriage may be quite different, so try to take it in.

"This is all my fault." (GUILT)   Blaming yourself is as unproductive as blaming your partner. Terry Farrell left her husband, Charles, because she fell in love with another man whom she planned to marry. Charles was furious; realizing he couldn't have Terry, he at least wanted their sons, so he sued her for custody. Terry said she felt so guilty about "breaking up the family," she decided she "owed" Charles the kids. Within six months, however, she had second thoughts; a several-year battle over their sons ensued, during which time the couple was virtually incapable of co-parenting (more on their story in chapter 3).

By the way, don't be surprised if you have the urge to blame the other person *and* feel guilty at the same time. Ambivalence is the hallmark of separation and divorce. Sometimes, after a period of finger-pointing, you finally get in touch with your role of responsibility; then, you go overboard, dousing yourself in a shower of "if only's" and "what if's." Either way, you lose. You're suspended in time, as fall guy or betrayer. Either way, the process of healing is thwarted.

Guilt is as damaging to kids as blame. In a hundred little ways, a guilty parent does penance for breaking up the family—by buying the kids too much, not putting the brakes on when they get out of control. You just don't know how to say "no." The so-called Disneyland Dad (or Mom) Syndrome is rooted in guilt. But you can't compensate for a child's emotional losses with expensive toys, extravagant outings, or by allowing kids too much slack. In fact, you'll compound the damage. Children need parents to set limits and to create what my good friend and colleague New York City family therapist Ron Taffel refers to as an "empathic envelope": an invisible safety net that holds kids and makes them feel secure.

Guilt also stops you from being able to talk to the children about divorce. "I sidestepped the kids' questions, because I couldn't bear to talk about it," admits Gail Winsor, whose ten-year-old son started becoming aggressive in school about six months later. "My daughter, who was three years older, seemed better able to handle it; maybe she talked to her friends. He was always more close-mouthed." The school counselor set Gail straight: "She told me that I'd better start looking at *my* issues, because otherwise I'd never be able to deal with my son's. The therapist she sent me to helped me realize how horribly guilty I felt. I finally saw I didn't end the marriage on my own, even though I said the words." The more the mother was able to put her own issues into perspective, the more available she was to her both her kids.

"There was nothing good about him/her or our marriage." (BITTER-NESS)   This kind of negative thinking not only poisons you, it also contaminates the children who feel the tug of conflicting loyalties. They—especially boys—often identify with the absent parent. Beryl Cohn, who railed on endlessly about her "no-good" ex-husband, also compared her teenage son to him whenever the boy argued with her. Finally, her son screamed at her, "Don't tell me how much I remind you of Dad—you *hate* him!"

Luckily, Beryl was ready to really "hear" her son's comment. She reassured the boy that she had been under such stress, both emotionally and financially, that she wasn't thinking clearly. "I'm ashamed to admit, but it was easier to blame his father than to take responsibility for changing my own life." Talk about swallowing a bitter pill!

Bitterness can be ameliorated when you focus on positive aspects of your divorce: No more late-night arguments, no more second-guessing your spouse's motives. If you married young, this may be the first time that you're truly in touch with your own identity. You have time to pursue interests that your spouse never liked, to take a course, to sit and read quietly.

"I'll get him/her for this!" (ANGER AND REVENGE)   She's afraid of being exploited; he's afraid of being a wimp. She withholds information about the children or, worse, stops him from seeing them; he withholds money. No one wants to let go of the rope in this tug-of-war. Even in the age of "no-fault" divorce, adversarial lawyers often feed the fury, inspiring clients to cite "reasons" why the marriage ended; why he or she is a bad person, and, therefore, why he shouldn't see the kids so much or why she doesn't "deserve" so much money.

Anger may seem like your best friend. It comforts. It makes you feel good; it certainly feels better than vulnerability. But anger and revenge can also propel you on a destructive course that cripples you and maims your children:

Because she couldn't admit to—or let go of—her anger, Elena Costos became what family therapist and divorce mediator Isolina Ricci calls a "junkie"—a person who is hooked on anger, depression, grief, blame, guilt, hostility, revenge, or any strong feeling that keeps her obsessed with her ex-partner. Ricci explains, "A junkie doesn't work out the feeling in safe or structured ways; he or she wants to keep the [negative] feeling."

Elena now realizes that going back to court to deny her ex-husband five extra days a month with his children was simply a matter of rage: "I just wanted to win—not because another custody arrangement was better for the kids. My anger was something I couldn't just stop."

Whether it's anger from the past or rage tied to your marriage, the feelings bubble up inside—unless you find positive ways of releasing them. Some parents discover that it's far better to channel the anger into other areas. Tony Palumbo took up acting. Harold Silverman pedaled his way to marathon bicycling after his divorce, and Dorrie Murphy became a racquetball player. Evelyn Kravitz, who took long drives to let off steam and sort through the pain, said she found herself screaming one minute and laughing the next. And some simply cry a lot, which Judith Wallerstein notes, "reduces the anger to human size."

It doesn't matter if you're the leaver or the left. "I had a lot of anger," admits Arlene Steinberg, who divorced her college sweetheart, Peter Levine, when their kids were three and five. At first, Arlene's anger was funneled into her new relationship—the guy she left Peter for. When that relationship ended because of Arlene's temper, she knew she finally had to deal with her rage. "I went into therapy. I joined encounter groups. I screamed; I pounded pillows! Today, I feel like I finally know how to express my anger." (See also "Dealing With the Anger," pp. 79–84 and "How to Manage Conflict," pp. 86–88.)

Also, think of it this way: "getting" the other person always works against co-parenting. Rather than give in to her own selfish impulses, Yvette Hoving, a psychotherapist in New York City who divorced when her son was five, says, "The day Bart walked out of the house I said to myself, the only way I'm going to make sure this boy has a father is if I put away my anger. I allowed myself to be angry at Bart in private, but not around my son." Yvette adds, "Fortunately, I had a former husband who was very devoted to his son, but if I had acted out the anger, he would not have come around too frequently. I can see where some men can be driven away."

You may want to obliterate your ex, but your children love him or her. A good exercise might be to weave your worst fantasy in intricate detail—he is jilted by his new love, she loses her job or for some other reason suffers tremendous financial losses, she contracts some dread disease, he dies. Now, after reveling in your fantasy, imagine for a few minutes the effect it would have on your children. If that doesn't silence that little revenge devil who sits on your shoulder, you're not making your children a priority.

"I'm going to be financially devastated." (FEAR)   "Money is the root

of much of if not all evil in divorce," observes Marcia Lebowitz, M.S.W., director of the Children's Divorce Center in Woodbridge, Connecticut. Money problems resonate throughout the dissolution of a marriage, during divorce, and often long afterward. Next to anger, squabbling over money is at the top of the list of factors that inhibit the development of a cooperative co-parenting relationship (see pp. 199–204); often, in fact, the two are intertwined.

The Pisanos' divorce process was initiated in 1989, when Marjorie told Nick that she had retained a lawyer. For the past four years, they had been seeing a marriage counselor, so Nick was "devastated" when he realized that Marjorie was serious about ending their twenty-year marriage. The couple, whose life together had all the middle-class trappings of success—he was a dentist, she a full-time mother who was active in the community—agreed that they would do whatever they could to protect their three children and to keep their feelings about each other separate from their parenting responsibilities. But money kept getting in the way—money for the lawyers, money for additional counseling, money for a mediator, money for filing fees every time their lawyers went to court, money for photocopying financial records. "It disrupts everything," says an anguished Nick, three years later and still not legally divorced, even though he and Marjorie have already spent $17,000 in legal fees!

Both men *and* women fear financial devastation after divorce—and with good reason: *It costs, on the average, 30 percent more than your family income to set up two new households.* Women more often feel the pinch. Professor Lenore Weitzman, a sociologist at Harvard University, found that in the first year after divorce, women with young children experience a 73 percent decline in income, compared to a 42 percent increase in their husband's standard of living!

Although some dispute such a gross inequity, pointing out that Weitzman's northern California sample was extremely small and the study conducted before new child support laws were enacted, other studies done since that time also have found that many women are forced to cut back financially after divorce. Some also have to go to work for the first time, or increase the number of hours they put in. In pressing economic times, however, so do many men, especially those who are shouldering even partial expenses of a second family and who are conscientious about paying child support—as the majority of dads who co-parent are.

It's not easy to put money fears in perspective, but it's crucial for children that you do so. Arguments about money have a devastating effect on them. When they hear "Where's the child support?" or "How do you expect me to pay for Johnny's school clothes?" kids are likely to feel guilty ("They wouldn't fight if it weren't for me.") and rejected ("Daddy must not care enough about me if he doesn't want to pay for my clothes."). Fighting about money probably won't change the dismal financial reality of your divorce, but it will change your children's perspective forever. Children of divorce report that insecurity about money plagues them long into adulthood.

"He/she is not hurting as much as I am." (SELF-PITY)   Granted, divorce is usually not a mutual decision. At the outset, the one who is left feels abandoned, enraged, shocked, or all of the above. The initiator feels guilty, and it *seems* as if he or she is in better shape, especially if there's a new love interest waiting in the wings. But, after a year, researchers observe, you often can't tell who the "injured" party is.

Neil Kalter points out, "The one who has had his or her pride and sensibilities most wounded generally has a harder time in the beginning, but it's simpleminded to think that the one who leaves or the one who does the filing will have fewer problems."

It also depends on *when* you look at a divorcing couple. Kalter offers a composite case in which the man has an affair, and his wife files for the divorce. When he first moves out, he may be feeling a bit guilty and "trying to be fair" to his wife. To an outsider, at that point, the man might seem like the stronger, less-wounded party.

"The balance flips the other way," notes Kalter, when the couple tries to work out the details. She ups the ante by asking for more money (because she thinks he "owes" her for what he did), and suddenly he begins showing signs of emotional stress. Enraged, he then sues her for custody, knowing that will wound her. In the thick of it, both partners are hurting in their own way.

Furthermore, several studies indicate that in general, women find the initial separation and earlier stage of divorce more painful than men, whereas men's adjustment problems tend to crop up further down the line. This may be because of their different vulnerabilities. Economic issues are usually a struggle for women, whereas "social dependency tends to be more of a man's problem," contends clinical psychologist Marla Isaacs, author of *The Difficult Divorce*. Children frequently get the fallout from both.

If you believe your ex is "better off" than you are, take another look. You're bound to see that although he or she may be functioning efficiently in certain areas, you're more competent in others. More importantly, *keep the focus on yourself.* Give yourself "assignments," and take small steps. For example, if you're deficient in the social arena, start by reaching out to just one new person, or join a group; you only have to commit to going once. If your finances are bleak, jot down five strategies that might improve your situation—get advice from a person more knowledgeable about money than you are, write a new résumé, start saving five dollars a week—and, for openers, do one item on your list. When you begin to concentrate on where *you* have to go, where the other parent is won't seem half as important.

"My lawyer will take care of everything." (A RESCUE FANTASY)   Abdicating responsibility to a professional—or to your parents or a new significant other—might feel like a quick and easy way out of the pain. Dan Barron, a divorced father who had been involved in a bitter custody dispute for many years, confided to an audience of newly divorcing parents in Los Angeles: "My attorney is handling my divorce; my accountant tells me what kind of financial shape I'm in; and my therapist says I'm depressed. I used to have this fantasy that someone would go to court for me and tell me how I did!"

Because men and women usually have different vulnerabilities after divorce, their fantasies often differ, too. A man is more apt to long for a new partner who will take care of him and his children—an instant new family. And a woman thinks "the answer" is money—with or without the man to go with it, which is why a lawyer who holds out the promise of a huge financial settlement is immensely appealing to so many women. In reality, when these fantasies must end, most women are disappointed by their financial settlement, among other reasons because no amount of money can buy confidence and self-esteem. And when men remarry to fill the void, many quickly discover that living out the dream only means trading old problems for new, more-complicated ones.

Nip such delusions in the bud by recognizing them for what they are and by concentrating on your self-esteem. Divorce has been known to make the strong appear weak, the healthy sick, the emotionally stable unbalanced. The best "medicine" is realizing that you can stand on your own. Of course, when you're despondent or perpetually anxious, it's hard to remember that adjectives like "energetic" and "enterprising" could have once been used to describe you, and it's hard to believe that you'll ever feel or seem that way again. So, let good friends be your mirror for a while; see yourself through their eyes.

If you put your mind to it, you have the ability to rescue yourself. Barry Hubert admits that it took him several years. "I felt that the only way to make it all right for my kids was to put another woman in the family." Several bad relationships later, he realized what all who cling to rescue fantasies must come to terms with: *He* had to be his own savior. Until he worked through his anger about the end of the marriage and his insecurities as a parent, nothing (and no one) could make him feel better or improve his relationship with his children.

"I'm all alone in this." (ISOLATION)   People rarely *have* to be alone after divorce. They choose it. When Margaret Daly walked out on her husband after a thirty-year marriage and moved into her own studio apartment, she says of family and friends, "No one called for two years. Everyone decided I wanted to be left alone." At the same time, Margaret admits, "I realize now, I never set them straight." Margaret felt guilty about leaving. She believed she "deserved" to be abandoned.

It's one thing to do as Dan Barron advises—"take control and responsibility for your own life"—it's another to seek support. When you're in the thick of separation and divorce, especially if you feel hurt and humiliated, you're positive that no one has ever felt this way or gotten *through* it and that no one wants to hear or see what it's like.

The jolt of rejection you have already experienced can make the idea of reaching out for help even more daunting. "That first year, I hardly went out. I'd get the kids off to school and go back to sleep," recalls Janis Moley, whose husband of thirteen years announced one day he'd "met someone else." He had been Janice's high school sweetheart, her whole life. Luckily, she finally realized she didn't have to be alone. She says she was "a zombie" when she walked into her first meeting of Parents Without Partners, a support group for single parents (see Resources, p. 319). "It was my ace in the hole."

"I'll never have a family again." (A CULTURAL STEREOTYPE)   Having grown up with the term *broken home* as a synonym for divorce, it's no wonder so many of us whose marriages end have the idea that we're missing a vital part. Think of the idioms we use, like "my better half." After divorce, you're not half a person, and the family doesn't self-destruct. A mother and a father and children still exist—except now they live in two households. The family "system"—the constellation of adults and children that combines to make up the whole—is simply rearranged to form a family apart.

"I had to rethink my childhood conception of family—build a new structure with the old ingredients," admits Yvette Hoving. "My childhood models were from my own family and the fairy-tale version." Yvette points out that if you look around today and count only families that fit the traditional mode, "that seems to make families an endangered species!"

More to the point, if parents see their family apart as a "real" family, so will the kids. And, believe it or not, the sooner you change *your* thinking on this one, the faster you will realize that a good life is indeed possible after divorce. Dawn Carver, whose parents divorced when she was four, can't remember anything other than life in a family apart, which is true of many children whose parents split up when they were young. "Having two homes, with one parent in each one, is just the way it is," she says matter-of-factly. Even older kids, like Adam Hartman, now in college, who groused that the traveling back and forth between two houses during high school was "a pain"—a common complaint among preteens and teens—agreed that the bottom line is to have *a family.*

"I'm absolutely fine—after all, I wanted this divorce." (DENIAL)   Divorce always involves a mourning period. As with Elisabeth Kübler-Ross's stages of death and dying, everyone goes through denial and isolation, anger, bargaining, depression, and, after they've traversed that terrain a few times, acceptance.

Thus, even if you feel you're "better off" without the other person and you quickly take steps to get yourself on track, it still takes time to achieve an "emotional divorce," which usually happens long after you're physically or even legally separated. Sure, some people have better coping skills to begin with—they call on family and friends for support, they get professional help when they feel "stuck," and they try not to let their feelings be inflamed by a legal inferno in which both are likely to be burned. Still, no one can dissolve a relationship, especially one with children, without feeling more than a twinge of regret and sorrow.

You may be good at hiding it—by throwing yourself into your work or social engagements, by immersing yourself in a new relationship. But you can't submerge your feelings forever. They often come out in insidious ways. You have accidents or get sick; you have trouble sleeping or concentrating; your appetite changes; you're short with people, particularly when they show *their* feelings. Unwittingly, you might also delay the legal process (holding on to that French provincial armoire in the living room may be a symptom of holding on to the past), or you may avoid being with your kids, who seem painful reminders of what was— and what might have been. Finally, the unfinished business of this divorce will also come up in your next relationship if you don't work on it now. Even worse, it will come up in the form of subtle back-stabbing and double messages that you give to your kids about the other parent (more about that in chapter 3).

Get a Life!

"When we separated I was forced to grow up—I had to learn to stand up on my own two feet," admits Barbara Palumbo, who was twenty-eight when she confronted Tony about his extramarital affair. At first, he promised to end it, but eventually Tony walked out on her. "The love just wasn't there anymore. I was hurt, devastated—all the cliché words. I had wanted the marriage to work." Still, Barbara knew she had to get on with her life. "I found things to concentrate my efforts on instead of sitting there pouting!"

That was twelve years ago. Today, Barbara sums up her healing quite simply: "I got a life! Once I could say 'I'm still a whole person with a life ahead of me,' I wasn't angry anymore."

The truth is, no matter what strategies you use to help yourself understand what went wrong in your marriage and get over the pain of your divorce, the best "medicine" is to get yourself out there, be with people—and get out of yourself. Introspection is fine, undoubtedly a necessary aspect of healing, but don't ruminate forever.

There's no such thing as a "road map" after divorce, but there are several avenues to getting a life:

Concentrate on finding out who you are.　If you married young, you may have gone on automatic pilot, playing the roles society laid out for a man or a woman, without really considering what you wanted out of life. Now is the time to reassess your identity and ask yourself the essential question, "Who am I?"

We all play many roles during our lifetimes. Right now you may be stuck in roles connected to your marriage (Wife/Husband) or the divorce process (Victim/Vengeful Ex). But continuing to play such roles not only holds you back, it also says nothing about who you are *today*. Take a step back. You will not always be A Divorcing Person. And in the infinite scheme of things, other roles you play—Loving Parent, Loyal Friend, Sociable Woman/Man, Career Person—will become far more important. If you have a consistent and reliable picture of yourself, you're better able to make decisions, withstand criticism, and adapt to change.

A study of midlife women's changes in the wake of divorce conducted by the National Center for Women and Retirement Research indicates that the process of divorce has an unexpected benefit, especially if a marriage of ten years or longer ends in midlife: Divorce can be a springboard for personal growth. It can help you mature into a more self-assured individual. Eighty-four percent of the women in the study said divorce led them to new feelings of achievement and self-confidence. "It's grow-up time after divorce!" exclaimed one of the women surveyed.

One woman, whose husband left her for a younger woman, began to see that she had never done anything with herself—or for herself—during her marriage. At first she wondered if "that would have made me a more interesting person to him," and therefore "saved" her marriage. But once she began to figure out what she wanted out of life, the woman realized that all that mattered was being interesting *to herself!*

One way to focus on who you are and what *you* value is to find a cause that you believe in. I have to credit Patricia Greshner-Nedry, a divorced and remarried writer in Santa Monica, who is now very active in the Stepfamily Association of America (SAA), for her "windmill" theory. It's based on the mythical Man of La Mancha, Don Quixote, who wanted to right the world's wrongs: "It's a way of asserting yourself and establishing a separate identity. I took on the U.S. Postal Service," says Patricia, explaining how she chose her particular "windmill" cause.

One day, the mailman just slipped a book Patricia had ordered under her fence, rather than making a second trip to redeliver it. Her dog got to the package before Patricia did and tore up the book. Patricia had found her windmill. "I really didn't care about the book—I just had to stand up for my rights . . . somewhere!" Telling the story, Patricia notes that she has heard similar windmill stories as a peer counselor for SAA. "One woman I know went to school to defend another woman's child!"

Reading books might help, too. If ever there was a time to sample self-help literature that can help you take your emotional pulse, it is now. Several parents say they were guided and made more hopeful by reading books about relationships, family dynamics, grief, negotiation, motivation, and change (for recommended reading, see Resources, p. 319).

"I've never been in therapy," says Tony Palumbo. After his divorce, he schooled himself in acting techniques and says, "It helped me get in touch with who I am—and that took the emphasis off what was 'out there,' so to speak." Tony also started listening to motivational tapes and reading books, and he makes a very important point about self-help techniques. "I didn't just listen to them, I experimented—I put the ideas into action. You can listen or read all day, and if you don't *do* anything, what the hell's the difference?"

Mend your body, as well as your soul. Research bears out that divorce takes a physical toll. A person who is in a constant state of anxiety, ruminating on the past or dreading the future, is more prone to develop "nervous" conditions like headaches, ulcers, and skin rashes. Somehow, though, tending to such ailments or even taking care of the basics seems like one responsibility too many!

"My teeth needed cleaning, but I never felt I had time to get to the dentist. And I suddenly got 'too busy' to run every morning. Eventually, I stopped all together," admits a woman whose marriage fell apart over her husband's alcoholism. "Shortly before we broke up, I joined Alanon [a self-help program for families and friends of alcoholics], and I had seen a therapist a few times, but as soon as the divorce got in full swing, I felt I didn't have the time or money to indulge myself."

If you lose or gain an inordinate amount of weight, if you don't function at your usual energy level, or if you're constantly tired, pay attention. What seems like "self-indulgence" may be a matter of survival. And in the face of so much that you *can't* control—how long the legal process actually takes, what your ex will do next, your family's disapproval—you can at least be vigilant about the things you *can* control. Go to a doctor, if necessary, or just take better care of yourself. Don't ignore little aches and pains until your entire system goes haywire. Only you can accurately gauge what's "normal" for you—which is why it's so important for you to tune in to yourself and to know what you need and want.

This may also be a good time to invest in an exercise videotape, go to a gym or health club, take up a new sport, or renew your interest in an old one. You might also consider investigating meditation, yoga, or other mind-body disciplines.

Rethink your career options. This is particularly important for women, because their financial security can be shattered by divorce. Don't wait until your legal divorce is finished to make career decisions, find work, or change jobs, even though a lawyer might advise you to "look poor" on paper. The longer you keep a low financial profile, the longer it takes to build up economic reserves after divorce. Groups such as the Displaced Homemakers Network and the National Association for Female Executives offer career counseling, job training, and networking opportunities (see Resources, p. 331). Throwing yourself into a new job or taking steps to advance your career by going back to school also helps redefine your identity. "It got me out there, feeling different about myself," said a woman who revived an ailing career in journalism after she got tired of making a career out of being A Divorcing Woman! "For the first time, I felt as if I was worth something—not just as a wife and mother."

Broaden your interests. Take a course. Build a tree house. Read those books about Chinese history that you've always been meaning to get to. Enroll in a lecture series. Go to the theater. Learn how to play a new sport. "Even though I had never played racquetball in my life, I joined a women's racquetball league," recalls Dorrie Murphy, forty-two. "That first year I got the Worst Player award!" But Dorrie, who had kept her true self under wraps for the nineteen years she had been married, got another kind of prize when she immersed herself in this new interest: the joy of living her own life. "I'd bring Micky with me to the club, and he'd play with the other mothers' kids, and I'd take whirlpools and have lunch—I felt like a person for the first time in my life."

Join a support group—or start one. Divorce often separates you from family and friends. In Barbara Palumbo's case, she had done a lot of socializing with Tony's big Italian family. After the divorce, when they stopped calling, too, the loss seemed even more profound ("It felt like an arm was cut off"). About a year later, however, Barbara's mother showed her an article about Parents Without Partners looking for members. Barbara filled the social void in her life by throwing herself into the new, struggling chapter.

Within a month, she was elected chapter president; she helped to bring her group from seventeen members to more than four hundred. She met new friends there, of course, but she ended up getting a lot more than the new social life she was looking for: "I was able to look at myself in the mirror and say, 'My God! There *is* something you can do! You can be successful—you're not a total failure.' That gave a tremendous boost to my sense of self-worth."

Some divorced parents get this kind of support from self-help groups modeled on the "twelve-step" philosophy of Alcoholics Anonymous. Helen Rogand notes that attending meetings of Alanon helped her understand her "control issues." When she feels as if she's losing this important perspective, she remembers AA's Serenity Prayer:

> *God grant me the serenity to accept the things*
> *I cannot change, the courage to change the*
> *things I can, and the wisdom to know the*
> *difference.*

Like 15 percent of the parents I surveyed, she says that sharing her situation with people going through similar trials allowed her to take a step back and see her situation more clearly. "They taught me I can't change anyone except me." Helen, who often counsels women going through the process, adds, "Healing after divorce takes longer if you hold on to the control and try to change what you can't change." The antidote is a healthy awareness of your own identity and an increasing sense of independence. "My need to control was tied into my low self-esteem. I had no feelings of control over my life, so I tried to control everyone else's."

Author Vicki Lansky didn't join a support group—she created one. On the first Father's Day she knew she was going to be alone, she made lots of phone calls: "I just invited every single mother I knew, and everybody they knew." The group, FDW—Fabulous Divorced Women—met monthly that first year. They had some laughs—especially over their Superman-inspired FDW T-shirts—but they also had a more serious agenda: healing. "It was kind of like group therapy. We'd go around the room, and as each person talked, we all learned from one another."

Sometimes support groups create themselves. In the late seventies, Phyllis Diamond was a divorced mother with a four-year-old son living in New York City. Hungry for the company of others who had been through similar experiences, she thought that a few impromptu social gatherings of single parents might help ease the loneliness of her new life. She promptly discovered that Kindred Spirits, as she called her group, provided the social nourishment she longed for. "It became a lifeline for me," remarks Diamond. "It's a lot easier when you're not alone—and single parents can offer a lot of comfort to one another when there's no longer a spouse to rely on." The group started informally, with Sunday-morning brunches, blossomed into sharing summer houses and winter retreats, and, in time, became an ongoing social and educational program for divorced parents sponsored by the Ninety-second Street YMHA.

Barry Hubert, an early member of Kindred Spirits, remembers those first few get-togethers. "When I met those people, it was wonderful. They were co-parenting, too, so I felt supported and, most important, it felt like what I was doing was normal."

With the explosion of self-help programs during the eighties, support groups for virtually every malady or life situation became much more plentiful, including groups for divorce. Such groups now range from worldwide organizations like Parents Without Partners to a wealth of local divorce groups like Kindred Spirits, church- and synagogue-affiliated groups, as well as those sponsored by family centers. Look in the local paper or your phone book, or ask friends who have been divorced. Some groups are pointedly social, sponsoring dances and lectures for parents, picnics, Saturday afternoon movies, and other family outings. And some have a more therapeutic bent. Decide what you need and go for it!

Get involved.   Not surprisingly, divorce support groups have a big turnover. As people heal, they tend to move on. According to Dawn Aikens, the director of Kindred Spirits after Phyllis Diamond retired, women tend to stick around longer than men (many of whom come mainly to fill the social void). Some people do continue their affiliation with a support group even after they have passed the crisis stage or they've gotten involved in new relationships, because they reap other benefits: it's gratifying to know they can guide a newcomer through this difficult transition, and it also helps them gauge their own progress.

Such involvement need not be centered on divorce. Be a volunteer in your child's school. Participate in activities at a community center, a church, a synagogue. Teach reading to someone who is illiterate. There are plenty of good causes out there to which you can give your time. Helping others takes the focus off yourself and shines a spotlight on the many who in fact are less fortunate than you. In short, if getting out is good, and getting out of yourself is better, then volunteerism—helping people who can't get out or can't help themselves—is often best.

Get professional help. If you can't get a grip on what's happening and sift through your feelings on your own (or with a little help from your friends), you might consider professional intervention. Impartial eyes and ears can sometimes help you get through the rough spots. Of my respondents, nearly half named individual therapy (25 percent) or family therapy (20 percent) as factors that enabled them to take responsibility for their part in the postdivorce conflict, taught them how to de-escalate the battles, and helped them shape and maintain the co-parental relationship.

Certainly, not everyone *needs* postdivorce counseling or therapy, but for some, it simplifies, even speeds, the process. Therapy doesn't have to be long or extremely costly. And in the long run, advice from a competent therapist, counselor, or other type of mental-health expert can save you a lot of heartache. The earlier the intervention, the more efficient it is—emotionally and financially. Many family centers throughout the country specialize in divorce counseling and provide services on a sliding scale. Some of these are private, run by psychotherapists (usually clinical social workers or psychologists); others are government-supported arms of local family courts, which sometimes are known as conciliation courts. Schools, Y's, and community centers may offer helpful services for divorced parents and children too. Family therapists are often better prepared to handle divorce issues than other types of mental-health professionals, who are taught to help individual clients deal with problems. In contrast, family therapists are trained in "systems" thinking—that is, to look at the family as a whole. Rather than dwelling on what's going on inside one person's head, they focus primarily on the space *between*—that is, the relationships among the cast of characters in the family drama, regardless of whether everyone is actually in the room. Not just your current family, either. A good family therapist can help you see those all-important connections between your experiences as a child and the choices you make as an adult.

Whatever type of therapist you choose, make sure he or she is familiar with family dynamics and the process of divorce. Equally important, pick someone to whom you can relate comfortably, someone who can recognize and respect your concerns. Remember, too, that gender, ethnic background, and values come into the room with any type of professional and may influence that person's perceptions of you and what you're going through.

Make a symbolic gesture.   Family therapists sometimes encourage clients to create a ritual that will help them achieve closure. Betty Carter told one man literally to "bury a hatchet" in his backyard. She asked a woman, who had been legally divorced for over a year, to build "a shrine" to her divorce—the court papers, her legal bills, the receipts she had so meticulously catalogued for her attorney. When it was all in front of her, the women realized it was time to let go emotionally, so she set her shrine on fire. (No one knows what she did with the ashes!)

Sometimes, people unconsciously create healing rituals. Mark became an avid rooftop gardener after our divorce; I'm sure that by ministering to his flowers, he also repaired something inside himself. I had a "Forty and Free" birthday party which, though I didn't realize it at the time, was a way of celebrating my new status. At the suggestion of her therapist, another woman had a "house-cooling party," inviting family and friends over to "give the house new energy" after her husband moved out. A third, a family therapist who had "prescribed" rituals to many of her clients, had a "divorce party" at her new house and invited her ex-husband! "It let our network of family and friends know that no one had to take sides. We were talking to each other, so no one had to feel polarized." (It's also where her ex-husband met his next wife!)

Set your family straight—and your friends, too.   Parents who divorce or are in the process usually beat themselves up for one thing or another. No need to let other people use you as a punching bag, too. Even if you are well on your way to healing, others—especially parents and other older-generation family members who didn't have any experience with divorce in their day—may not be ready to acknowledge your new status. "Divorce was something that happened to someone else, according to my parents," recalls Steve Posner. "My family took it very hard, and they felt that for Brian's benefit we should have stayed married."

Similarly, Loretta O'Brien's family was appalled. "I was the first one in my family to ever get a divorce. My mother thought it was horrible." Loretta realized that the sooner she set her parents straight the better. "I told them that I hadn't planned on getting divorced when I got married. But now that it was inevitable, I was at least going to make our divorce work—and that meant making sure the kids still saw Bill."

Sometimes you may have to cut certain "well-meaning" friends out of your life—or at least tell them to keep their opinions to themselves. Evelyn Kravitz, a fifty-two-year-old woman whose husband suddenly abandoned their twenty-two-year marriage, saw her own situation quite clearly. Despite her pain and the deep feelings of betrayal she felt when Arthur left, she silenced anyone who tried to "console" her by telling her what a louse she'd been married to. "I resented it, and I'd tell them, 'I spent all those years and had three children with that man, and if you call him a jerk, then I'm a jerk for having stayed so long!' "

Have a fling.   Kept in it's proper perspective (and not used as an escape fantasy), a new relationship can be just what the doctor ordered. "Nothing helps an adult as much as a good love affair!" agrees Judith Wallerstein. A vital caveat goes along with that suggestion: Try to resist the natural urge to idealize the new relationship or to start planning another wedding! At first, it will undoubtedly seem as if your new lover is everything that your ex was not. But once you get beyond the "romance" stage, every relationship takes work. "Take what you have learned from your first relationship, so you don't repeat it," counsels Wallerstein.

That may be hard if you dive into a rebound relationship without doing your postdivorce emotional homework.

Be the best parent—and co-parent—you can be.   Believe it or not, being a responsible, mature parent and having the mind-set to co-parent *will* help you heal from the trauma of your divorce. "When parents start to deal with their children, it has a stabilizing effect," says Judith Wallerstein. "And there's an immediate payoff. When they put in the time, they can protect their children." Besides, Wallerstein points out, the opposite tack takes its toll on a parent. "After all, nothing is more upsetting to parents than to see a child going to pieces."

Comparing the experience of 201 divorced families in which parenting was shared with 194 families in which the mother was sole custodian, the 1984 Toronto Shared Parenting Project indicates that co-parents are also more likely to take responsibility for their own behavior, which is imperative for getting through the fire. The co-parents in the Toronto study were less likely to feel guilty over the breakdown of the marriage than sole-custodian parents (46 percent compared to 61 percent) and more likely to indicate that the decision to separate was mutual (37 percent compared to 25 percent).

In the 1988 Joint Custody Study Project, forty-eight joint-custody families from all walks of life in the greater San Francisco Bay Area and their sixty-seven children were examined a year after the legal divorce. Each adult and child was assigned to one of three adjustment groups—the parents being classified as "successful," "stressed," or "failed," and the children as "doing well," "stressed," or "at risk." The parents who were judged "successful" were able to cooperate and make decisions concerning their kids with a minimum of conflict; they also felt good about the arrangement. They probably felt good about themselves, too, because the vast majority of their children fell into the "doing well" category—and those who didn't were only moderately "stressed." The researchers concluded, "[Those] parents could focus on their [children's] needs and concerns while working to resolve the ambivalent feelings from the marriage."

The experiences of cooperative co-parents in other studies mirror those of co-parents interviewed for this book. As a whole they are able to coordinate plans and to get along well with one another and to make parenting decisions jointly. They report "very extensive" involvement in child rearing. And while many parents recall incendiary incidents, when it is necessary for them to act on their children's behalf, they usually are able to put on the brakes and deal with the matter at hand.

This point is crucial, the foundation on which the rest of this book rests: *Cooperative co-parenting can help children withstand the hard knocks of divorce.* You may not believe that it's possible, especially if you're still floundering in the aftermath of your divorce. You may have to grit your teeth and act "as if"—as if you really are capable of cooperating with your ex-spouse on a mature level (see page 148). And miraculously, modifying your behavior also changes your attitude.

Yvette Hoving says that when she and her husband of eleven years split up, "I kept talking to myself, saying, I messed up my own life. I'm not going to mess up my son's life any more than I have to. He did *not* ask for this. He was guaranteed a mother and a father when he came into this world, and *I* broke the contract."

It's your job to reassure your children—by your actions, as well as with words—that even though these are tough times, you're strong enough to be there for them. Most important, Sally Brush says, promise your kids *two* parents after the divorce: "The best help parents can give children is to let them know that each parent deserves a space in their lives. Both parents have to work to make that happen."

The best way to reassure your children is to spend time with them. "That doesn't mean taking them to Disneyland or to see a Muppet extravaganza," points out Ron Taffel. Spend quality "moments," says Taffel, by doing simple, everyday things with your child. Read her a story at bedtime, have a chat while she's taking a bath, ask him to help you with a project (one you really need help with, not just busywork and not a regular household chore). Be with the child—and let him be. Don't try to make it a therapy session in which you constantly explain, teach, or try to excavate your child's feelings. Just spend time.

This can be particularly hard if your co-parenting schedule

gives you less time than you'd like, which may happen because your child is young and you've both determined that she needs a "home base," or because you and your ex live too far away from each other to share time almost equally. Even though you know that the arrangement is based on what's best for the child, you still might feel lonely and cheated. And it's only natural that you'll want to try to make every moment count. The truth is, just by being emotionally stable and a dependable force in your child's life, you *are* making every moment count.

Even when life seems bleak, remember that your children learn from your every move. "Kids imitate instability," says Neil Kalter. "When things go bad, you have an option of sitting around—or you do something about it." Having watched their parents triumph over difficult times, says Neil Kalter, children of divorce often learn a very valuable lesson. As young adults many of these kids look back on their parents' experience as one that gave them a greater sense of responsibility. They are more mature and better able to deal with life's hard knocks, says Kalter. "They think of themselves as more realistic—not dewy-eyed kids. And the girls certainly will protect themselves better economically."

So if, in the thick of the legal process, you're inundated with details, overwhelmed by emotions, and confused by the changes in your life, it helps to think of yourself as a shining example and to remember that your kids *need* you to be in good shape. The bottom line is that even on days when it's tough to get out of bed, look at your children. You'll see the best reason to get on with your life.

— 3 —

GROWING UP AFTER DIVORCE

Key #2: Act Maturely

A Television Healing

Have you ever wondered why people who are fighting with each other would agree to appear on a TV talk show to air their dirty laundry? I found out by interviewing members of the Farrell/Brown/Wilson clan, who credit their much-improved relationships to an appearance on "Good Morning America." (Follow the diagram below to keep the players straight.)

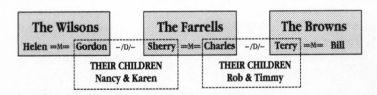

The Wilsons	The Farrells	The Browns
Helen ==M== Gordon –/D/–	Sherry ==M== Charles –/D/–	Terry ==M== Bill
THEIR CHILDREN Nancy & Karen	**THEIR CHILDREN** Rob & Timmy	

KEY: ==M== MARRIED   –/D/– DIVORCED

Charles and Terry couldn't even talk to each other, let alone cooperate as co-parents. Charles was bitter because Terry had fallen in love and was planning to marry Bill Brown. The first summer after their separation, he insisted that Rob, thirteen, and Timmy, eleven, live with him; he then decided to fight for custody. Feeling guilty and worn out by their battles, Terry finally agreed. "I never thought he'd actually *keep* them."

But he did—and moved four hundred miles away with his new wife, Sherry* and her daughters, Nancy and Karen, eleven and seven. Sherry's ex-husband, Gordon Wilson, had left her for Helen, who had never been married. Perhaps because she, too, got involved with someone else fairly quickly, Sherry says that despite "a few disagreements" with Helen, she and Gordon were able to co-parent fairly well almost immediately—to communicate civilly with each other and to make joint decisions about their daughters' welfare.

Meanwhile, the relationship between Terry and Charles continued to deteriorate. Terry admits, "It had gotten to the point that Bill and Sherry [the respective stepparents] were the only ones who could talk and make arrangements for our kids." Terry was miserable about her decision to relinquish custody. She missed the boys desperately and feared that their father and stepmother were turning them against her. Heartsick and tortured by the implications of being "a mother who gave up her children," she wrote angry letters, begging Rob and Timmy to come back to her. The boys just happened to leave her letters lying around the house. Reading them, Charles and Sherry viewed Terry as unstable; clearly, Rob and Timmy were better off with their father.

Not surprisingly, the girls, Nancy and Karen, seemed to be doing okay in the new "Brady Bunch" arrangement, but Rob and Timmy were floundering in the wake of their parents' battles, especially Timmy, the younger one; he was getting into trouble in school and becoming increasingly hostile toward his stepmother.

It was at that point, five years after Terry and Charles split up, that the producers of GMA were looking for "families like us who would actually go on the show and have counseling," explains Terry. An entire week of program time would be set aside to air portions of their session. Thus, on a cold Monday in December, the Browns came to New York from Idaho, the Farrells from North Dakota, the Wilsons from California.

Once the videotape cameras started rolling, they were off and

*Even though these are pseudonyms, in real life, Charles's two wives' names also rhymed!

running. Sherry remembers, "The minute the therapist asked, 'What's going on here?' Charles jumped right in, talking about the letters and how he thought Terry was trying to sabotage his parenting efforts. "The issue didn't matter—we just needed to get the feelings out."

And to hear each other's perspective. Terry told the story from hers: "I thought everyone was going to look down on me, because here was this mother who let her sons go live with their dad. I was still living with the feelings of guilt. I grew up in an era where you just don't do that." When the therapist acknowledged just how painful it must have been to give up her sons, Terry broke down—in front of fifty million TV viewers.

"Sherry looked at me and said, 'If I had had to give up my daughters, it would have killed me.' Suddenly, I thought, *My god! She's a human being! She understands how I feel.*' That was the first time I looked at her as another woman—not just my sons' stepmother," admits Terry. "That's where it started changing for me. At the same time, they all found out that I wasn't a horrible monster either. I just wanted to spend more time with my kids."

Of all the sound bites, it was the kids' dialogue, particularly sentiments articulated by the boys, that had the most profound effect on the six parents: "You're scared . . . too scared to express feelings—you don't know what's going on," explained Timmy. "You just want to jump in a hole and have the ground cover you." His older brother added, "If you're in the middle, anything you do is going to hurt one of your parents."

"All those years of anger and hate don't just evaporate, but they were starting to go away. By the time we left New York, we were all feeling a lot different," recalls Terry. "We actually thought we weren't putting our kids in the middle," Terry remarks. "I'd like to take back everything we did in those days; I wish their younger years had been more pleasant." Today, four of the adults—Terry and Bill, Sherry and Charles—often conduct workshops for stepfamilies.

They are truly an example of what stepfamily experts Emily and John Visher call a "parenting coalition"—a committee of responsible adults who work together cooperatively and jointly look out for the children (more about parenting coalitions in chapters 8 and 10).

Why Children Need Us to Call a Truce

It's not their parents' divorce that upsets children; it's the ongoing conflict that threatens their world and diminishes their self-esteem. When parents battle with each other—verbally or physically, on the doorstep of one's home or via long-distance phone calls— children are always affected. This family was no exception; Rob and Timmy Farrell kept their pain locked inside them, behavior that is typical of children, especially boys, who don't want to do or say anything further to upset their parents. Timmy was having trouble in school, but he never asked for help: "My dad was unstable. I didn't think my problems were as bad as his."

The Farrells' TV awakening may seem dramatic, but other divorced parents recount similar episodes, related to health or behavior, that forced them to take off the gloves and focus on their children's welfare. Often, children unconsciously become red flags when their parents are in trouble.

The connection is clear: the family is an interrelated and inter- dependent "system," and when one of the parts of that system changes, breaks down, or is removed altogether, the other parts are affected, too. The child may be the "identified patient"—the one who evidences symptoms of the distress—but closer scrutiny reveals that the whole family is ailing; and the problems have simply trickled down from parents to kids.

All families are susceptible to this trickle-down phenomenon. Marital status aside, *adult problems affect children.* If parents argue or if one parent is depressed, loses a job, has an affair, or grapples with a substance-abuse problem, the kids feel it, too. Among the families I interviewed, the adult crisis just happened to be di- vorce—particularly ongoing conflict between the parents—that threw the whole system and all of its parts into utter chaos. In effect, when their parents rock the boat, the kids, feeling as if they're about to drown, often start to cry out for help—until someone tosses them a life preserver.

"It really affected her," admits a mother whose daughter was four when her parents declared war on each other. "She began to lisp, had nightmares and stomachaches, and she wet her bed." Another mother said that her children, then twelve and nine, were so fed up with their parents' behavior that they asked point-blank, "If you two can get divorced, why can't we?" So unsure were they about their parents, they figured that being their own parents was safer!

It's an indisputable axiom: *The longer we act like children, the more ways our own children will show (or tell) how much they need us to "grow up."* Certain kids are more resilient than others, but even the strongest will eventually wither under the strain if their parents aren't adult enough to call a cease-fire and travel the road to maturity. In fact, if we don't pay attention, kids' cries for help can translate into increasingly serious problems.

But a mature co-parenting relationship doesn't just happen. Even if both of you agree to cooperate about the children, arrangements rarely fall into place without a hitch. Money, lawyers, in-laws, friends, and your own ego often get in the way (and not necessarily in that order) . . . until you begin to act maturely which, in turn, enables you to put your children's needs, your emotions, your personal priorities, and the whole divorce process into perspective.

In this chapter we look at what it takes to get there and what pitfalls parents commonly encounter along the way. For some, the turning point is a sudden crisis; for others, a slowly evolving set of circumstances ushers in growth and change. Either way, given time and willingness, and with increasing maturity, these co-parents were finally able to focus less on their grievances and more on their children. Eventually, they learned to deal with their feelings, communicate with each other, and put legal and financial issues into a healthier perspective.

Turning Points I: Crises

Valerie Ford can pinpoint precisely when she and her ex-husband began to co-parent. She was standing in a hospital corridor with her ex-husband, Dave Gilbert, as their almost four-year-old son was being hoisted onto a cold, metal gurney. Helpless, she watched her little boy disappear behind the doors of an elevator that led into an operating room. When those elevator doors closed, Valerie knew that Johnny was more important than anything else in her life, and now his future would be decided by a high-powered microscope. In that moment, the fears, the jealousies, and the anger toward Dave began to melt away. "I said, 'What are we doing? This kid needs *both* of us to get through.'" Valerie and Dave collapsed into each other's arms. It was an important beginning.

Married for seventeen years, Valerie and Dave had been in a constant state of siege since separating a year and a half before. They each hired no fewer than three big-guns lawyers, who only inflamed and escalated their war. Valerie hoped Dave would drop off the face of the earth; he fervently wished the same about her. Bitterness aside, the only thing they had in common was their love for a towheaded little boy named Johnny, who was only two when the couple separated.

"We had the time, the money, and the inclination to fight over our child." Valerie, like many others, transformed by the passage of time and greater maturity, cringes a little when she remembers the crisis period surrounding her divorce. "We were awful to each other, and we were awful to our son. We weren't meeting his needs at all. We were only meeting our own selfish need to punish each other for all the hurts we thought we had suffered at each other's hands." And through it all, Valerie admits, "I, of course, thought *I* was the better parent."

Then one morning, Johnny came toddling into Valerie's bedroom and fell over. He couldn't walk. She rushed him to the family pediatrician. He sent her to a rheumatoid arthritis specialist who, in turn, referred her to a leukemia man. Yet another specialist, an orthopedic surgeon, finally took the X-ray that revealed a tiny, ominous shadow on Johnny's leg. The doctors told her Johnny's leg might have to be amputated.

Valerie and Dave's nightmare ended where their family apart began. When the surgeon emerged from the operating room several hours later and told them their son was going to recover, she says, "As he spoke, Dave and I realized that though we didn't want to be married, we both wanted to be the parents of that little boy!"

Over 15 percent of my respondents, like Valerie Ford and Dave Gilbert, noted on their questionnaires that "a particular incident or crisis" led to a significant change in the co-parenting relationship. One couple saw their situation in a new light when the woman was diagnosed with cervical cancer; another was forced to co-parent when their son had a manic-depressive episode. More often, however, the scenarios were not so spectacular.

Turning Points II: Evolutionary Awakenings

It's usually not *one* particular anything that inspires increasing maturity and converts battling spouses into cooperative co-parents but a rather unpredictable mixture of time and events that modifies the relationship and motivates parents to "have the guts to transcend our own craziness," as Charles Farrell put it. For three out of ten parents, "realizing my ex was 'good' with and for the children," helped them adopt a more grounded attitude toward the other parent. Twenty-seven percent said "a change in my ex's attitude/circumstances" made the difference. Patricia Davenport explained that her husband's anger toward her for initiating the divorce "miraculously" dissipated when she announced that she had no intention of "taking his children."

Predictably, an overwhelming 83 percent cited "the passage of time" as a key element in changing their co-parenting relationship. Time is not only a great healer; it allows you to view your situation from a new vantage point. When Bill Paterson saw that having a "successful divorce" could help him heal from the pain of an *un*successful marriage, he recognized the benefit of letting go of his animosity. Barry Hubert became aware of a shift in his attitude when he realized he was a good father. Tom Gorman was reassured because he saw that his ex-wife still needed him on one level: he often acted as a mediator between her and their son when the mother/son bond began to strain in the boy's teen years.

A number of respondents also noted that a milestone event, such as a birthday party or graduation, seemed to mark the beginning of more positive co-parenting. For me, Jennifer's Sweet Sixteen party was such a moment, but it was not the moment or the party *per se*. Five years had passed since our divorce; we had already co-hosted several birthday parties for our kids. But Jennifer's sixteenth was the first time I allowed myself to feel our connection and to give Mark a tentative hug. My eyes welled up as I admitted, "I guess we did *something* right." Such events can remind others, as it did Mark and me, that they are in this thing for the long haul—whatever they feel toward each other.

A pivotal point for Lana Berk was seeing sixteen-year-old Charlotte, her "baby," getting dressed up in a long gown: "Here she was, growing up to be a pretty young lady, going to her first prom. I had to call my ex." It had been almost a year since Lenny Berk had ended their twenty-six-year marriage, and, until that moment, their contact had been limited to angry phone calls and letters sent through their lawyers. "I called him and said, 'I think it's time we talked. But, also, what I really want is for you to see how beautiful your daughter looks in her prom dress.' " Touched by Lana's sensitive gesture, Lenny came right over. That special moment not only moved the warring couple toward peaceful co-parenting, it also inspired them finally to settle their legal divorce.

Mutual love for the children can be a most powerful healer. Sue Carver's comment captures the sentiments of many parents in my survey: "A love for my daughter and wanting her to have a close relationship with both parents necessitated my 'getting along' with my ex-spouse."

My respondents' experience closely mirrors the Toronto Shared Parenting Project, which found that although most parents wanted to share parenting and were satisfied with the arrangement, only about a third are able to do so immediately—without a hitch. For most, the process takes one to three years, given the proper motivation—and help: "Our children's happiness has been more important to each of us than being right. We were in family therapy after our separation, which helped lower the reactivity between us."

Undoubtedly, many whose turning points come sooner rather than later already have a repertoire of coping strategies that have served them well in other life crises. But even parents on somewhat shaky emotional ground when they first separate are able, in time, to inch their way along the road to maturity. A critical factor is what they do when they encounter some of the roadblocks that tend to work against a cooperative co-parenting relationship: anger, an inability to communicate, the legal process, and the influence of "well-meaning" outsiders.

Dealing with the Anger

Some parents are immediately able to recognize the importance of dealing with their anger: "My former husband and I were angry, and we didn't know how it would be, but we decided at the onset of our separation that our son was the most important person in our lives. We worked very hard from Day One to put aside our anger toward each other so that we could co-parent well together," says Yvette Hoving. Perhaps because Yvette is a family therapist who had seen the damaging effect of conflict on other people's children, she was inspired to act maturely in the wake of her divorce. Her husband's questionnaire indicated a similar willingness and wisdom.

For a variety of reasons, other parents take longer. Judith Wallerstein notes, "Years later, the love goes away, the longing goes away, but the anger has a capacity to endure because it wards off the hurt and humiliation." At the same time, nothing harms children or poisons a co-parenting relationship more than ongoing anger. So, if you don't take the time to examine these feelings and to find appropriate ways to vent them, you're likely to explode when you interact with your ex-partner, even though, admittedly, he or she probably deserves some of it!

Marla Isaacs has helped many warring couples work through their anger so that they can put their kids first. In *The Difficult Divorce,* she describes the two most common types of fighting styles: *Sporadic and scared* describes couples who periodically have fiery, furious, unproductive arguments that are punctuated by periods in which they attempt to avoid conflict by steering clear of each other and battling through the children. *Frequent and direct* fighters never let up on each other and, Isaacs says, "they seem to thrive on the very process of chronic frontal fighting." She believes that in both cases, arguments are easily incited and escalate quickly. And in both cases, the children suffer. Worse still, because the partners usually are not in touch with the underlying causes of their anger, the children are often the "subject" of their battles when, in fact, arguments only serve to cover up other issues that aren't being addressed.

Some people are able, on their own, to excavate what lies beneath the surface of their emotions; others seek out professional help, be it in individual or group therapy, postdivorce couples counseling, or a support group. "It's a matter of recognizing that a lot of the feelings come from your own personal problems—not your ex," admits Gabe Delaney, a father who says that therapy helped him see how his family background inhibited his communication in marriage and influenced what he was feeling after divorce. "Eventually you need to say, 'I'm an okay person; you're an okay person.' And if you really look at yourself, it allows you to have a better relationship."

With professional help or on your own, it's important to see how much incessant fighting hurts your kids and to look at what's driving your anger. Below are some therapeutic questions you can ask yourself. The goal is to understand *why* anger often leads away from relief and toward more pain, and to use your new understanding to work toward a healthier, more productive co-parenting relationship.

What's behind the anger you feel toward your ex?   Admittedly, there are many times, particularly in the initial stages of divorce, when you have lots to be angry about. Still, you might also be harboring an old grudge, rather than reacting to something happening at the moment. Are you still angry at him for all the years that, at least in your view, you tried to get him to talk about his feelings? Do you still resent the fact that for years, at least from where you sit, she seemed to value everyone else's needs before yours? Many of my respondents, given three to five years of hindsight, realize that some of their grievances date back to the early days of their marriage. They just swept them under the rug.

Also ask yourself who you were *before* you got married and what kinds of yellow-brick-road expectations you brought with you to the altar. You may be angry at your ex for letting you down. "There's always a prince," points out family therapist Florence Kaslow. "He used to come on a white horse, and now he comes in a white Jaguar or on a white motorcycle!" Kaslow also describes the counterpart fairy-tale scenario for men: "Even if some wicked witch turns him into a frog, when he meets his sweet princess, her kiss will break the spell and he will reemerge." From early on, says Kaslow, we are brought up to believe that when we get married, we'll be rescued. "Our fairy tales do not tell us how to live happily ever after—only that we're entitled to that expectation."

Anger can also camouflage other feelings—like sadness and fear. Sue Carver realized that fears and feelings of dependency were stopping her from moving ahead in her life, but they emerged in the form of anger toward her ex. Therapy helped her regain her confidence after they separated and strive toward independence. "I could not depend on someone else until I could be my own person." Another mother now realizes that she felt guilty for leaving the marriage—and very vulnerable. "I was the one who wanted out, and I was the one who cheated on him." She, like many others, let anger fly, because that's the emotion that *feels* best; it's strong and assertive—a perfect cover for other, more vulnerable feelings. And a father admitted, "I thought if I let myself really feel how sad I was, I'd be destroyed. It was better to rant and rave at her than to admit how scared I was."

To determine where your anger comes from, at the top of a piece of paper, write several headings: *My Ex Now, Historic Grudges, Present Grudges, My Expectations, My Fears,* and *Other Feelings.* Whenever your anger precipitates an argument with your ex or spills over onto the children, try to figure out where the rage really belongs. Ask yourself what—or whom—a particular conflict reminds you of. We all have feelings of déjà vu when we're angry; paying attention can yield very helpful insights. Sometimes you might use more than one heading per outburst! Add your own headings, if you need them. For instance, one of my pet peeves was the legal system, and I now realize that whenever I felt impotent with my lawyer, who was supposed to be supporting me, I had my worst arguments with Mark.

In the quiet after a storm, think about the accusations you hurled at your ex, and switch them into what Harriet Lerner, in *The Dance of Anger,* calls "clear, nonblaming statements." That is, instead of focusing on your partner's lack of consideration, self-ishness, neglect, meanness, or passivity, identify exactly what a certain behavior makes *you* feel and need. This isn't easy. But it's a step toward having a strong, well-defined sense of identity, which will ultimately enable you to disengage from unproductive fighting and, instead, concentrate on the important business of co-parenting.

Does your ex remind you of a parent whose critical voice still echoes in your head?   Although you may be legitimately angry at your ex-spouse, you also might have residual rage about abuse (real or perceived) that happened long before he or she came into your life. What was your relationship with your own parents like? Did you marry someone just like Mom or Dad? Unconsciously, you may have been trying to replay the drama of your early childhood, hoping that it would come out better this time. If so, the feelings you experience in divorce will be amplified. One woman recalls, "My father was very controlling, and whenever Stan started yell-ing, I felt like a five-year-old." This is not to say that her hus-band's criticism didn't bother her, but that it felt doubly intense because of her own history.

To gauge whether anger is rooted in the past, picture yourself as a child and recall interactions with your parents. Think about negative adjectives that you would use to describe your parents— cold, distant, explosive, critical, unpredictable, harsh, punitive, angry, depressed, pessimistic—as well as what kinds of words they might use to describe you. How many of the same traits also paint a picture of your ex? You may be surprised to discover that you unwittingly chose a marital partner with the same traits as one or both of your parents, who now helps you reenact those old scenes.

Are you projecting your own feelings onto your ex-spouse?   Often, a mate represents an aspect of oneself that has been "disowned" because parents thought it inappropriate ("That's no way to talk to your father") or because it wasn't socially acceptable ("Big boys don't cry"). In some marriages, for instance, the guy expresses all the anger and the woman does enough crying for both of them. Each is frightened and can't bear it when the other person expresses the disowned emotions. In divorce, she must learn how to feel her own anger, and he has to get in touch with his sadness. Otherwise, their conversations are bound to deteriorate into escalating emotional spirals, and it will feel safer to argue about money or the children, rather than confront themselves.

Make a list of what you like most about yourself; then make a list of what you like least. If many of your least-favorite traits describe your ex-spouse, you may need to work harder to take responsibility for your own feelings.

Is your anger hidden under a coat of self-righteousness?   Everyone has a different emotional style. Some people don't *appear* angry, but their actions are loud and clear. They convince themselves that they are not acting out of revenge—but out of justifiable outrage—when they label the other parent "crazy" or "unstable," warn the kids about his or her behavior, or keep them away from that parent altogether. Children can be deeply wounded by parents who act in this way . . . in the name of "protecting the children." The experts are unanimous: It is extremely harmful to badmouth or belittle the other parent; and except in the very rare cases in which a parent is extremely disturbed or violent, one parent is *never* justified in denying children access to the other.

Beneath the surface of righteous anger, you often find fear, competitiveness, dependency, or a combination of these feelings. If you feel insecure or overwhelmed, the other parent may loom as a threat. If you haven't worked on making a new, separate life for yourself, when children talk to or spend time with the other parent, you may fear that your ex is going to turn the kids against you or that they will never want to come back.

However, children are at grave risk when, out of righteous anger or dependency, a parent holds on too tightly, becomes overly solicitous, or, worse, makes a child (often, the oldest) a confidante and a co-parent (see pp. 116–118, for more on "paren-tifying" children). No child should be a substitute for a support-ing adult. It's perilous for you, too, because it prevents you from being with your peers, getting adult input, and developing a new social life and new interests.

To check the urge to belittle the other parent, Ron Taffel suggests keeping track of the snide comments you make—per-haps by keeping a log. Note how many times you bad-mouth your ex. Look at what else is going on inside you when you get angry. "If parents keep an honest list, they'll know how many times they say things that are genuinely for the children, how many are out of anger," notes Taffel. "And when you stop, you'll see the color come back to your kid's face!"

Clues from Your Marriage

Even if you're divorced, when you have children, there is no way around the fact that you still have to deal with your ex-spouse's views. That might seem overwhelmingly difficult. In fact, over a quarter of the co-parents in my survey checked "things that bothered you when you were married," among causes of conflict after the divorce.

"If you didn't like something about your ex when you were married," warns author and divorced mother Vicki Lansky, "you're certainly not going to change it when you separate!" The truth is, whatever ranked high atop Your Hit Parade of Pet Peeves when you were married—his sloppiness, her forgetful-ness, his temper, her control, his stubbornness, her laziness, his financial irresponsibility, her compulsive neatness—will probably be intensified a hundredfold after you separate.

"I have to mold my reaction to him," recognizes Nancy Blake whose ex-husband, Todd Dresdin, continues (in her view) his attempts to "bully" her. "When we were married, it was like the giant coming home—everyone quaked." Nancy has since become more assertive, but she concedes, "I have about as much chance of changing Todd as I do of changing the curve in my street. It's just that way; I have to accept that I can't do anything about it except steer the car!"

You can't control your ex-spouse's reaction, but you can look at how *you* usually react to differences of opinion. Because your old style of dealing with conflict probably got you nowhere most of the time, it's important to ask yourself:

Did I try to win? If every disagreement was seen as a conquest and every difference as an opportunity to reform, you weren't happy until you got the other person to do it or see it your way. You probably tried to solve disputes by bullying, dominating, or manipulating. In your marriage, you needed to feel that you were calling the shots, that you "won" or were "right." The problem with making everything a contest is that someone always loses.

Did I placate? If you tiptoed around hot spots and made concessions in order to avoid confrontation, you probably gave your "self" up. Your needs, your point of view, and your desires took a backseat to your spouse's—and that's no way to run a relationship!

Did I deny? If you pretended that his or her annoying habits didn't bother you, or that you didn't really disagree, you were probably adept at sidestepping confrontations. The problem with avoidance is that deep down inside, you're ready to explode. Meanwhile, the chasm between you continues to widen . . . until one day you turn into The Terminator!

Did I bargain? If every disagreement turned into *Let's Make a Deal* ("I'll do the dishes, if you vacuum and take the kids out on Saturday mornings"), you may have come up with temporary solutions, but you probably didn't deal with the underlying issue ("He thinks of himself as my helper when it comes to housework and the kids, but I'm always in charge"). With bargaining, everyone gives a little, but no one really gets what he or she needs.

You still may be using one of the above styles of conflict resolution to deal with postdivorce differences. But none of them will help you and your ex-spouse achieve a long-term postdivorce détente. You will need to learn to handle disagreements more productively. The following section will point you in the right direction.

Learning How to Manage Conflict

Most of us don't know how to express anger constructively, because *we never learned how.* A number of courses, workshops, and seminars throughout the country help couples learn how to argue, manage conflict, and problem-solve more effectively. The participants are typically married couples trying to salvage relationships and engaged couples or newlyweds who want to inoculate themselves against problems in the future. But why shouldn't people who divorce also learn how to argue constructively and how to avoid escalating spirals of conflict?

In a study conducted in 1991, Cheryl Buehler, a researcher at the University of Tennessee, looked at how divorced parents handle conflict. "People are scared of conflict; but in any social relationship, conflict is inevitable and natural," points out Buehler. It's how people *handle* conflict that makes the difference. "If parents get into a power struggle, it will manifest itself in everything from toothpaste to child support. They set themselves up to fail."

The good news is that throughout the country, conciliation-court counselors, family therapists, and other mental-health practitioners now recognize the importance of teaching *all* parents how to communicate, regardless of their marital status. Consider enrolling in a conflict-management or postdivorce parenting course with your ex (see Resources, p. 330). Broach the subject in a quiet moment—when you both realize that your fighting has got to stop because it's hurting the kids. Sadly, many spouses only realize this when kids get into trouble at school or when another child's parent points out that the child has been unusually aggressive on the playground.

Obviously, both parties need to be willing to de-escalate; in some cases, taking a course together might not be feasible until one or both of you get *individual* counseling or therapy to find out why you're holding on so tightly. If your ex won't agree, you can still take a communications seminar on your own or read books on the subject. Even if *one* of you is determined to control yourself during discussions and gains some insight about effective communication techniques, your conflicts are bound to become more manageable. You'll learn constructive ways to solve problems and gain new skills, which will help you stick to "ground rules" for discussions such as the following:

- Listen without interrupting. Many communication courses suggest "mirroring" what your partner says—that is, repeating out loud what you think you heard. It forces you to listen and cuts down on misunderstandings. Under no circumstances, should a speaker be interrupted.
- Use "I" messages. Starting sentences with "I" gets you out of the accusatory mode. For instance, a statement such as, "You always yell at me," becomes "I get nervous when you raise your voice."
- Be polite. Talk to your ex-spouse as you would a business acquaintance and under similar circumstances. Be courteous and respectful, and, until you both learn how to restrain yourselves, meet outside either of your homes, perhaps in a public place. Name-calling, cursing, or using abusive language should neither be allowed nor tolerated.
- Don't "kitchen-sink." Separate issues when you have discussions. Too often, a single issue careens into a discussion of other issues, precipitating a barrage of old, unresolved conflicts. If you stick to one subject, stay in the present, and avoid blame and sweeping generalizations ("You always . . ." or "You never . . ."), your discussions are less likely to escalate into unproductive, emotionally charged exchanges in which neither of you can remember what you were talking about in the first place!
- Agree on the right to call a time-out but never to walk out. It's important to make a commitment to improve your communication but, at the same time, you also need ways of stopping discussions from becoming hurtful, ineffective, or overly intense—for instance, by giving the other parent a hand signal or by saying the words "Time out!" Taking a break is not the same as avoiding a discussion or walking out on one. Don't leave the other person hanging too long. Just take enough time to allow yourself to simmer down—never more than a day.

- Don't "mind read." Before you jump to conclusions, get all the facts. Never assume that you know what the other person is thinking. Instead, listen carefully; and ask questions to clarify.
- Keep conflict between the two of you. It's best not to bring in "ammunition," by repeating the opinions of family members or friends when you two are trying to make a joint decision ("My Aunt Esther, who has been teaching for years, thinks The ABC Day School is the best place for Peter") or when you hit a brick wall ("Even your mother thinks you're stubborn!").
- Take responsibility. Learn how to apologize and to accept your part in what goes wrong. Pay attention to the way *you* react under stress. Instead of focusing on what your ex does that gets you crazy, figure out what *you* do that pushes his or her buttons! Some people get hyper-emotional and begin to scream, but others withdraw or become very logical. The two are flip sides of the same coin. The visibly angry person is not "causing" the spiral—what each of you does incites the other!

Adversarial Divorce: Be Wary

If there's anything that works against the principles of good communication, it's the legal system. How often I wished I had listened to veterans of divorce who advised Mark and me early on—while we were still in the cooperation zone: "Don't put this in the hands of lawyers. They'll only make things worse, and you'll end up spending more money on them than you'll get in your settlement."

Unfortunately, for far too long, I couldn't see beyond my rescue fantasy (see pp. 55–56). By the time our divorce was finalized, I had hired three lawyers. I fired the first one because he was too paternalistic and, I thought, slow; I hired the second because I thought he was more aggressive. He ended up firing me! And on the eve of "going to court," I had to plunk down $10,000 borrowed from my family to hire a last-minute heavy hitter (who would later represent Donald Trump). In retrospect,

I often refer to my divorce as "my second college education"; it actually cost much more. It was a lesson in greed (the lawyers') and humiliation (mine, not, as I had hoped, Mark's).

I can't believe how naive I was. For example, I allowed my second lawyer to file for sole custody, even though I had every intention of sharing both legal and emotional parenting with Mark. Despite the lawyer's reassurance that it was a "strategic ploy," it turned out that this move only served to escalate our battle, prolong a final settlement and, of course, put more money into his pocket. That was the same attorney who dropped my case right before we were supposed to go to court and sued me for nonpayment, although I had already paid him thousands of dollars in fees!

It has been somewhat reassuring to hear similar stories from other women—whether they had court-appointed lawyers or high-priced legal barracudas whom they chose. Women are particularly vulnerable to lawyers, willing ourselves in their hands, only to discover that they are not the knight in shining armor we had hoped for—far from it. Many women felt that their attorneys—mostly male, but some females as well—were condescending, failed to protect them, and didn't understand (or couldn't care less about) the needs of their children.

Men sometimes fare better with lawyers, but only if they are better at speaking up when a lawyer's actions are not in their best interest. That wasn't the case with Nick Pisano, a dentist. Dismayed that he and Marjorie had spent $17,000 in legal fees and three years later still didn't have even the germ of a separation agreement to show for it, Nick asked his lawyer what to expect. "Oh, it'll cost between $25,000 and $30,000 by the time you're through," said the lawyer without skipping a beat. And when Nick bellowed an incredulous "What?" the lawyer assured him, "That's cheap for a dentist!"

Marjorie notes that even though Nick was "furious," he didn't switch attorneys. Man or woman, when you've already paid thousands of dollars to one attorney, the idea of having to pay an additional retainer to another one often paralyzes people.

Nick and Marjorie, still in the thick of the legal process as this book is being written, are painfully aware of how lawyers and money are getting in the way of cooperating, even though both have the best intentions when it comes to the kids. Many others who are long past that point comment in retrospect that legal tactics senselessly intensified conflict with their ex-spouses.

"Kids simply can't do well if the legal battle drags on," claims Ron Taffel. "If that's lurking in the shadows, there's a continual reopening of the old wound." Taffel says he always advises clients to seek a mediator who will take a less adversarial approach or, at least, to get the legal proceedings over ASAP.

Cindy and Dick Danzer agree. "Our most emotionally divisive issue was the continuous court battles over 'child support.' This kept us angry at each other for six years!!" according to Dick. "Our anger always heightened around the times of court appearances, and those were the few times that we'd both sometimes be guilty of speaking negatively about each other to the kids." Once they stopped the legal battles, the Danzers' co-parenting relationship improved. "I realized that fighting for financial equity wasn't worth the emotional price," says Dick.

Mediation: A Saner Alternative?

It would be spurious to claim that *all* matrimonial attorneys take an unproductive approach, but in many cases, lawyers do prolong the process and, not so incidentally, fatten their own purses in the bargain. A more sensible first step might be to seek mediation. A hybrid creation—part psychological support, part legal advice— the profession emerged from a growing awareness of the complex demands of a legal process that is also a highly emotional trauma. Parents seek out a qualified mediator *together,* who, in the best-case scenarios, helps them design an agreement equitable to both parties.

In fact one of the major differences between a divorce mediator and a lawyer is that the former is hired by both parents and the entire family is the focus, whereas an attorney is only concerned with the interests of one parent—the client. Although some lawyers insist that they do keep children's needs in mind when they counsel clients and that they try to help clients reach agreements that are equitable to both parties, many lawyers don't.

Mediation, at least, puts you in the same corner with your ex, rather than immediately squaring off at each other from opposite corners of the ring. Therefore, mediation can be a very constructive first step—one that benefits both you and the children. It works best when each parent accepts the inevitability of the divorce, sees cooperation as a high priority, and is at least willing to listen to an impartial third party.

Amicable parents usually require three to eight hour-and-a-half- to two-hour-long sessions with a mediator; angry, warring parents may take two to four months. In any event, even if you can flush out the division of property and a parenting plan with a mediator, you still need a lawyer to look over any agreement you come up with. Nevertheless, mediation can serve to iron out decisions (and teach partners better decision-making skills)—a process that usually feels overwhelming at first because you both feel so vulnerable.

Buyers ought to beware, however: this is a young profession. Some mediators or mediation teams are not as well trained or experienced as others. The best are mental-health professionals well versed in matrimonial law, or lawyers who perceive mediation as a more human alternative to the traditional adversarial approach.

Isolina Ricci, Ph.D., now the Statewide Coordinator and Administrator of the Statewide Office of Family Court Services in California, is concerned about mediation being "oversold." Few states have outlined official standards for this new profession. Ricci says it's crucial to ask about a mediator's training and personal biases. And don't make a decision hastily or on the basis of having talked to only one person. "It's like surgery—get a second opinion," Ricci suggests. (See the Resources section for more information on mediators, p. 330.)

Arlene Steinberg and Peter Levine went straight to the horse's mouth. A northern California couple, they split up in 1982, not long after Ricci published *Mom's House, Dad's House*. "Peter had seen the book, and then I read it," recalls Arlene. "When we realized that Isolina had a private mediation practice in the area, we went to see her."

Today, Arlene and Peter still don't agree on much. Both are

remarried, enjoy quite different lifestyles, and, except for their children, have even less in common these days than they did ten years ago when they first split up. However, both parents have the same opinion about their choice to seek mediation: It was shorter and less costly than negotiating through lawyers, and, most important, if problems arose, they knew they always had a referee they could go back to. "That was really important," says Arlene, who acknowledges she has learned a lot about the art of negotiation.

Other parents in my sample who used a mediator parallel the findings of the Divorce and Mediation Project, to date the only long-term study on mediation. Its principal investigator, Joan Kelly, a psychologist and divorce mediator who runs the Northern California Mediation Center, reports that when provided by "trained, experienced mediators familiar with family law and the complex dynamics of the divorce process," mediation was more effective than the traditional adversarial process. Participants who mediated their divorce agreements were better at containing and limiting conflict, communicating, and cooperating.

Kelly reminds us that mediation is neither a panacea nor a salve for ongoing problems. Staying on relatively good terms with each other is, for all couples, a ticklish and tenuous proposition. In fact, two years down the line, Kelly points out, divorces that have been mediated look pretty much like those that have gone through the traditional process. But there is one advantage to mediation: If the lessons learned during the process are incorporated into daily life, parents are better about accommodating and supporting each other.

Dealing with the Experts

Annie and Wes King segued from marriage counseling to divorce therapy, which then led to mediation. For nine months, they had been seeing a family therapist originally found through a local family center, Annie explains. "But when I saw that there wasn't an equal commitment on Wes's part to carry out the counselor's suggestions, I couldn't take it anymore." The counselor was asked to switch gears.

One session was about making the decision to divorce, and the next several focused on how to handle five-year-old Willy. The counselor sent Wes to his own therapist and continued to see Annie alone for a few more sessions; he also sent the couple to a mediator. Although Wes was "very angry—and it took three times as long as it should have," in Annie's opinion, mediation was by far the most expedient route for the Kings.

"I know we're both trying to do the right thing for Willy," says Annie today. Heaving a sigh that speaks volumes about the strain of the last two years, she admits, "You know, every time I think we're on the right road, something changes."

Because of the incredible emotional stress during what is known as the "legal divorce"—a time when difficult, often wrenching decisions are made regarding finances and child care—Bonnie Winter, a divorced mom who now works as a counselor/mediator at Beech Acres' Aring Institute, a family center in Cincinnati, Ohio, contends, "Mediation is not enough!" She also advises joining a support group (see pages 62–64) and/or seeing an individual or family counselor or therapist (pages 65–66) to help you get through this difficult period. Although it can be costly to avail yourself of so much expert advice, some family centers that specialize in divorce offer the services of mediators and counselors on a sliding scale; conciliation courts can also help you find appropriate professionals who charge reasonable fees (see Resources, p. 330).

Whether you opt for a lawyer or a mediator, take responsibility for supplying what that person needs to function most effectively on your behalf—for example, organize and label financial records and other important documents. Also keep in mind that specialists view problems through their particular professional lens. It's expensive—and fruitless—to ask a lawyer to act like a therapist; stick to the facts and vent your emotions elsewhere.

With any expert, know what you want, be sure *you* set the agenda; put the person through the same kinds of "tests" you would expect any professional to pass. What is his training, her experience with divorce, his feelings about co-parenting, her concerns about the well-being of children? Do you like or at least respect the person?

Above all, don't accept any advice as gospel; trust your instincts. Even if a third party helps you write an agreement, you and your ex-spouse are going to have to *live* it. As Isolina Ricci puts it, "The best parenting agreement is the parents' agreement!" You know what your children need, and you know what you're capable of handling—and how fast and what kind of changes your particular family can accommodate.

By the way, just about everyone, nonexperts included, will offer free advice—your Great Aunt Tillie, Uncle Mortimer, and a gaggle of others who, divorced or not, "only have your best interest at heart." In divorce, the road to Hell is populated by the well-intentioned. So, if you're determined to improve your relationship with the other parent, chose very carefully whose recommendations you take to heart.

Advice to—and from—women and men tends to differ. "Thank goodness, I took steps from Day One to be my own person. I remember other women who had small kids telling me I was crazy to let Mitch 'have' the kids as much as I did," says Helen Rogand. It wasn't exactly fashionable to co-parent when she and her ex separated in 1982, but from the beginning, Helen not only allowed her ex-husband to visit, she says, "I *insisted* that he stop by every day." Then, when he settled into a place of his own, the co-parents designed an alternating two-day schedule. "In the back of their minds, I could imagine some women thinking, 'It's really selfish of you—you should be with your kids all the time.'" By *not* listening to the prevailing wisdom, Helen is convinced, "I was better able to get along with him *and* be a better mother."

Men's choice tidbits of insight for their divorcing buddies typically center on the business end of the divorce—the deal-making tactics. *Be careful about what you tell her. She'll take you to the cleaners if you don't watch out.* Several fathers encountered prejudice as well. Stuart Mercurio, a New York City attorney who has been an active co-parent for the last decade—since his daughters were six and nine—recalls, "The guys at the office couldn't understand my saying 'I've got to leave to get home to my girls.'" Luckily for his family apart, that never stopped him.

Keeping *Yourself* on Track

With all that works against divorcing couples, it's a wonder that any of us manages to create new kinds of postdivorce relationships (more on how we do this in chapter 5). You may not be able to sidestep the legal system; and you may not be able to silence the well-intentioned, but when two co-parents work together, at least they have a sporting chance.

On the other hand, if your ex-spouse is not ready to cooperate, you can't change him or her. *You can only change your own behavior.* For a while, you may have to be mature enough for both of you! Even if your co-parent continues to be controlling, ornery, or overbearing, if you take responsibility for your own actions, the balance has to shift. After all, the other parent can't continue to play the game if you refuse to step onto the playing field. Here are some other helpful reminders that can keep you on track by focusing on yourself:

Get comfortable with who you are.   When you begin to establish a separate identity (see pp. 58–61), you begin to act and think for yourself, and you develop what Dudley Weeks, author of *Conflict Resolution,* calls "positive self-power." And the more you become comfortable with your own needs, priorities, values, and goals, the more you will be inspired to reach for the same in your partner. You will also become more empathic and receptive— which is far better than being angry and closed; in turn, your co-parenting relationship will become more trusting and collaborative.

When you adopt this kind of attitude, you will find that you don't just share problems or limit your focus to mistakes. You tend to concentrate on the things you do well together and that each of you does best. "Everything changed between us," admitted one mother, "when I started to see him as part of the solution, instead of part of the problem."

See each interaction with your ex as an opportunity to show your best self. Co-parents often make heroic decisions . . . for the sake of their children. Primarily, they filter their own feelings through their children's needs. "I realized this was something I had to get through, whether I liked it or not," says Sue Carver. At some point during her initial separation, she decided that life as a single mom would be easier if she were back in her native Hawaii. "He put his foot down. Although I was angry, I finally had to come to terms with it. I had to get on with my life, but Dawn had this relationship with her father, and I knew that seeing him once a year wasn't enough." That was in 1982; Sue is still living in New York, cooperatively co-parenting with her ex; Dawn, who sees her dad every other day, has never had to worry about losing him.

Accept some loss of control.   When you're a parent in a house undivided, you're constantly aware of your children's comings and goings, and you know whether they're watching too much TV, eating junk food, or hanging out with new friends. Not so in a family apart. "Most parents are afraid of losing the child's love and losing control of their lives," contends Bonnie Winter. "In marriage there's often fighting over control, and in divorce they think they can still control."

Being in the throes of divorce and feeling utterly out of control, you're apt to grasp at anything that gives you even the slightest illusion of power. But engaging in power struggles can precipitate a major regression in your postdivorce relationship, not to mention tearing apart your kids. While women tend to heighten their sense of control by limiting, or stopping, visitation, men tend to do so by withholding money. Often, they are related actions; both alternatives hurt children *and* parents.

"Look at your own issues. Why do you need to control?" asks Winter, who also believes that even when one parent is "flawed," children need access to both parents. "Most kids are more attracted to the healthier parent, anyway.

"You have to mature with the process of divorce and learn to let go," says Winter. Besides, as a parent's need for inappropriate control diminishes, not only does the co-parenting relationship usually improve, the environment also frees children to learn how to be in appropriate control of their own lives.

Remember the adult benefits of cooperative co-parenting.   Advantages to the children aside, a number of studies indicate that sharing parenting is better for adults, too. In the Toronto Shared Parenting Project, for example, 83 percent of those who co-parented reported "satisfaction"; 88 percent recommended it to other parents. And they were more likely to feel closer to their children than parents with sole custody. My respondents claim similar gains and more: time off from the rigors of parenting and time to pursue adult interests. "I have a life, and I know my children are getting the best of both parents," explains one mother. And a father, who was afraid that he would lose his children, admits, "I'm sure I never would have spent this much alone-time with my children or done as much hands-on caring for the kids. I had no idea how fulfilling solo parenting would be."

Look into Your Children's Eyes

The best gauge of your increasing maturity—and the most important beneficiaries—are your children. To know whether you're really on track, listen to what they hear (directly or indirectly) and look into their eyes. "If parents are sensitive and watch their kids, they'll *see* physical clues," insists Sally Brush. Some children will wince visibly when they see one parent shoot an arrow toward the other parent; others will just look sad, or even blank. In any case, when you're really focused on your child, you're less likely to let the arrow fly in the first place.

Suppose your ex is late to pick up the kids, and they're getting edgy about it. You have two choices: You can try to divert their attention and make excuses for the other parent ("She/he must have hit traffic"). Or you can mutter obscenities under your breath and use the opportunity to point out (once again) that the other parent is a no-good sonofabitch! Even if every bone in your body aches for the second alternative, stop yourself for your child's sake.

Learn to recognize *what* it feels like when you're about to lose it. You may get a knot in your stomach, a twitch in your eye, or break out into a cold sweat; that's your body telling you that your mind is on red alert, and that it's time to excuse yourself. Go into your room or take a walk—anything that provides a kind of time-out. If your child is too young to leave alone, put her in a safe place, playpen or crib; give her an engaging toy that will occupy her until you've composed yourself.

Also figure out *when* you're most likely to slip up. For instance, if phone calls are a problem, make them when the kids are not around. If you get angry when kids are dropped off or picked up, make yourself scarce or invite a friend over as a buffer. And if you don't catch yourself in time, *apologize*.

Bertha Samuel, divorced five years ago, recalls that during the first six to nine months, she "knew" she should remain neutral, if not supportive, when it came to talking about the children's father, but sometimes it was impossible for her to contain her rage in front of the kids, then four and eight. "I was angry at him for what he did to me. Whenever I'd say something nasty, I'd tell them, 'I'm really sorry. The fact is, he is a good daddy to you.'"

All parents have lapses; the most damage is done when you don't admit to yourself—and to your child—that you've had one. Don't go into a long-winded explanation; a simple statement will do, like the one Sally Brush suggests: "Oops! I'm doing it again. That's because I'm sad/mad about the divorce and sometimes my feelings spill out. But those are *my* feelings. I know you love both of us, and we love you."

If you're unsure what a particular statement sounds like to your child, Vicki Lansky also suggests a good strategy: Imagine what it would have felt like to hear your own parent saying the same thing to you as a child—how wrenching to have been enlisted as your parent's messengers or spy, to be pumped for information about the other parent, the parents you love. How unfair, how hard!

This paradox bears repeating: *Keeping your mind on what your children need not only mitigates the harmful effects of divorce on them, it also helps to diffuse your own feelings of loss and self-pity.* Moreover, your children will learn valuable lessons as they watch their parents mature and strengthen their ability to cope with each other's differences, shortcomings, inconsistencies, and imperfections. They take these lessons into their own lives and into their own relationships.

"I was amazed at how my parents changed over those first few years," says a college senior, looking back eight years since his parents first separated. "We had some rough times. They were both nuts! But by the time I went to college, both of them helped me move into the dorm—even Dad's girlfriend was there!" The young man notes that his parents "still argue sometimes, but probably less than if they were still married. Maybe they wouldn't have seen as many therapists or tried as hard if they hadn't divorced."

It can also help to keep the long-run perspective in mind. "Take at least a five-year look at the reality of your life and of your children's lives," suggests Neil Kalter, asking parents rhetorically, "Do you haul your ex-wife into court because she spent the child support on herself or took her boyfriend on a vacation. Or, do you go out and buy your child the hundred dollars worth of clothes you think she spent?" If you can't be objective, says Kalter, get help from professionals who can.

When divorcing couples come to her for advice, Constance Ahrons recommends that they imagine life fifteen years down the line: "What will happen at your child's wedding?" she asks. You don't even have to look that far ahead. One mother, whose child was taking piano lessons, imagined how distracting it would be for her daughter to have hostile parents at her recitals.

Also, look around you. That's what Gloria Shannon did. By paying attention to other families going through divorce, particularly the kids, Gloria discovered plenty of examples of what *not* to do. When she was going through her divorce in 1989, Shannon, a preschool teacher, notes that two girls in her class were living in joint-custody arrangements. "One girl's parents cooperated, communicated, and even did things together. Their little girl did very well. The other child's father not only didn't allow her to travel back and forth between the households, he didn't even want her to mention her mother in his presence. It was devastating! The little girl began exhibiting severe behavior problems at school. I was determined not to put my son into that kind of situation."

Gloria, who felt deeply wounded by her husband's affair—the event that precipitated the divorce—says that professional intervention also helped her muster the strength and maturity to shield her son. "We had been in marriage counseling, which turned into divorce counseling, then individual. It didn't take long to realize it was more stressful to be angry and hostile than to work things out with my ex-husband."

Postdivorce maturity doesn't come easily for anyone. The road is long and arduous, but if you stay on course, you begin see the scenery change. You improve your attitude little by little, you let things go by that might have irritated you in the past, and you take small steps that sometimes feel unsteady. You may not notice anything particularly spectacular at first, but one day you realize that you've traveled farther than you realize. A lot of the animosity is gone, your relationship with your ex-spouse has become more rewarding, and, day by day, your children's and your lives are getting better.

—4—

A DELICATE BALANCE

Key #3: Listen to Your Children

The Children's Perspective

Children's views of divorce are often quite different from their parents'. I found this out in a wrenching conversation with my own son, Jeremy, nineteen and a sophomore in college at the time we talked. Explaining that I was writing a chapter about how important it is for parents to heed their kids' perspective on divorce, I asked, "What bad things do you remember about Dad's and my divorce?"

"You mean, the fighting?" he asked.

"Well," I hesitated, suddenly timid, sorry that I had asked the question in the first place; perhaps I should have stuck to interviewing other people's children.

"Yes, I guess," I wavered. "But I didn't think we fought *that* much around you." I wondered if I sounded as defensive as I felt.

"I don't remember that much. Whatever I remember, I've tried hard to forget," he said and then paused. "I guess I do remember that I always thought that there was really poor communication between you and Dad. You'd say, 'Didn't Dad tell you?' and he'd say, 'I thought Mom told you.'"

His voice grew stronger. "And all that moving around. You and Dad probably thought it was a very organized schedule, but I don't think either of you realized the impact on Jen and me. I never felt settled; neither house felt like home, because I was always thinking, 'Soon I'm going to have to move to the other house.'"

My "interview" with Jeremy, which lasted no more than ten

minutes, left me reeling. I'm sure parents who participated in my research would be equally astonished to hear *their* kids speak about how they behaved during the divorce process—parents who were sure they never fought in front of the children, parents who thought they always made the kids feel wanted and loved, parents who'd swear they never made their kids choose sides, parents who believed that they kept the lines of communication open.

The trouble is, children don't often tell us how they feel directly; in turn, we are all too eager to assume that their silence means that they must be doing just fine. But it's not that simple, not even in the best situations. To strangers, many children of divorce complain about their parents' pettiness, selfishness, and childishness. Some are bitter; others are relieved to be out of the direct line of fire, though sad nonetheless; almost all remember the conflict. When recounting their family sagas, though, most of these kids exhibit sensitivity and understanding beyond their years. They have given divorce a great deal of thought, because it was the defining event in their lives.

The children's side of the story has much to teach us. I wish I had known then what I know now about Jeremy's feelings. One mistake, I realize, is that *I never really asked him!* I felt guilty, frightened, and defensive. Not wanting to face the children's sadness and anger definitely colored my ability to communicate with them.

I'm not alone. Other parents report that dealing with children's feelings and talking to them about divorce is excruciatingly difficult; it brings up their own feelings of sadness and anger. In fact, one study, reported by child psychologist Edward Teyber in *Helping Children Deal with Divorce,* indicates that 80 percent of the time, children are not even given explanations for their parents' divorce.

Often, parents offer cursory statements ("Dad and I are getting a divorce") without realizing that children need both an immediate, age-appropriate, detailed explanation *and* thoughtful, ongoing conversations about how their families will change. Parents assume that one BIG conversation is sufficient. And then they fail to pay attention when their kids' behavior cries out for more. Parents may feel that they're "protecting" their children or "not burdening" them by "sparing" them the details, but for kids, it's devastating when they're kept in the dark. Consider the ramifications while listening to kids who have been there:

Kids blame themselves.   Children are *never* the cause of a divorce, yet many suffer years of guilt feelings if parents don't tell them that—clearly and firmly. "I figured because my parents argued so much about my problems in school, that it was my fault that they split up," says a boy whose parents divorced when he was ten. "My little sister and I fought all the time. Our parents always said, 'You two are driving us crazy,' so when they said they were getting divorced, I kept thinking that maybe if we hadn't fought so much . . ." remarks a wistful fourteen-year-old girl whose parents split up five years ago.

Kids fear that they'll lose both their parents.   When parents don't explain carefully (and repetitively) how both will continue to be present in their children's lives, they often assume the worst. "My parents went to counseling, but they never brought us kids into it. I never knew what was happening, or whether we'd have any kind of family," says a twenty-one-year old whose parents separated when she was a teenager.

Kids feel rejected.   "It took me awhile to realize that my father still loved me even though he didn't love my mother anymore," admits one boy, now in his early twenties; he was eight when his father moved out. "No one sat me down and said, "Look, I will always be here for you. You are my child, and I will always love you.' I wish my father had."

Kids worry.   They worry about being taken care of, about being left alone, even about having their basic needs met. And no wonder! With all sorts of change swirling around them and, even worse, with parents constantly battling about time, money, and responsibilities, everything really does feel tentative and bleak. Might they starve, be homeless, even loveless? Some conclude that *their* needs don't count. "I'm not sure my mother wants to talk about it," one teenager confided to divorce counselor Marcia Lebowitz, "but the reason my younger brother doesn't go to birthday parties is because he's afraid Mom can't afford to give him money for a present."

Kids feel torn.   Children feel confused and ripped apart when the two people they love and need the most are at each other's throats. A psychology major, now a junior in college, recalls the time five years ago when her parents were separating, "They fought constantly, and I remember when my older brother was at college and my mother moved into his room. She wouldn't speak to my father. So, if my father had to tell her something, he relayed messages through me." A classmate of hers, age twenty, says of her own parents' tumultuous marriage and divorce, "I've been aware of the fighting ever since I was really little—five or six. They always argued, always brought me into the middle of it. I don't remember a time when they really got along."

Kids grow up too fast.   The same young woman, whose parents' on-again-off-again marriage finally ended after more than a decade of their battling and her pain, also laments, "I found out about my mother having affairs when I was eight or nine. They were fighting, and my father shouted at my mother, 'Why don't you tell your daughter what you did?' I know more about them than any child should know about their parents."

Kids think they have to protect their parents or, worse, take care of them. "I thought I'd always have a mother, but still . . . I was terribly insecure for a long time. I was afraid to leave my mother alone," admits a twenty-one-year-old girl, echoing sentiments I had heard from many teenagers and young adults. Some have mixed feelings about the responsibilities foisted upon them by irresponsible parents. In one breath, a college student complains about her parents, who "took away a lot of my childhood," and in the next, she defends them, by saying, "I know that they couldn't help it. I see them as children."

These childhood themes run through many accounts of divorce. Although in some cases more than ten years have passed since the initial separation, many of the children in my study ask not to be identified with or linked to their parents' stories. They still fear hurting their parents or burdening them with their feelings!

For the Sake of the Children

As it turns out, what we parents think we're doing "for the sake of the children" is often really for ourselves—to protect *our* feelings, to make *our* lives easier. Some parents can admit this—at least in retrospect: "We wanted to satisfy our needs. Instead of fighting over him, we often fought over the time we got to spend *without* him," owns a mother who began co-parenting in 1977. "I regret some of the things I did, but there wasn't much around to guide me. I read a few books, but they were very superficial and had very little about co-parenting. We've gotten a lot smarter since then."

Sadly, as in my case, some of us find out years later how inadvertently hurtful we had been just because we didn't ask the right questions. And now, with a nascent maturity, even Jeremy is able to say, "Besides, look where both of *you* were mentally. That didn't help."

Granted, it *is* difficult to be steady in the midst of your own chaos, to exercise restraint in front of the children when you're in emotional turmoil, to be generous when you're feeling robbed, to be open when you feel like crawling into a deep, dark hole, or to help your children express their feelings when you're over-whelmed by your own, but the truth is: parents don't have a choice if we want our children to come through intact.

A college student comments, "I hated it whenever my parents assumed I was too young to realize what was going on. We kids always figured things out." This was a frequent complaint among the children I interviewed. Kids shouldn't have to "figure it out." That's a parent's job.

Children of divorce confirm what virtually every researcher has found: Kids fare best when parents help them understand and handle the changes in their lives, are rigorously attentive to both their verbal *and* behavioral clues, and continue to talk to them about the divorce—day after day, month after month, even year after year. Learn how to "read" your children and discern what they need. The information in this chapter will hone your awareness of typical responses and vulnerabilities at particular ages and stages of development—to help you break the news and structure appropriate conversations with each of your kids as time passes.

Remember that this is an ongoing and very individual process. Children change; and priorities, rules, and schedules change with them. The idea is to build a realistic foundation so that your family apart is suited to your children, preserves the sense of "family," and facilitates open, continuing communication among all its members.

The Developmental Picture: Ages and Stages

What children learn about divorce is primarily in your hands and mediated by your example, but they also bring their own baggage to every life situation. A number of observational studies have documented that even very young infants evince their own style of interacting with the world. Different infants react differently to the same stimulus, which would include the impact of their parents' divorce.

A child of any age will perceive and process an event in a variety of ways unique to that child. Difference is mediated by several factors: chronological *and* emotional age, gender, temperament, and coping skills—that is, a child's ability to handle unexpected or stressful situations. All these elements should be thought through carefully before you break the news. And then, it all must be reviewed—again and again—in the coming months and years as you continue the discussion.

Had I thought about it more at the time, for example, I would have realized that Jennifer, twelve (on the cusp of adolescence), and Jeremy, eight, would have completely different responses to the co-parenting plan Mark and I devised. She was a child who always adapted easily to change; he was ruffled by the slightest alteration in his daily regimen—even before the divorce. I also would have realized that the schedule, which suited our needs for almost equal time with the children and, we thought, had the virtue of being consistent, was completely unsettling from Jeremy's perspective. Living at Mark's every Thursday and on alternate Mondays and weekends had no logic for him and disrupted his sense of order. In retrospect, I really shouldn't be surprised that he "never felt settled" or that he was so upset because Mark and I always seemed to "spring" things on him, while Jennifer appeared to roll with the punches (or didn't overtly express her discomfort in the ways Jeremy did at the time).

Hindsight makes us wonderfully wise. The trick is to look at these kinds of issues *in advance*. Reading books and getting expert advice will only take you so far; you have to understand and adapt all this information to your own children. *You know them best.* Step back, take a good look at your kids, and mentally climb into their skin. Think about how she deals with change, how he reacts to strangers; remember how they handled transitions in the past, like going off to school for the first time.

Although it's important to evaluate each child's unique personality and history, don't overlook the importance of her developmental stage. Allowing for individual differences, the broad guidelines that follow can be useful in structuring sensitive, age-appropriate conversations and routines that will help children feel safe:*

Infants and Toddlers (Birth to Age Three)   Cora Portino, whose daughter was a toddler when Cora and her husband split up, doesn't remember telling her little girl anything. "It's kinda hard to tell a fourteen-month-old about divorce." But within two months, even though Cora's ex-husband was a frequent visitor, Cora's little girl communicated her fears. "She was standing by the window, watching him leave. I was right behind her, and she whirled around, smacked me on the face, and shouted in a very accusing tone, 'You make Daddy go away!' That was when I tried to explain to her what happened."

Cora Portino is correct: It's quite difficult to "tell" an infant or toddler about divorce. Compared to other age groups, researchers know less about their reactions. And what complicates matters is that these little ones change almost monthly; the needs of a six-month-old are vastly different from those of an eighteen-month-old.

---

*Ages for each grouping are approximate, based on generally accepted definitions of child development. For an extremely detailed picture of children's needs and reactions at various ages, you might also want to refer to Neil Kalter's *Growing Up with Divorce*, listed in Resources (p. 322).

In general, however, parents should be aware that such young children have a very limited ability to keep people "in mind" and to understand time. Therefore, you can't very well tell them what divorce is or expect them to understand a schedule. In fact, a very young child who doesn't see one parent for two or three days is bound to feel, as Cora Portino's daughter did, that the parent "went away."

When children are very young, it's not so much what you say about divorce; it's what you do and how you do it. Younger, more dependent children will sense, and be affected by, a parent's emotional state. They are highly susceptible to anger, sadness, and anxiety. Additionally, the younger child will be more upset by changes in routine. Thus, parents can best protect these little ones by making sure that they—the parents—are on an even keel emotionally and by minimizing disruptions in the child's life. As consistently as possible, stick to the usual schedule and avoid unfamiliar caretakers. If Dad wasn't a primary caretaker before the divorce, even his feeding the child or putting her down for a nap might be confusing in the beginning. The co-parenting plan should take these possible reactions into consideration (more on this in chapter 6).

Very young children will "tell" their parents they're upset; but you may have to watch for, rather than listen for, their message. They sometimes regress: an infant who sleeps through the night suddenly becomes restless and cranky at 3 A.M.; a toddler who drinks from a cup wants the bottle again. Admittedly, it can be difficult for parents to determine what is "uncharacteristic" when children are naturally changing in so many ways. At least, be aware of what's typical at this age and be mindful of your own child's pattern. If he was "late," in development terms (to hold a bottle, sit up unassisted) before you split up, don't panic if he seems "slow" afterward; just watch for other signs that might indicate anxiety.

Even if your child seems too young to understand, begin to explain the divorce, offering constant and loving reassurance. Psychiatrist Richard Gardner contends that if a child is old enough to recognize a parent, he is old enough to be told "at whatever level of communication . . . that the parent will no longer be living in the home."

He makes a good point. It's impossible to know precisely when a particular child will understand. After all, you begin to sing lullabies long before they understand words, because children gain a sense of well-being from a parent's soothing voice. You point out a "cute little doggie" before the child can grasp "cute" or "little" or even "doggie," because you want to sharpen senses and develop cognitive skills. In the same way, long before an infant or a toddler begins to understand what divorce actually means, saying "Mommy/Daddy loves you, even though she/he doesn't live here" will reinforce the child's connection with the absent parent and gradually initiate his awareness of the divorce. In the long run, communication may be easier for parents who start talking to very young children; by the time the child is old enough to ask questions and answer back, the parent has had lots of practice!

Sandy McGee reports that when within a few months after she separated from her husband, she began to read *Dinosaur's Divorce,* a book for preschoolers, to Julia, who was nine months old when her parents divorced, she thought it would help her toddler understand what "going to Daddy's house" meant. It didn't matter that Julia could barely understand the content. And at eighteen months, when Julia began to live at both houses, Sandy kept reminding her, "Mommy is always in your heart when you are at Daddy's." At one, Julia couldn't respond; at two, she could point to her heart, and by three she could acknowledge, as she went out the door, "You're in my heart, Mommy."

Preschoolers (Three to Five) Preschoolers make great strides in acquiring cognitive and physical skills. They can walk, talk, solve puzzles, climb the jungle gym. They are more independent, willing to play on their own for longer periods, and able to spend time with friends in play groups or nursery-school settings. Still, their understanding of time and space remains limited as does their ability to comprehend cause and effect. Three- to five-year-olds have trouble grasping a statement such as "Daddy will come here tomorrow." This is also an age when fear of abandonment is particularly acute; these kids really identify with Hansel and Gretel! When a preschooler is told that her parents are "getting divorced," and she realizes that one parent is going to move out, she may also fear that the other parent will leave, too.

An added complication is that these kids don't always know how clearly to distinguish fantasy from reality; their fears increase, and they attribute "magical powers" to themselves and others. Regardless of how well parents try to minimize a child's worries, each "brings his own private agenda to situations," warns Neil Kalter. He recounts the story of a four-year-old whose mother took care not to change the nursery-school routine that the boy seemed to love. When he became clingy and fearful anyway, the mother found out why: "You're going to leave me and go far away to live!" The little boy's dad had moved only ten miles from the family home, but for this preschooler that was "far away," and he feared losing his mother, too.

Most preschoolers' ability to articulate is still somewhat limited; behavior is the best clue to a child's reaction, even with very verbal kids. If a divorce is initiated when a child is an infant or toddler, signs may emerge a year or two later. For example, although little Julia had been living in a family apart for more than two years, the formerly affable child didn't begin to express her resistance—and pain—until she was three. Her mom, Sandy McGee, who admits that she and her ex-husband were still hostile, recalls, "Julia would look at a kid on the playground and just shove him for no apparent reason."

Whether during the initial weeks or months while the news sinks in or a year or two after their parents separate, preschoolers can regress, demanding more time and attention and exhibiting sadness or anger, particularly if they witness their mother and father fighting, as Julia did. Other parents report previously outgoing preschoolers becoming withdrawn and capable kids needing help dressing or feeding themselves or crying for a seemingly long-forgotten pacifier. Toilet-trained kids can suddenly start wetting the bed, and children who once seemed easygoing can throw tantrums.

Preschoolers may be overwhelmed not only by their feelings but perhaps even more by their inability to express them. Look at books or magazines that have pictures of people (or animals) who are sad, afraid, angry, and happy. Or, get out the crayons and draw pictures with the child. Suggest why the child in a picture might be feeling a particular way: "I think this boy might feel sad because he is moving out of his house into a new one. Maybe he's scared, too. What do you think?" Help the child connect what she's seeing, drawing, or feeling with a word used to describe it. Constantly link events with feelings and then with words: "Were you sad when Mommy went shopping? Are you as glad as I am that I'm back now?"

Reading stories or looking at pictures with preschoolers and talking about how *the characters* seem to feel is a classic "displacement technique" used by child therapists. *Dinosaur's Divorce* is an excellent book because the illustrations portray a range of emotions, while the story is reassuring: "The bad feelings won't last forever . . ." and "It helps to talk about these feelings and let them show."

Also help your preschooler see what his or her family apart looks like. Again, anything visual or tactile—picture books, photos, dolls, action figures—can help transform vague concepts into more concrete and therefore more understandable ideas for young children. Read appropriate books, play with dolls, make a collage, draw a picture, or start a scrapbook showing the new family structure.

Because of their limited ability to process and retain information, preschoolers will need repeated explanations and assurances, sometimes every day (which may require more time and energy than you expect). One co-parenting couple came up with a unique solution: They wrote and illustrated a bedtime story and made one copy for each parent's house, which helped their kids, two and five, understand their new family apart.

Be aware that even young children can feel guilty; some convince themselves that Mommy or Daddy went away because they were "bad." These little ones may be solicitous, too; they think that they can make Mommy or Daddy "feel better," perhaps by being on extra-good behavior or keeping their own feelings under wraps.

Sally Brush, who runs groups for parents and children of divorce at Beech Acres' Aring Institute in Cincinnati, Ohio, suggests that parents talk about their own feelings as well. It's important to get "real" with your kids and to admit that you're having an emotional reaction to the situation. Saying "Mommy is sad sometimes" or "I get angry, too" gives children permission to feel and express what *they* are feeling. It's okay for a child to see a parent cry, as long as the parent demonstrates that he or she can cope with these feelings. The message is that it's acceptable to have emotions and that adults can handle them. You should also exercise good judgment and restraint. Some children are innately more sensitive than others, so you have to know what your child is capable of handling.

School-agers (Five to Nine)   These kids need specific information and explanation about the divorce. Some studies claim that children, particularly boys, are hard hit at this age. They are old enough to understand what the divorce means and to pine over memories of the family together but young enough to feel completely defenseless. These children may feel angry when they first hear the news, but more often, intense sadness is the overriding emotion.

This is difficult for most parents, especially those who are struggling with their own sadness; the kids' pain magnifies theirs. Therefore, even though it feels (understandably) as though your children's sorrow might be the straw that threatens to break your emotional back, address it. You might begin with, "A lot of kids your age feel sad when their parents split up, and it's easy to understand why."

As with preschoolers, you can also help these children sort through feelings by using displacement techniques. Read books with them; they're probably still not too old for some picture books, like *Dinosaur's Divorce, I Think Divorce Stinks,* or *Divorce Is a Grown-up Problem* (see Resources, p. 324); or use symbolic activities—hand puppets, dolls, action figures, storytelling, and storywriting about imaginary children.

Create a character that enacts some behavior that you see— and worry about—in your child. For example, if your daughter has stopped playing with kids in the neighborhood, set up a similar scenario, ask what the imaginary kid feels ("Is she sad? Is she lonely?") and offer reasons why that may be happening to her

("Maybe she's upset because her parents are getting a divorce, and she thinks that means her father is going away forever"). Be sure to say that such feelings are "okay." Finally, you might suggest better ways to cope with painful feelings ("She could tell her mother what she's sad about, because talking about it will make her feel better"). Try to get your child involved, by asking questions such as "What do you think she's feeling?" or "What happens next?" Don't worry if your child doesn't talk much; most children will get the message anyway.

One mother told me that she used "little people" (small wooden figures that come with many Fisher-Price toys) to help her five-year-old daughter talk about the divorce. "We played some games using kids on the school bus, others using a doll house. She sort of practiced telling her friends about the divorce and what it meant." The mother also helped her daughter see, more concretely, the ways in which her daddy would still be in her life. "We only had one doll house, so we made a second house out of a cereal box—and that was the apartment building where her father had just moved."

With kids of all ages it's helpful to remember (and to remind them) that you can have many conversations—small talks—so that neither of you has to bite off too much at once. Kids will need continuing, broader explanations as they get older and understand more. Sometimes they'll come to you; but sometimes, you'll have to reach for them.

Pay attention to school performance and to relationships with peers. Some kids may have trouble concentrating in school—in Wallerstein's study 50 percent did—or they may refuse to take part in normally pleasurable activities. They may feel the need to take care of their parents, rather than themselves. Anxiety, guilt, or fear of abandonment may inhibit children's enjoyment of being on their own or with friends and unconsciously impede their ability to move up the developmental ladder.

Parents often report that their school-aged children seem to be surprisingly mature; one mother referred to her eight-year-old son as "my little man"; a father talked about his seven-year-old daughter offering to cook dinner. Be wary of such "pseudo-maturity" in a school-age child. These kids who seem so grown-up may start having nightmares, balk at ordinary routines, and develop physical problems, like stomachaches and headaches, that keep them out of school—and require care at home. Children should never be allowed, and certainly never be asked, to assume adult roles vacated by a departing parent (be sure you read about the dangers of "parentifying" children, pp. 116–118).

As is true of their younger counterparts, these children should be shielded scrupulously from parental conflict, negative comments about the other parent, or worries about the future. Look for and lean on adult support, not your child.

Preteens (Nine to Twelve)   These kids are keenly aware of what's going on around them. They're immersed in their own culture, moving toward increasing independence, trying to make sense of the world. Divorce upsets the order of things. Preteens are concerned about "fitting in," and although divorce is increasingly commonplace, the event and its repercussions may make them feel uncomfortably different.

Whereas their elementary-school counterparts generally react by feeling powerless, preteens are likely to strike back powerfully at the news of divorce. They may express anger, verbal and sometimes physical; they can be contrary or blatantly rebellious. As Neil Kalter puts it, "It is as if they are saying, emotionally and behaviorally, that they refuse to take the divorce lying down." Children of this age may have more sophisticated responses at their fingertips than younger children; these older kids can deny, displace, intellectualize their feelings, or, like younger kids, turn them into symptoms. Preteens may mimic an absent parent, rather than admit to feelings of loss. They may take out their anger on their peers; their schoolwork is likely to suffer; they may even get into more serious trouble—like lying and stealing—which, if parents do not heed the red flag, can portend a stormy adolescence.

Gender-different reactions are particularly noticeable at this age. Studies show that boys are usually more literal when they express their anger. They may pick on younger kids or siblings or defiantly refuse to follow a teacher's orders or a parent's rules (especially a mother's!). Just because a girl doesn't show open signs of distress, however, parents should never assume that she's not hurting. Judith Wallerstein identifies this phenomenon as the "sleeper effect"—when children (usually girls) submerge their own feelings about the divorce for many years, only to have the anger or sadness or insecurity reemerge in later adolescence or early adulthood, when they first attempt their own intimate relationships.

The best antidote is parental time and understanding. Preteens are torn between acting grown-up and needing their parents, but they'll never admit to the latter. And you don't have to force them to! Simply engage them in activities *they* like—playing backgammon, going to a movie you'd never choose to see, or having them show you how to play Nintendo! It doesn't have to be a trip to Disneyland or a week in the Bahamas, just something that lets them see that you're taking time.

Feeling conflicting loyalties toward parents is hard for any child; but at this age, in particular, it can be deadly. You need to be aware; don't "pull" on children, overtly or subtly asking them to take sides. Sometimes, we do it in roundabout ways: by making snide comments about the other parent ("Just like your father to forget to make you a sandwich," when the child remarks that she bought lunch at school), by denigrating a new love interest ("Your mother sure didn't wait long to find a boyfriend"), by pumping kids about the other parent's behavior ("I thought your mother's car was broken down. Whose did she borrow to take you away this weekend?"), or by unwittingly encouraging the child to lie ("You don't need to tell your mother about this").

As children get older, maintaining communication with them is probably the most formidable task for parents, and the most crucial. Most preteens—as adolescents in training—are already figuring out clever ways of dodging heart-to-heart talks with their parents, but that doesn't mean you shouldn't try. These kids will make it hard for you ("You already talked to me about the divorce"), even make you feel guilty for trying ("All you think about is the divorce—give me a break!"). *Don't* expect to sit a preteen down or take her out to dinner for a meaningful talk. If *you* have trouble talking about your feelings, imagine her distress!

So as not to put an already confused preteen on the defensive, use everyday opportunities to spark short conversations. The next time you're engaged in a side-by-side activity—preparing dinner, sorting socks, driving in the car, try asking the child directly, "Sometimes when their mothers and fathers divorce, children feel like they did something to make it happen. Do you ever feel that way?" You may get an abrupt "No," or "I don't want to talk about it." Offer a quick reassuring sentence ("I can see this is not a good time, but I just wanted to make sure you know that our divorce is not your fault and that I'll be here when you do want to talk about it") and then change the subject. But don't give up. Try it again another time, perhaps more indirectly by talking about someone else ("Other children your age some-times feel [guilty/angry/sad]"). Or you can discuss fictional chil-dren on TV shows or in movies about divorce that you see or rent, such as *Rich Kids*. (Make sure *you* screen movies before you rent them, so that you know what you're in for and that the content is suitable for your child.)

Finally, expect tantrums, moodiness, and testing from pre-teens. Even as you cut them a little slack through these trying times, you must set limits. These kids want to know that parents won't let them fly out of control. Classic is the preteen who begs, whines, and finally throws a fit because Mom won't let her go to an unsupervised party. A half an hour later, she's cleaning up her room without having been asked. Why? Because she probably was scared to go in the first place but didn't know how to get out of going to the party without losing face!

Adolescents (Twelve to Eighteen)   Different pictures of ado-lescent reactions to divorce emerge from the research. Some observers hold that because adolescents are about to flee the nest anyway, they react better to the news than younger children. Others maintain that divorce inhibits teenagers from taking that expected developmental leap. The truth is, every adolescent is different, and reactions can run the gamut between the two extremes. Understandably, some adolescents become preoc-cupied with their parents' problems and worry about adult vul-nerability: how is Mom going to pay bills on her own and how is Dad going to cope with loneliness? Others rebel entirely—fly the coop prematurely, which is often most frightening for par-

ents; older kids can get into serious trouble, abusing alcohol or drugs, acting out sexually, running away, even committing petty crimes.

The pitfall with adolescents—who often seem quite "grown-up" in the physical sense—is that some parents rely on them too much and, at worst, "parentify" them, asking the child to meet adult needs. Child psychologist Edward Teyber notes that parentification usually occurs in one of three ways: when parents rely on children for a sense of security (the child takes care of the parent), for emotional needs (they're best friends), or for practical needs (the child runs the household and takes care of younger siblings). Children often enjoy the role; it makes them feel special. But, as Teyber points out, this role reversal—which can also happen with younger children—is always harmful.

Of course, that doesn't mean you can't ask teenagers to do more around the house, shop for food, or run errands. Such responsibilities actually help most children become more capable and self-reliant. What you want to avoid is going overboard; don't turn your teenager into your counselor, constant companion, confidante, or co-parent. Take care that you don't ask her to be concerned about adult issues, that you don't consider him your "lifeline," and, most important, that you stay in charge. Single parents *can* run a family. If you think you can't, do something other than relying on your kids. Take a parenting course or get help from a professional who will help you become a *balanced* parent—my term for one who doles out plenty of love and nurturance and yet can set appropriate limits and controls (see chapter 10).

This won't necessarily stop your teenager from worrying about money problems, their parents' sex lives (which they'd rather not think about!), or their own romantic future. Many of the teenagers I spoke with mentioned being "very cautious" about relationships. They said it was hard to see their parents cry, argue, or appear weak. One gets the feeling that although fears of making it in the real world weigh heavily on all young adults, they can be overwhelming for those whose parents divorce. This occurs especially when their parents continue to clash or are so immersed in their own problems that they can't see their child's reality.

Not surprisingly, many of the parents I interviewed noted

"problems" when their children were in junior or senior high school. Their kids started lying, ignoring curfews, cutting school. Some experimented with drugs; others ran away from home. One couple was forced to unlock horns when they were called down to the local precinct to bail their teenager out of jail. This is the extent to which some older kids may have to go to get their parents' attention.

The summer before he turned sixteen, Jeremy ran away from home; he drove cross-country with older friends. That crisis turned out to be a real turning point in Mark's and my co-parenting. The reasons (conscious or unconscious) for Jeremy's departure are not clear: Was it his need to pull his parents together or his desire to get us both to be more mindful of his development instead of our own problems? Both are probably true. In any case, the incident made us realize that we must not be in synch; and if we didn't pull together, we could lose our son.

Teenagers can be very threatening to parents. They tell it like it is for them, and we often don't want to hear their truth. Sometimes, it feels easier to give in to a rebellious or smart-alecky teen rather than put up with the flack. But in the end, we do the kid a disservice. In order to flee the nest properly, a teen has to experience it; he has to know that it's there, feathered and secure, a place to come back to if necessary. Parents who are too weakened or too preoccupied to set rules sometimes force teenagers to be prematurely independent; they grow up too fast. Even in the face of a teenager's outright defiance, parents must continue to set strong, reasonable, but expanding limits—until their teenagers demonstrate that they're really ready to be independent.

Telling the Children

Clearly, divorce is a process that must be dealt with differently at different times. For the children, it all begins when you tell them that you've decided to get divorced. Consider this moment with care; most children will remember it for the rest of their lives.

Ideally, both parents will have planned for this conversation in advance, and both should be present. Be prepared to say that the decision is final, so that the kids won't think they can say or do anything to change it. "Keep it as much out of the child's life as you can," says a young woman, twenty, when asked what advice she would give parents who divorce. "It's very personal between the two grown-ups, but kids don't get that. You have to encourage them to see that the divorce has nothing to do with them. I always felt I could change the situation. There was a ton of guilt."

Although the prospect of breaking the news is agonizing, parents have to be able to set aside their own feelings if they are to focus clearly and carefully on the kids. Timing is important—for example, it's best not to tell kids when they're tired, sick, or about to leave the house for a basketball game. Equally important is the amount of time that you allot to the conversation; children need this time and the chance, at this moment, to work through their feelings. Disregard the (understandable) impulse to break the news quickly and "get it over with." You will need time, too—to listen to them, to observe their reaction, and to answer their questions.

Most experts suggest that this conversation should take place a week or two before one parent plans to move out. If the change is too sudden, children are taken by surprise and access to both parents is too limited; if the change is too drawn out, there will be unnecessary confusion and anxiety—for your kids and probably you, too.

The most productive discussion happens when parents practice beforehand—going over the points they want to cover, writing them down if necessary—and when they try to anticipate their children's reactions. Be sure to let kids know that this is only the first of many discussions. Reassure them that you will be available when, as time passes, they will have other questions and concerns. If you have more than one child, explain that the two of you are telling them the news together but that later, when they are ready, each child will have separate time to talk with each parent. Being open and responsive now will encourage the children to come to you in the future. If you're not, they will quickly get the message that they're not to bring up the subject again.

Explain with age-appropriate information and language *why*

you're getting a divorce. Agree in advance that whatever reasons you give the children, you will present the divorce as a mutual decision. Keep in mind that many children worry that the divorce is their fault. Emphasize that this is *an adult decision:* they didn't do anything to cause the divorce—and they can't do anything to reverse it. Help them see that there are certain decisions that can only be made by adults—for example, whether or not to have a child or to buy a house; even though children might have an opinion about such matters, adults call the shots. Contrast that with making other types of decisions, such as the location of a family vacation or the kind of family pet to get. Make it clear that divorce falls into the first category.

Many experts think it's a good idea to tell children that you don't love each other anymore, because that will prevent reconciliation fantasies. But be sure to stress that *you still love the child and you always will:* "We loved each other when we got married, and we are both so grateful for what came out of that love—you! But we just don't want to be married anymore."

Voice some variation of "We can't get along with one another." You shouldn't burden children with adult details, but you can say that each of you has changed in terms of what you want/expect from the other. Always stress mutuality ("We *both* think it's a good idea for us to live apart"). And never point a finger ("Dad moved out because he's angry at me"), because there's a good chance that the child will turn such a statement toward himself ("Dad is really angry at *me* ").

If for some reason, your ex-spouse is not available, and you have to tell the children by yourself, act as you would if the absent parent were sitting beside you. Keep in mind that the children will be wounded by name-calling and blame, not your ex.

Assure them that both parents will continue to be in their lives. If you and your co-parent have already come up with a working plan, share it with children who are old enough to understand: "You will have two homes now, so that you can spend time with each of us. You will be with Mom [name days or amount of time] and Dad [name days or amount of time]. This may take some getting used to, but you'll always know where each of us is and how to reach us. When one of us is not with you, we can always talk on the phone."

If you don't know all the logistics—one of you is still looking for an apartment or plans to move into a relative or friend's house on a temporary basis—you can still reassure the children that they will always spend time, if not live with, both parents (more about living arrangements in chapter 6). Remember to stress that you will always be a family and that nothing—different homes, schedules, rules—will change that.

Judith Wallerstein also reminds parents to apologize, to let kids know that you're aware of how upsetting this decision must be. "Put simply, parents should tell the children they are sorry for all the hurt they are causing." At the same time, she says, make it clear that this is a crisis that the whole family will face together.

The parents I interviewed who had taken steps to educate themselves about the effects of divorce insisted they would *never* blame a child. Not knowingly, perhaps. They probably would not say anything as obviously harmful as "Our marriage fell apart because of you." However, more subtle messages can have long-term effects too. A comment such as "I left your father for your sake" may seem "loving," from a parent's perspective, but it may weigh heavily on the child. Children who believe that one parent left the other for them not only feel guilty, but they also may develop a distorted sense of their own power over their parents' lives—and, later, other people's lives.

Even though you break the news to all the kids together, in the weeks and months that follow, try to focus on each child's individual responses. Be sure to notify children's teachers, guidance counselors, and others who have regular contact with them. Even better, if your school system has a program like Banana Splits, steer your child toward it.

Banana Splits is a peer-support program for kids whose parents have died, divorced, or remarried—to help them process family change. It was launched fifteen years ago by educator Elizabeth McGonagle in the Ballston Spa, New York, school system. The name is derived from the fact that when a child joins, he gets a paper banana with his name on it, which he then hangs with all the other "bananas" on the tree. "Thus, to any parent, teacher, or child, there is an immediate visual impact of the number of kids involved," says McGonagle.

"It's pure Band-Aid, but it works," says McGonagle, likening the program, which serves kids from ages four to fifteen, to Weight Watchers and Alcoholics Anonymous. "In other words, the kids quickly realize they are not the only ones who feel alone and in need of help, and they have the shared experience of their peers." The program has been replicated in many school systems, at family centers, and by support groups (see Resources, p. 328).

Even if children are fortunate enough to have other adults to talk to and peers to commiserate with, it behooves parents to continue to be observant of the various changes each child experiences and expresses, and to keep an eye out for potential problems. Children need empathy and reassurance that their reactions are normal and understandable. They don't need to be "fixed" or "answered" when they cry out of sadness or rage that the divorce isn't "fair." From their perspective, it isn't.

Naturally, it's wrenching to witness your children's anger or sadness, to watch a child sob when the other parent has forgotten to call. It's even harder still at those times to resist the impulse to agree that the other parent is bad or that the child is "better off" without him. Still, you must allow your children to express what they feel and help them resolve their feelings without adding your own to the situation. In time, they will put the hurt in perspective and learn that loving the other parent (or anyone, for that matter) involves acknowledging and coping with flaws.

Beyond the Formulas: What Children Need/What Parents Can Give

I have to credit family therapist Ron Taffel, for reminding us about what he calls the "myth" of child development. He observes that although children generally fit the composite at various "stages" of development, the old models don't ring true all of the time. Because of the fast-paced, media-saturated world we live in, a six-year-old who sees an MTV video can sometimes sound like a teenager; and a teenager who is overwhelmed by confusing choices that confront today's adolescents can act like a baby. So if you purposely skipped some of the foregoing sections on stages of development, reading only the one pertaining to your child's current chronological age, it might be a good idea to go back and read *all* the sections. Under stress, children rarely act their age!

Besides, it's not only a matter of where the child is in developmental terms; family dynamics are also defined by where the parent is in the ongoing process of adult development. Just as a child must learn to drink from a cup, dress independently, and climb stairs, adults must master difficult new tasks, too—to be financially independent, to maintain healthy adult relationships, and to be a nurturing parent. As with children, adult mastery is not related strictly to age; some grown-ups are not "ready" for certain challenges, no matter how old they are. And as with children, development doesn't necessarily occur in neat, orderly stages, or along a linear path.

Parents and children clearly influence each other. And nowhere are the connections between adult/child development more evident than during the divorce process. The very foundations of the family are shaken; homes reorganize; roles, rules, and relationships change. During relatively stable periods, adults and children often take one step backward for every two steps forward. And during periods of stress, the drama of development is even more suspenseful—and intricate: adults can act like children, teenagers like petulant toddlers, and school-age children like little adults. Thus, figuring out what's best for a particular child, or what a child's behavior means, is not just a question of recognizing the child's development stage; you also have to pay attention to where *you* are—and what kind of nurturing you're capable of giving at this time.

When Doreen O'Hare separated from her husband of eight years, their son, Taylor, was only two. Her ex-husband, Ken, had been seeing another woman, but Doreen realizes that wasn't what was "wrong" with their marriage. "He was a carpenter; I was the upwardly mobile New York City career woman of the seventies." The only thing Ken and Doreen agreed about was that Taylor's needs had to come first. They determined that Taylor would live with Doreen during the week and spend weekends with Ken—an arrangement that continued for three years without much conflict.

Then Doreen, a fashion designer, was offered a plum position on the West Coast which, for her future, she felt she couldn't refuse. "I became a bi-coastal Mom. It was the hardest thing I ever did, but I couldn't uproot Taylor. I knew that he'd have a more dependable life with Ken. By then, he had remarried the woman he was seeing before the divorce. She was wonderful with Taylor, too, and I knew that she and Ken could give him a more stable home life."

Doreen commuted cross-country for the next several years, seeing her son once or twice a month and speaking to him almost daily. She often longed to "have" Taylor, but she knew that her frequent trips to the Orient didn't make for a secure environment for any child, let alone one Taylor's age.

She never really considered her long-distance mothering a permanent arrangement, but, "I wasn't in a good place to give him what he needed." However, she worked hard to remain an important presence in his life. Over the years, as Taylor asked different questions about the way his family lived, Doreen kept the lines of communication open, telling him as much as he could handle at each age. "I said his father and I had loved each other very much when he was born, but our goals had changed. No matter how angry I ever was at Ken and his new wife—the 'other woman'—I'd never, never say anything bad about either one."

A few years ago, when Taylor was nine, Doreen relocated to the East Coast. "I wanted Taylor back, and I was finally in an emotional and financial position to do it. But then I couldn't. I knew he had a bond with his father and stepmother. I had to ask myself whether I really wanted to put him through the emotional changes. He's approaching adolescence now, and the good news is that it's getting better all the time."

But What About Me?

Balancing your needs with your child's is a tricky business; most parents wrestle endlessly with this issue. Todd Dresdin, who has been divorced since 1985, contends, "Guilt is without a doubt the root of all evil when it comes to effective parenting. When you move out and leave your children behind, that becomes a new burden." Todd left his wife after thirteen years of marriage; their daughters were eight and four at the time. "In the beginning, I only picked activities—usually expensive ones—that I thought the kids would like and only spent time with friends who had kids. I turned myself into a one-man entertainment committee, two nights a week and every other weekend."

Todd admits that his greatest fear was that the girls "weren't enjoying themselves and they wouldn't want to see me anymore." As a result, he had no life of his own. After a while, he "started to realize that there were other things I wanted to do with my evenings."

Todd's experience is not uncommon; parents sometimes turn their feelings of guilt into a distorted sense of responsibility toward their kids. Putting your children's needs first does not mean obliterating your own! But it may take time and greater maturity to know the difference. Asked whether they "put their children's needs first," the vast majority of my respondents answer "almost always" or "usually," which indicates that they have a healthy handle on balancing adult needs and children's needs.

The point is, if you don't take care of your own basic needs, you won't be able to offer your children the sustenance they need. You feel too empty. You risk feeling resentful about the kids *and* leaning on them. Nurture yourself. Pay attention to your physical and emotional well-being, your new status and life circumstances, your need for adult support, and your social life. Besides helping you "get a life" (see pp. 58–70) when going through a divorce, over time, stability in each of those arenas also has parallel advantages for you *and* your kids:

Your Physical Health Physical well-being will not only revitalize you, it will also give you the energy you need to be with active kids. By example, you'll also teach your children the importance of taking care of themselves: Waiting on the sidelines of a high-school track for her fortyish mother to come around, a slightly overweight eleven-year-old girl told me, "My mother never did any exercise in her life. She took up running after she and my dad split up. That was about a year ago. Now she's in great shape. I can't quite keep up with her yet, but I'm trying!"

Your Emotional Well-being   Parents who are in touch with their emotions—and who learn to cope with feelings rather than shun them—are better equipped to help children experience theirs. As a result, everyone heals faster. If you can recognize the emotional ups and downs of divorce as inherent and necessary, you will be able to help your kids go through their own process. Your rage, loneliness, sadness, and feelings of betrayal will ebb, especially if they are allowed to flow naturally.

Your New Status   Try to check the urge to overachieve or underachieve. Don't exhaust yourself trying to prove you're not as bad or as weak as the divorce made you feel, but don't give in to those feelings either. Research shows that either extreme can retard the healing process. Give yourself a break! If you can be easier on yourself, you will be easier on your kids. It's also okay to tell children that you have been overdoing it or that you've been vegetating, as long as you explain how you were able to stabilize yourself ("I realized that I was trying to do everything on my own and do too much at once—looking for a new house, finding a better-paying job. It was overwhelming, so now I'm just taking on one thing at a time, and I'm getting help from . . . "). This is a valuable lesson in coping.

Let your kids know that they are part of the process. Their tasks are often parallel to yours and equally daunting: You have to get used to being single again; they have to get used to having parents in two homes. You have to move to a new house and, possibly, get accustomed to a new (or first) job; they have to move to a new house and, possibly, get used to a new school. Each of you needs time and space to accept and understand what "divorce" means to you and to the family as you once knew it. It will help *you* (as well as them) to walk them through a new apartment or house you're considering, to tour the new neighborhood, to look at a map and trace the new routes you'll have to travel to work and to school.

Your Support System   When you bend a friend's ear, find a good therapist, join a self-help group, or all the above, you're less likely to burden your kids with your troubles (or your anger). Deborah Nachum confided that she and her divorced cronies started a club called Ex-Wives of Assholes, affectionately known as "EWA" (ee-wah). They had three EWA "alerts": If a member called and said, "EWA 1 alert," that meant "Stop everything and listen." "EWA 2" stood for "Come over with donuts so we can talk face-to-face." And the most serious cry for help, "EWA 3," told a fellow member, "Come over and get me out of here!"

Having trustworthy, caring friends on board can also help you monitor what you say to or in front of the kids. Ask your friends to remind you to be cautious about what you say and to watch what they say when the kids are within earshot. When another adult isn't available, write a list of the things that enrage or annoy you and save it to share with a good friend, a support group, or a therapist. Just the act of writing and the promise of support can help protect kids from your turmoil. Date your lists and, after several months, review them. Chances are, over time some of your pet peeves will have paled to insignificance.

Your Social Life   Take time to have an adult social life and adult interests. Kids can be a convenient excuse—for your fear of taking the social plunge and getting on with your life. "The kids needed me," said one mother whose twenty-four-year-old daughter later told me how "clingy" her mom was after the divorce. Parents don't do their children any favors by monopolizing their time or asking them to fill the emptiness left by a departed spouse. Get out of the house; meet new people; develop new interests. Admittedly, with younger kids, it may be difficult—and costly—to find baby-sitters, so be creative. Ask family members or friends to pinch hit, or trade off with other moms or dads.

As Todd Dresdin found out, guilt benefits no one. Although he continued, for the most part, to make his adult plans on nights his daughters were at their mother's house, he eventually mustered the courage to hire baby-sitters. He stopped showering the girls with gifts and planning extravagant outings. "I realized that my children are going to love me no matter what. Now I do what's right for me *and* what's right for them."

Happily—or Sadly—Ever After

In the final analysis, parents do "owe" their children certain things: awareness of their needs, clear communication, and honesty. Which brings us back to this important key: *Listen to your children*. It sounds simple, but it's not. Too often we talk *at* children and tell them how they should feel. Take the time to listen to what your kids are actually saying about what's going on. Pay attention to their offhanded comments when they're playing with their friends, when they're talking about TV shows or movies, when they're fighting with siblings.

Encourage your child to talk to you, but don't play therapist—a common pitfall among parents steeped in pop psychology. I can remember Jeremy saying to me, time and again, "You can't read my mind" when I tried to tell him what *I* thought he was feeling. Maybe I was right, and he, at age nine or ten, just didn't know it. Or maybe . . . I was wrong. I'll never know, but I do regret not having been more of a listener. Even in the best of times, we parents tend to feel that our kids aren't communicating with us; there never seems to be enough *time*. Still, it's a good idea to work at being a little less desperate!

Talking is not the only way to connect with your child. You may have to leave conversations hanging for a day or two and be creative with new approaches. Most of all, you will have to be patient, keep your antennae extended, observe, listen—and listen some more (see also pages 223–231, "Setting the Tone for Kids: How to Spot Communication Problems").

By far the greatest listening challenge is when your children talk about life with the other parent. Don't editorialize or criticize, and don't cut your child off. Instead, provide an atmosphere in which your child feels free to talk about the other parent, and can even ask your opinion. It takes great self-control, but try to hear *the child's* needs without imposing your own agenda.

For instance, if she says something like "Daddy pays more attention to his girlfriend than me," resist saying "It figures!" Instead, suggest that it might be a good idea for her to talk to Daddy directly. Help the child structure her conversation, give her ideas about when to have a talk (when the girlfriend's not around), and, to help her script the conversation, role play—let her pretend she's Dad, and you be she.

If you're in the throes of a divorce or fear that you've already made some glaring mistakes, all these caveats and reminders may seem overwhelming. But it's never too soon to begin the healing—or too late to take your head out of the sand. Even today, fourteen years after Mark and I separated, when my kids and I speak about the divorce, it sometimes feels painful to listen their reactions. But I can apologize. In fact, after Jeremy's and my "interview," I wrote him a letter telling him how sorry I was for not being more sensitive and more mature when he needed me the most.

From your first BIG talk through the months and years to follow, you have to be there for your kids, encouraging them to communicate, allowing them to express their sadness, providing guidance and reassurance, setting limits . . . so that they still feel "held" by their parents. How you behave in the wake of your divorce—how you cope with stress, deal with change, resolve differences with the other parent, and view your new family apart—will set an example for your children. They will learn what you teach them in word and deed.

— 5 —

BAD SPOUSE/GOOD PARENT

Key #4: Respect Each Other as Parents

Transformations

Recalling the time, two years ago, immediately after the separation from his wife, Jason Stern says, "It was an instant transformation, almost as if Amy were saying, 'You were a schmuck as a husband, but you're a good father.' She definitely thinks more highly of me in this role." Their daughter, Diana, adopted as an infant, was two when the couple broke up. "Had there been no child, we never would have spoken after the divorce, but the irony is that now we talk every single day," reports Jason.

Though Jason was "infuriated" that his ex-wife, Amy Lutsen, didn't "make more of an attempt to save the marriage for the sake of our child," both tell surprisingly similar stories about their marriage and divorce. Co-workers in a graphic-design company and friends for several years before they became romantically involved, they lived together for three years. He admits, "We probably shouldn't have gotten married in the first place. By the time we made it to a marriage counselor, it was over."

Strongly motivated by their desire for a child, Jason was thirty-six and Amy thirty-nine when they wed. But they soon encountered fertility problems that seriously strained their relationship. Ignoring the increasing distance between them, the couple finally decided to adopt.

"Frankly, I knew from early on that the marriage was in

trouble," Amy says now. "We were living in a small two-bedroom apartment in New York City, both working at home. It was too much." She adds, "We're very different. I was raised in a pastoral village outside of Milwaukee. I think of Wisconsin as 'home,' and he's a city boy who thinks life only happens between Fourteenth and Ninety-sixth Streets! We also have very different backgrounds—my family is Norwegian, his Jewish—and there was a lot of ugliness from both sides."

Remembering her own parents' "miserable marriage," Amy says she also didn't want to subject Diana to a similar experience. Even though she wanted out, Amy recognized how much Diana loved Jason and how devoted he was to her. She vowed she would never deprive her daughter of a father. "We both got a really wonderful daughter out of this! *I* didn't want to be married to him anymore, but Jason is a very gentle, good, refined human being. He has really admirable qualities. And he's a good father."

In addition, Amy's memory of own father's death while she was in high school strongly influenced her behavior toward Jason after the divorce: "I knew what it was like not to have a father. And my mother barbecued the man, even after he was gone. My brothers and sisters and I became alienated from her because of it. So, when Jason and I split up, I decided you'd have to cut my tongue out before I'd say anything bad about him. I didn't want my child to feel about me the way I felt about my own mother."

For his part, Jason also began to see his ex-wife in a new light. His bitterness over the abrupt end of his marriage was ameliorated by Amy's supportive attitude. Since the divorce, he spends every other weekend with Diana and has two dinners with her during the week. His blossoming relationship with his daughter has tempered much of his anger.

"There are days when I miss her terribly. We speak on the phone for a half hour every night, but there are just so many things you can chat about to a four-year-old. Still, there's a lot of continuity; I don't feel that the relationship is in peril. And when the parenting part is going well, you're less frightened, less likely to turn things into a disaster with your ex."

Choosing a New Relationship: What It Takes

Amy Lutsen and Jason Stern's ability to see each other as co-parents instead of ex-spouses is echoed in other parents' stories. Although many transformations are not as "instant," the motivation to change is often the same. The vast majority of my respondents realized that no matter what *they* thought of the former spouse, it was important to be a regular presence in their children's lives. Consciously or unconsciously, these parents realized that seeing the ex-spouse in a different role would enable them to communicate with and support each other.

Granted, changing the focus from ex-spouse to co-parent often involves a greater leap of faith when the marriage lasted only a few years or was extremely contentious or if one parent is more resistant to the divorce and/or its terms. Likewise, if one parent is skeptical about the other's skills or sees the other parent as incompetent or irresponsible, the road may also be a bit bumpier. Still, by whatever route and for however long it takes to get there, respecting your ex as a parent is the basis of cooperative co-parenting, no matter how parenting time is actually shared. This change in perspective is *a conscious choice* you must make for your children. Mastering it involves three fairly difficult tasks:

Task #1: Separate the parenting relationship from the marital relationship.   Obviously, this is easier if you view your partner as a good parent to begin with and if he or she was active in a variety of ways before the divorce. But it can also happen when you see your former spouse in action—being a parent. Compared to mothers who have sole custody, the 1988 Stanford Custody Project found that joint-custody mothers report more respect for their former spouses' parenting ability—and perceived them to be more supportive and understanding. Nearly nine out of ten of the parents in my survey do as well. In response to the statement "I respect my ex as a parent," approximately half marked "almost always" (34%) or "always" (14%), and 35% marked "usually." It would seem, then, that even when there are profound feelings of betrayal related to your marriage and divorce, it is still possible to separate marital grudges from your children's immediate and long-term needs.

The clearer you can make this distinction, the sooner you will begin to see—and honor—the other parent's love for the child or children. You also may be surprised to discover that, as marital issues become less central, your views of each other will modify.

Pam Costanzos, who describes her relationship with her ex-husband as changing from "moderately angry" in the first year after they separated, to "civil but cold" in the second, and, finally, to "friendly," says, "Our differences were between us and could stay there. But we also shared a mutual feeling right away that we had to make the situation as easy on the children as possible. We always cooperated concerning the children, and we each trusted the other as parents. Eventually, the relationship between *us* changed, too."

Task #2: Acknowledge how much the children need the other parent and that the other parent has something to give. Concentrate on your common blessings as parents and your mutual love for the children. Identify, respect, and maximize the other parent's gifts and talents, rather than harping on his or her deficiencies. If you make a checklist of each of your strengths—related to the children's personal and social development, school, sports, music, art, and other areas in which a parent can help enrich children's lives and broaden their interests—you'll see how much you *and* your spouse can contribute. Ask for and appreciate the other parent's input and ideas. Being "better" or "right" about an issue is not the point. In nondivorced families as well, parents often have different but equally sound perspectives; and when both opinions are factored in, the result is richer, more thoughtful decision-making.

"When you have similar values, want the same things for your kids, when you value education and integrity, it's easier to come together as co-parents," maintains Yvette Hoving. Despite occasional conflicts and "different parenting styles," she knows that she and her ex-husband have the same interests at heart. She is more likely to listen to his opinions about their son and to consider him a resource rather than a hindrance (more about accepting a co-parent's differences in chapter 7).

Task #3: Find something about your ex-spouse that you can respect. After all, the two of you brought the child into the world in the first place. Reflect on those early years. Can you remember good qualities that were characteristic of your ex then? Is it possible that they are still present, if no longer evident to you? Are you willing to look for them and respond to them? Remember, neither of you is all good or all bad.

It may be easier to change your attitude if you try to see your ex through your children's eyes. A day at the amusement park may seem frivolous or indulgent to you, but to your children, it's just "fun." The other parent's forgetfulness, chronic tardiness, or sloppiness may drive you to distraction, but your kids may dismiss the behavior with a simple "Oh, that's Daddy—late again!" or "Mommy forgot . . . for a change!" Listen and learn from them; their perspective may be best for everyone. Besides, individual behaviors don't define the whole person.

The stories in this chapter, which show how some parents move along the co-parenting continuum by changing themselves and changing their view of each other from bad spouse to good parent, may help inspire your own transformation. You may have to give up your old ideas about what families are *supposed* to look like or how ex-spouses are *supposed* to relate after divorce. You may have to look beyond your own resentments or quell the urge to compete for the children's love. And you may have to work harder, exercise restraint, and consciously *look for* positive traits in your ex-partner. These difficult assignments may seem easier if you always remember that in all but a few, very extreme cases, *children need both parents.* A child who feels estranged—divorced— from one parent will suffer undue and far-reaching consequences.

Beyond the Stereotypes

When Jason Stern reflects on his co-parenting situation, he notes that "what might have been or should have been is totally irrelevant. I often use the analogy of having a handicap. Sure, divorce is a detriment, like a handicap, but this is the hand you're dealt. You face it; you don't wallow in it. You just have to work a little harder.

"Take the holidays. Amy and I divide them fifty-fifty. So? Is that bad? As far as Diana is concerned, this is the way *we* do holidays!" Jason resents the implication that people think Diana is "deprived" because her parents split up. "Society assumes that. But I don't think about it or feel bad—until someone reminds me that I should."

Jason's view of societal resistance to a more "normalized" understanding of divorce as one of many challenges faced by families is, unfortunately, quite accurate. And whether they are aware of it or not, those rigid images of "family" can limit the possibilities of parents seeking a different way to relate after their marriage ends.

Contrary to the stereotypes, a family does not have to be decimated after divorce, nor must children be contaminated by the fallout. It's far more constructive for divorcing parents and their children to think—and act—in terms of the nuclear family transforming into a different but whole *family apart*. Roles modify, positions shift, and relationships change, but the family endures; it reorganizes into two households with a parent at the center of each. The structure changes, but each home can provide a nurturing environment for the children's development, as well as for the parents' growth.

Prior to 1978, when Constance Ahrons began to collect data for her Binuclear Family Study, few researchers had bothered to study relationships *after* divorce. It had been assumed that divorce meant the end of a relationship and the severing of ties. At its worst, Mom got the kids, and Dad disappeared. Ahrons discovered that these assumptions didn't hold up; listening to couples one year after the legal divorce, and then three and five years later, she concluded that while some relationships between ex-spouses continued to be volatile or distant, just as many were not.

"In reality," Ahrons points out, "each of the ninety-eight divorced couples [in my study] was unique, and all formed an unbroken continuum of relationship styles from very angry and hostile to surprisingly friendly, with the majority falling somewhere in between."

Since Ahrons's study, a number of researchers have validated the diversity of divorced couples and the fact that, over time, their relationships can change. I found a similar continuum among my co-parents. Although they were angry and bitter after they first separated, today Elliott Brower and Linda Stein, who divorced in 1975, exemplify a postdivorce relationship that falls at the very friendly end of the continuum. They meet for family vacations with each other's current spouses and visit in each other's homes. Linda was a guest at both of Elliott's subsequent weddings. (She even addressed the invitations for his second one!) And after their son moved to Michigan to live with his father, Linda says, "That first Mother's Day, Elliott sent me $1,000 to come for transportation."

If the Brower/Stein divorce sounds unusual, it is. Such couples made up less than 10 percent of Ahrons's sample. It is rare that divorced partners are able to have intimate and sustained contact almost from the very beginning; more often, they start out at the "extremely hostile" or "moderately angry" end and move toward "friendly" and or even all the way to "very friendly" (see below). The Brower/Stein family apart is not meant to be held up as an ideal (although it is important to know that it *is* possible). Rather, it shows how insidious and limiting the old divorce stereotypes can be. "To get written off as 'weird' makes me uncomfortable," Linda wrote in a letter to me. "Initially, people thought I was just kidding myself to remain friendly with Elliott, and that our co-parenting arrangement was a way to hang on. Read: *unhealthy.*"

Table 5.1 **The Co-parenting Continuum**

	EXTREMELY HOSTILE	HOSTILE	MODERATELY ANGRY	CIVIL BUT COLD	FRIENDLY	VERY FRIENDLY
Year 1	19%	19%	33%	19%	9%	1%
Year 2	8%	13%	19%	34%	22%	4%
Between 2 & 4	3%	5%	9%	45%	34%	4%
After 5				26%	61%	13%

Note: Of 84 respondents, 74 had been divorced long enough to describe their relationships between the second and fourth year, and only 61 had been divorced for five years or longer.

Parents who characterize their relationship anywhere from "civil but cold" toward the "very friendly" end of the co-parenting continuum are able to create the best workable co-parenting arrangements; they also defy the stereotypes of how divorced partners are supposed to relate to each other. These couples highlight their abilities as parents while downplaying their disabilities as former spouses. Even if the necessary proximity to the other co-parent feels uncomfortable, they forge ahead.

"Both of us might have preferred more distance, but we really thought staying close was the right thing to do," says Helen Rogand, whose three children were six, three, and one when she and her husband first separated after thirteen years of marriage. "The kids always came first with us, so co-parenting was important from the start." Still, it's obvious that they had to work to make it happen: Helen's questionnaire indicates that their relationship went back and forth between "hostile" and "moderately angry" during the first year, but every year after that their relationship improved; after five, they traversed the "friendly" to "very friendly" zone.

Many couples who have hospitable co-parenting relationships say that friends frequently ask, "If you get along so well, why did you ever get divorced?" The answer is simple and consistent with researchers' findings as well: *you can respect someone as a parent but not necessarily want to be married to that person.* "We now have four healthy people, instead of four crazy people living together," maintains Cindy Danzer, mother of two, who separated when her son was ten, her daughter seven. She adds, "I would say Dick wasn't great to be married to. But he's a good father and a good person to be divorced from!"

Moving Toward the Positive End of the Continuum

If you and your ex are still quite antagonistic, don't despair. Most relationships change over time. Some parents admit that, at the outset, they were determined to "beat" the other parent, by "winning" the children—an attitude that, upon closer inspection, is usually a manifestation of their own insecurity: *If my child loves me more, than I must be better than the other parent.* Or, the other parent may be seen as an annoyance, if not a disruptive influence in the children's lives: *We would be doing fine, if only the kids didn't have to spend time with him/her.*

Gradually, however, the adults stop focusing on themselves and their spousal grievances, and they start to take care of the children's greater, more imperative needs. Of the mothers and fathers I surveyed, 65 percent note that "the need to co-parent" improved their relationship over the years; and three out of ten say that "realizing my ex was 'good' with and for the children" was a significant factor in successfully restructuring the family.

As I mentioned in chapter 3, sometimes a crisis shakes parents out of self-centeredness and makes them see that the other parent has at least some redeeming aspects when it comes to the children. Consider what happened to Gail Conners and Carl Bosco, whose acrimonious divorce seemed to obviate the possibility of their ever being able to cooperate. They wed in 1971; it was Carl's second marriage, Gail's first. In 1974, nine months after their son, Evan, was born, Gail was diagnosed with cancer.

"Carl couldn't handle it," recalls Gail. "He was convinced I was going to die, and he was shopping around for a new mommy for Evan." Gail notes that the following year was a whirlwind of surgery, chemotherapy, and sessions with a psychotherapist, punctuated by angry exchanges with her errant husband. Ultimately, she realized that she had to end the marriage.

Over the next four years, Gail, the custodial parent, blocked Carl's attempts to see his son, except for sporadic, time-limited visits. She was still furious about his behavior before, during, and after their separation. And she didn't approve of Carl's heavy drinking or his party-hearty lifestyle. She refused to let him keep the boy overnight, and when she later suspected that Carl's third wife was a substance abuser, she refused to let him see his son at all.

Then one morning, eight-year-old Evan woke up paralyzed. Waiting in the emergency room, Gail knew she was morally obligated to contact Carl. They were together when the doctors told them that Evan's paralysis was the result of a transient bone condition called legg perthes; fortunately, the disease had been caught early. Carl and Gail were told to keep Evan off his feet and also to help him do prescribed regular exercises, so that his bones would not become brittle.

Both parents understood that they had to pull together for their son's sake. Carl came to Gail's apartment twice a day to help Evan exercise. The boy eventually learned to walk again, thanks to his parents' willingness and ability to work well with him and with each other.

As their son recovered, so did Gail and Carl. Seeing each other in action helped them move along the co-parenting continuum. Gail remembers Carl's devotion to his temporarily paralyzed son. "Carl was a champ. He rallied; he was really there for Evan. That year, we shared parenting for the first time. And a lot of the bitterness went away."

Carl and Gail's story is a testament to parents' ability to change their views of each other. Carl had a few wild years; his parenting record was far from stellar. But when Evan got sick, Gail turned to him, needing and hoping for support, caring, and sharing. Carl responded. He was older then; he had divorced his third wife and was in therapy. Meanwhile, Gail was also seeing a therapist and had been working on *her* growth. "I had matured," she admits, which helped her set aside Carl's past indiscretions, "and I also saw that I could trust him more."

Today, Gail and Carl no longer view each other as adversarial ex-spouses who caused a marriage to fail. Now they are simply Evan's parents. Oddly enough, by 1984, they even became partners again—this time in their own law firm. "Sometimes it's hard to believe I was ever married to him," Gail remarks, "and sometimes I can't believe we were ever divorced."

Crisis is not the only thing that can motivate parents to change their attitude. The co-parents I surveyed cited various other factors that helped them transcend their own egos and move toward the positive end of the continuum: feeling love and concern for their children; observing the effects of atrocious divorces in other families; avoiding a repetition of their own, often painful, family history; seeking and using advice from counselors; reading books on divorce; and, most important, the passage of time and their own growth.

That Ol' Demon Competition

Although motivation and process may vary, change and growth are far more likely to occur in a positive environment. But a warning is in order: If you can move toward the friendly end of the co-parenting continuum, you can also slide back—especially when competition gets in the way.

I have to admit I felt a twinge when Mark traveled cross-country with Jennifer to help drive her car to Colorado—a trip that she, with her inimitable wry humor, labeled "a bonding experience." In the same way, perhaps Mark felt a bit cheated when I flew out to Portland to help Jeremy get acquainted with the city and set up his freshman dorm room. Undoubtedly, such experiences are typical in nondivorced families as well. In subtle ways, most parents compete for their children's love, but when you're married, the terms are not as absolute, the stakes not as high.

"As I was filling out your questionnaire," admits Barry Hubert, "a voice in my head was telling me to put down the answers my ex-wife would have written." Although Barry sees himself now as "calmer and more resilient," competition with his ex-wife is a dominant theme in his story. "Having girls and being a parent of the opposite sex was hard. They didn't talk to me about the same kind of stuff." In addition, he now realizes that he was in mourning when Judy left. "The thing that hurt most was that I wasn't going to grow old with the woman who had given birth to my children."

The first summer they were separated, Barry remembers visiting day at daughter Laurie's camp. "Judy and our younger daughter, Daisy, came up, too. Old friends of ours—Judy's and mine—were visiting their daughter, too. And because they invited Judy, and not me, out to dinner with them, I felt like I had lost. I remember running around the lake just to work off the rage.

"The whole day was about competition. There we were at camp—it was supposed to be a joyful time. If Laurie decided to spend a half hour with her mom, I felt hurt. If she wanted to spend a half hour with me, I felt victorious. If I had it to do all over again, I'd have gone up another time."

For a long time, Barry compared his *external* circumstances to his ex-wife's, and he always came up short. "Until recently, that continued to be an issue. I always felt this either/or thing. My life didn't seem as stable as hers. Judy remarried, she was making good money in a new business with her new husband, and when the kids were with me, we had to squeeze into a small apartment."

Judy notes that Barry's attitude was particularly troublesome when they changed the schedule. "He took a lot of things personally. He had a hard time seeing things from the kids' point of view. He was always suspicious and hurt, even if it was for the kids' benefit." When she realized how "competitive" her ex felt, Judy changed the way she gave him input. "I always felt that he was critical, but I realized that part of his behavior is defensive. Now I take a deep breath and walk him through my ideas in a different way."

But Barry has changed, too. Therapy, reading books, talking to other divorced fathers, and time have helped Barry conquer the feelings of insecurity. Not surprisingly, his need to compete has also abated. "Now I don't need Judy's approval, which I was always looking for. I don't want her to be the enemy, but I also don't want her to be the boss."

Because competition often belies feelings of inadequacy, it's only natural that men and women would attempt to win, control, or take an absolute position where they feel most capable. Even if she's a working mother, Mom may have trouble relinquishing authority in the parenting domain, because that's where she feels more confident and in control. So, she looks over Dad's shoulder, criticizes his every move, belittles his efforts, or tries to limit his access to the kids. She convinces herself that because Dad isn't dressing the kids, monitoring their diet, setting limits, or talking to them the way *she* does, it's "wrong." In worst-case scenarios, Dad believes that he's not competent, he stops trying, or he fades out of the picture altogether.

Meanwhile, fathers who want to "win" often use the weapon they're more comfortable with—money. They withhold it, or they criticize how the ex-wife spends it. Marcia Lebowitz of the Children's Divorce Center observes that many fathers are certain that their ex-wives "squander" child-support payments on themselves. They may malign a child's grooming or the appearance or condition of his clothing as proof that the money is obviously not being well spent. Lebowitz recalls one father who threw away his ten-year-old son's sneakers and sent the boy home barefoot to "teach his ex-wife a lesson." Of course, it was the child who learned the painful lesson—that Dad was so angry at him, he didn't even care if the boy had no shoes.

Roll back those videotapes. In both instances, *the parents could have made different choices,* governed not by a desire to "win" but by their children's needs. The mother can step back, live her own life when the kids are away, and let the children and their father build their own relationship. The father can stop thinking of child support as "his" money; and if he thinks his son's sneakers are in such bad shape, he could buy the kid a new pair. These options take maturity and no small degree of self-restraint, but, importantly, they won't take a toll on the children.

A modicum of competition, even a little bit of jealousy, between parents is inevitable. However, if divorced parents are *preoccupied* by one-upmanship, their kids may engage in their own form of competition. All children are skilled manipulators and instinctively know how to play one parent against the other. Children in divorced families often elevate this ability to an art form. "That's not the way Mommy cooks my hamburger," is bound to make Dad feel resentful, hurt, jealous, or inadequate. "Why can't you take me on vacation like Daddy does?" is likely to make Mom feel the same. Such feelings can be mediated by a sound identity; knowing who you are and being confident about your own self-worth can deflect even the sharpest criticism. A parent who is psychologically grounded is also less likely to "bite" (or bark) when a child drops the bait. Feeling centered, Dad would know that he's a good father even though he doesn't cook the same way as his ex-wife, so he would simply come back with, "You're right—Mom *is* a great cook. Maybe she'll give me her recipe." And Mom, knowing that she gives to her children in other ways, would calmly explain, "I wish I could take you on vacation, and maybe someday I'll be able to afford that. In the meantime, I'm so glad that you have a father who can."

You also might want to address the child's manipulative behavior directly: "You know, a comment like that could hurt a person's feelings [or if it really did hurt your feelings, say so]. I know that you love both of us, but there's no reason for you to compare us. We're two very different people, and we both try to give you the best of whatever we have to offer." Even if your child is not aware of the game she's playing, this kind of approach is likely to end future fishing expeditions! Also inject some humor in the situation—your version of "And thank goodness I don't do everything like Mom. Imagine how silly *I'd* look wearing high heels to work!"

Years after the fact, competitiveness and envy can linger; what you *do* with these gnawing feelings is the issue. "It's gotten easier, but I still feel some jealousy, especially when it comes to friends," admits Gabe Delaney, divorced eleven years ago. "For a time I was like a kid, feeling like I didn't get picked for the team. I used to be angry at her, but the jealousy is really anger at friends." The difference these days, thanks to a great deal of introspection and therapy, is that Gabe gives more attention to other, more important and beneficial feelings. "I feel Sally's a good mother. She's been there for our son; she really loves him."

Don't chastise yourself for feeling competitive; just keep it to yourself—and make sure that your actions are not motivated by "winning," but by your children's interests. Interestingly, professor of sociology Gayle Kimball, author of *50-50 Parenting,* suggests that a good argument can also be made to *support* competition between parents: it can inspire disinterested or inexperienced fathers to spend more time and energy with their kids! "Children try to use competition between divorced parents to their advantage, but if the contest has positive results, and parents are not critical of each other in front of the children, this can be an effective motivator for fathers."

Elena Costos would agree. Her son and daughter were three and four when she left their father, Jim Miller. "Jim is *not* the same since the divorce. When we were married, he was irrelevant—he disappeared into the wallpaper. He was involved with the kids, but I was always the quarterback. Only after we got divorced did he start to give me a hard time." Like many fathers who do more hands-on parenting once they're divorced, as Jim started to trust his own opinion about what his children needed, he became more assertive about the kids' clothes, their daily habits, where they should attend school.

While it's good that Jim became more involved with the kids, the escalating competition between the parents was *not* good. In fact, it ended up back in court, battling over custody. Fortunately, seeing the wear and tear on the kids changed both parents' perspective. Elena concedes that it was hard to relinquish the power, but, "I began to see that my entire motherhood did not hinge on his time with the kids. As they grew older, and I got a little smarter, I realized that our fighting was more damaging to them than it was worth. I was willing to give up more time with them than I had ever dreamed."

Elena then says what she was once too proud and too competitive to acknowledge: "I have to admit, he's a good father. And by letting go, we've both gotten closer to the kids."

Co-Parent/Better Parent

Research in the past has been limited about the efficacy of co-parenting, because most studies have looked at sole-custody situations. Certainly, *cooperative* co-parenting eliminates the one factor that virtually every study of divorce has identified as *the* major risk factor that compromises children's postdivorce adjustment: conflict. It is clear that when parents cooperate, children are less likely to feel divided loyalties, less likely to feel abandoned, less likely to feel that they have to support their parents. They are free to be children.

Hugh McIsaac, former director for Family Court Services in

Los Angeles and now Director of Family Service in Portland, Oregon, says "I've seen these kids. They sometimes have a greater range of abilities than children in intact homes and they're much more socially adept because they've had to deal with different personalities."

Co-parenting also eliminates another major risk factor: father absence. Although some fathers in my survey were active participants in their children's upbringing before the divorce, an equal number had relegated the parenting spotlight to their wives—until divorce forced them into center stage, too. A man who co-parents doesn't necessarily turn into "Mr. Mom," as one mother called her ex, when he became a born-again father after their divorce; but he will become more intimately involved in the details of his children's lives. Fathers who never paid attention to kids' table manners, how they dressed, or other mundane details are amazed to find themselves reading books on parenting, noticing more, and altogether caring more when they become homemakers for their children.

Even Jason Stern, a hands-on dad from the day of Diana's adoption, grants, "I actually see her on a one-to-one basis more than I ever did." His experience is common among fathers who co-parent. Many think they have "gotten to know the kids better" than if they had stayed married to the children's mother. Seeing how much they're needed, they're more likely to respond to their children; they set limits, offer guidance, take care of kids' day-to-day needs, nurse them when they're sick. Studies have shown that involved fathers are twice as likely to pay child support compared to fathers who are completely cut off from their children. And they are less likely to suffer the feelings of loss, loneliness, and estrangement that often plague distant dads.

Mothers, especially those who have been able to relinquish the need to control, also report that co-parenting makes *them* better parents. "I have more time to myself without the kids now, so I feel freer to give my time when the kids are here," says one. "I'm a better mother, because I'm a less stressed-out mother," says another.

For many women, a major postdivorce responsibility is to become financially self-sufficient. This may involve going back to school, working out of the house for the first time, or changing to a better-paying, perhaps more-demanding job. Co-parenting, and more time away from mothering responsibilities, may allow a woman to grow, not only as a parent, but as an individual as well.

"Divorce was good for me. I gained a sense of independence," says Helen Rogand, forty-two, whose situation is similar to that of many midlife women after divorce—women whose main "job" had been caring for the family. Like so many women who marched down the aisle to the tune of tradition, Helen spent years being the perfect wife and mother and then began to hear the clarion call of the women's movement; so she started taking classes and became increasingly active in the world outside of the family. "He would say he'd be home at such-and-such a time to be with the kids, but then he'd never show up. After we divorced, I wasn't willing to be at his beck and call any more. Fortunately, Mitch was very generous, and I had the freedom not to work and to go back to school full-time."

Helen feels that their kids are learning invaluable lessons. "I wanted to give them a role model. And I've found that communicating and working out changes in our family structure with Mitch is better than taking my anger out—on him or the kids. We're teaching them positive skills they will be able to use in their own lives."

Indeed, the most current data from a number of different studies conducted in the last ten years* indicate that both men *and* women may be better parents as cooperative co-parents, because co-parenting gives each parent more personal time and also allows more energy to be directed toward the kids. Co-parents report significantly less difficulty finding time to play or chat with their children, certainly more than mothers in primary-custody situations in which fathers see the kids sporadi-

---

*I am indebted to John L. Bauserman at the Children's Rights Council for bringing to my attention at least two dozen studies that point to the positive effects of co-parenting and to Joan Kelly's review of the research, which she wrote in 1988. All are listed in the Bibliography.

cally or not at all. These parents are also more satisfied with the arrangement, which certainly influences their general disposition.

Bill Paterson and Loretta O'Brien have shared equally in the care of Kevin and Gretchen, eight and almost six when their parents first split up nine years ago. Both parents see an overall improvement in their family life. Bill says, "It's better in a lot of ways. Each of us has time for ourselves. And with the kids, you never get to the point of their being around so much that you take them for granted."

Several couples also remark that splitting up alleviated the marital problems that plagued them (and, simply through proximity, their children) and, therefore, their new status—as co-parents—made their relationships more stable. Martina Davis and Harold Silverman, both mental-health professionals, were in constant conflict as spouses. Her gripe was the seeming disproportionate share of parenting that fell in her lap; in his eyes, different religious backgrounds put stress on the relationship.

"Parenting has actually been easier in many ways with the structure of two separate households," notes Martina, "because everything is clearly defined. Instead of my doing ninety percent of the child care and paying for half of Anna's expenses, we renegotiated, settling on sixty–forty time while maintaining the fifty–fifty money split."

"Things are much easier now," agrees Harold. "The religious—cultural—differences have been relieved by the separation." He feels freer to spend the Jewish holidays with Anna and to allow his wife to celebrate a nonconflicted Christmas and other holidays of importance in her tradition.

Paradoxically, by becoming co-parents, the ex-spouses have been able to come together, rather than argue and compete, over issues that pertain to their child. "Music has been a very strong forum for our joining as co-parents," says Martina. Anna, who has been taking violin lessons since she was a toddler, has inherited her parents' appreciation of music. "We both do a lot of music with our daughter—Harold plays piano with Anna; I play violin, too. And there are lots of times when we *enjoy* being together—for example, at concerts."

But This Won't Work for Us . . .

If all this sounds too idealistic or impossible, don't lose hope. Perhaps you're not quite ready. Maybe the circumstances that led to the end of the marriage were so painful that right now you both feel too raw to respect each other, let alone cooperate on anything. Sadly, not all couples are able to overcome their own issues or each other's. Still, just about everyone who divorces has a rocky beginning and then occasional painful backslides along the way (which are dealt with in chapter 10). So try to take small, intermediate actions that can ease the stress and at least begin to change *your* perspective.

Don't wait for your ex to "come around."   If your ex-partner doesn't respect you as a parent, why should you respect him or her? Because your children need at least *one* parent to act maturely. Instead of saving face or hanging on to your pride, be the leader. Treat your ex the way you want to be treated. As one mother told me, "I realized that I wouldn't want to be denied the joy of raising my kids—how could I contemplate doing that to him?"

Be polite.   A little courtesy goes a long way toward softening anger. If you have to be with the other parent, and you're still angry, keep conversations to a minimum, be businesslike, avoid vengeful looks, sarcasm, and baiting. Before your meetings, practice the following mantra—or write your own affirmation—and then repeat it (silently, to yourself) when you're in the other parent's presence: "I need to act civilly for my children. This has nothing to do with my feelings for my ex-spouse. I need to act civilly for my children. This has nothing to do with my feelings for my ex-spouse. . . ."

Do something different.   When the air between you is still thick with conflict and the same negative scenarios keep cropping up, allow yourself to visualize a situation ahead of time so that you can plan positive ways to *be* different the next time you see the other parent. In *Divorce Busting*, Michelle Weiner-Davis suggests several "uncommon sense techniques" that can help block destructive patterns of relating. Weiner-Davis suggests these tactics to save a marriage, but why not use them to save your co-parenting relationship? One strategy is to "act as if." Problems often occur because people expect them to, says Weiner-Davis. So change your expectations; act "as if" you expect the other parent to be friendly. Ask yourself, "How would I act if I thought that the children's father/mother would be cordial and cooperative at pickup time?" Your answer? You would probably *be* more cordial and cooperative as well!

Reassure the other parent that you won't undermine him/her. Say this out loud to the other parent, even though the angry part of you doesn't want to believe it: "I know that regardless of what I think of you, or what has transpired between us, our kids need two parents. I also know how much the kids love you and you love them. I won't stand in your way; in fact, I'll try my best to support your relationship with them and I hope you'll do the same."

Don't preach, or use an I'm-better-than-you tone, or expect the other parent to respond immediately. It may take time and may take the patience of a saint on your part, but even if the other parent belittles you or insults you in front of the children, stick to your guns. This kind of reassurance—and the behavior to go with it—will, in the end, help avoid the most damaging effects of divorce.

Change your vocabulary. Such terms as "my ex" or "my former spouse" carry heavy, judgmental, negative meanings, and words have a powerful effect on your psyche. Isolina Ricci has an entire chapter in *Mom's House, Dad's House* on how words can be used to change attitudes and help divorced parents move beyond negative stereotypes. More than a decade later, Ricci maintains, "Shifting to positive terms in everyday conversation is a simple, yet powerful, tool for change." So stop calling him or her "my ex." Use a first name instead, or say "my children's father/mother." If you concentrate on his role as the father of your children or hers as their mother, it's easier to keep parenting separate from conjugal issues, and you also won't be as inclined to think in destructive terms.

Our legal system and its verbiage doesn't help much. Terms like *sole custody* and *visitation,* imply that children are property and that one parent loses "rights" to them while the other gains. So, buck the system. Instead of buying into limiting legal lingo that regards children as chattel, think of and talk about yourselves as a family apart and create a "parenting plan" that sets out each parent's involvement and responsibilities (more on this in chapter 6).

Learn how to negotiate.   In Constance Ahrons's study, she found that the main difference between the parents who could at least cooperate and those who were still somewhat hostile was their "management and resolution of the anger." Anger is inevitable after divorce. It's impossible to keep legalities, finances, and emotions separate from parenting at all times. The best strategy is knowing how to manage conflict and negotiate compromise. Take a course, read a book, and learn strategies that can help you stop arguments from happening in the first place or at least contain them before they spiral out of control (see pages 79–88).

Build more structure into your co-parenting relationship.   Just because you both feel wounded and you don't trust each other, your co-parenting relationship doesn't have to suffer—it can be modified. In the early stages, in particular, if there's a great deal of animosity, there's not a lot of room for flexibility. You don't want to give an inch, because you're afraid the other parent will steal a mile. So you may have to be more specific with each other about expectations, rules, schedules, and monetary contributions. Get professional help from a therapist or mediator if you can't do it on your own. Difficult though it may be to believe in the beginning, as new trust and respect build, parents usually become more generous with and less suspicious of each other.

Trust the other parent's motives.   Many parents worry whether they can really believe their ex-spouse's intentions. Are they "pure" and child centered? They might not always be (and the same could be said of your motives as well!), especially in the beginning stages of divorce when parents typically feel so insecure. Co-parenting is a real stretch of faith, but the result is well worth it. So, try to give the other parent the benefit of the doubt. Besides, not all ulterior motives will necessarily harm the kids.

Gloria Shannon thought her ex-husband, Gary, was being too much of a Disneyland Dad the first few times he took five-year-old Matthew for the weekend. But she also understood why Gary felt insecure; he wasn't spending as much time with their son. Because she trusted that Gary's heart was in the right place, instead of acting on her resentment, she talked to him calmly, told him that he didn't have to "buy" his son, and reassured him that she *wanted* his participation. "He definitely has taken my suggestions."

For his part, Gary says that when he realized that in between visits Gloria talked to their son about him, he felt supported. He saw that lavish gifts weren't needed to keep his place in the family. He also owns up to the fact that prior to divorce, he wasn't much of a hands-on father, which added to Gloria's early suspicions. Like many moms, she was afraid of "losing control" over her son to an ex-husband who, by his own admission, is quite "controlling."

Keep a parenting diary for both of you. Think of Gary and Gloria Shannon's growth and change. Their transformation took time and faith, but it also involved recognition of change. A parenting diary can help clarify your own priorities and strengths as well as focus on what your ex-spouse contributes; it will help you measure your movement toward the positive end of the co-parenting continuum.

Every day, write down what you do with, for, and in the interest of the children; describe activities—both mental and physical—in which you invest time and energy. Appreciate your efforts and congratulate yourself on "showing up" for your children in spite of your own pain.

Now here's the tough part: Every day, also list the other parent's strengths and efforts. Be sure to keep in mind your children's needs and hopes—in other words, not what you think your ex-spouse *ought to do* with, for, and in the interest of the children, but what *your kids* would like. This kind of filter may help change your view of the other parent's time with the children. Before you immediately judge or devalue an activity, listen to the kids. You might discover, as Deborah Nachum did, that what seems like "a waste" from a parent's vantage point, is a wise investment of time and energy from the kids' standpoint.

One night, returning to her house, Deborah's then seven-year-old son, Davy, reported to her that Dad and he watched a football game all afternoon. During their marriage, seeing her husband glued to the set every Sunday drove Deborah crazy, but, she says, "For some reason, I suddenly realized that it wasn't the same experience for Davy. He told me they made popcorn together, cuddled up in front of the tube, and talked 'guy stuff' during the commercials. That was their way of spending time. Davy loved it—it had nothing to do with me or my feelings about TV football!"

Parenting is a tough job. Give yourself and the other parent the leeway to make mistakes. Kids don't come with instruction books, and you're only human. One miscommunication, one wrong decision, one incomplete or inadequate explanation does not add up to utter failure. You can always say "I'm sorry" to a child, bring up a subject for further discussion, or change your mind about a decision. Allow the other parent to do the same.

After you have made several entries in your parenting diary, reread "What It Takes" at the beginning of this chapter. Chances are, this will make it easier for you to separate parenting from marital issues; and you probably will see the other parent's contributions more accurately in the context of your co-parenting partnership.

Watch your entrance and exit lines. It's Sunday night, the doorbell rings, and the kids are back. This is a crucial moment in time for your family apart, so count to ten and *don't* say the following lines—or any variations on these themes:

"You could have at least given him a bath."

"More toys?"

"Can't you see that it's raining—where are her boots?"

"I'm sure he's too full of junk food to have dinner."

"Can't you ever be on time?"

Transition times are the most difficult for the children, and they're not so great for adults either (more about this the next chapter, pages 180–186). You may be tempted to lecture on the "best" way to do things (*your* way!), or to offer a litany of instructions whenever your ex picks up or drops off the kids. Restrain yourself. Try to be emphatic; act "as if" your ex is doing the best she can under the circumstances. If not, your criticism certainly isn't going to improve his or her perform-ance!

Imagine that something is seriously wrong with your child. This may sound like a morbid suggestion, but terrible things do happen to kids—sickness, accidents, problems at school—that often force parents to come together. Why wait for disaster? Imagine the worst and ask yourself, Who else is as important to your child? Who else wants, needs, and deserves to be involved, to help the child *and* you? *The other parent!* As grim as this little exercise is, it might help change your outlook.

"I wish that somehow we could make divorcing parents realize how important the other parent is to the children," says Sara Goodman, who separated in 1986; her children are now sixteen and twenty. In four years Sara went from feeling "extremely hostile" toward her ex to "civil but cold." Recognizing that the process takes time, she adds, "Most of us get it, sooner or later. If only parents could do it sooner, it would save them—and their children—so much heartache."

Consider the alternatives. If you can't imagine what will happen if you cut your children off from their other parent, read books or talk to a therapist. Listen to children of bad divorces; they will open your eyes. Identify with your child and imagine what it would feel like to have what psychiatrist Frank Williams, head of child and adolescent psychiatry at Cedars Sinai Hospital in Los Angeles, California, calls a "parentectomy." Research and experi-ence tell the same story: *Children need two parents.* True, there are rare situations, such as when a parent is mentally ill, violent, or has a long history of substance abuse or criminal behavior. "But such dramatic conditions are not typical," insists family thera-pist and mediator Isolina Ricci. You and your spouse ended the marriage; you couldn't live together. No matter how much you hurt each other in the process, you are probably not disturbed or incompetent, and neither is your ex.

Don't expect perfection. Nondivorced families aren't perfect, either! Sometimes the occasional ill wind will reappear, chilling the atmosphere of everyday life. Years after successful co-parents think that they have worked out all the kinks, arguments can crop up over money, old fears can creep in around the holidays or before a "big" event, such as a wedding or the birth of a grand-child. But if you keep in mind that you are protecting your children (and grandchildren)—it will help you weather these future storms and secure the foundation of your family apart.

— 6 —

NEW FAMILIES/NEW FORMS

Key #5: Divide Parenting Time

Homes Apart: What "Co-Parenting" Means

Like most parents who opted for co-parenting in the eighties, Mark and I made it up as we went along. We came up with a schedule that, we believed, gave Jennifer and Jeremy almost equal time with—and never too long without—each parent. Not having many families to compare notes with, we did the best we could on our own. Looking back, I see some things I would do differently and others that I'm quite proud of. Most important, I have learned that co-parenting is far more than a matter of sharing time.

Participants in my survey make it clear that "co-parenting" is defined differently in each family apart. But all agree on the definition used throughout this book: "Co-parenting" involves both parents' unremitting dedication to their children's care. This commitment exists regardless of legal documents, living arrangements, or allocation of time.

You and your ex-spouse—the co-parenting team—must work out a game plan that reflects the unique needs of your family apart. It must embody children's and parents' needs, distance and time constraints, financial considerations—complexities that would give King Solomon pause! The goal is to work toward *real* sharing—of rights *and* responsibilities, joys *and* hardships.

With time, effort, attentiveness and, literally, "response-ability," you can structure a new family form—a functional, healthy family apart. This chapter, which looks at both legal and practical options, can help you weigh the many factors you must consider when deciding what kind of arrangement might work best for your family apart.

Response-Ability: Being a *Real* Co-Parent

Divorce is a legal process that ends a marriage, divides property, defines custody, and enumerates financial responsibilities. It is unfortunate that *custody,* a term which implies that children are kept, given up, or passed back and forth like chattel, is part of the package, because children are then used as leverage. Even though only a fraction of divorces are actually litigated, the uncertainty of "What will happen when I get to court?" looms ominously and can cloud parents' perspective.

Co-parenting, which concerns parents' responsibilities, has little to do with custody, which concerns parents' rights. Elaborating on this important distinction, lawyer and divorce mediator Sam Margulies, author of *Getting Divorced Without Ruining Your Life,* explains, "What you do to insure your legal rights to the child may fall within the scope of *custody,* but what you do to insure the welfare of that child falls within the concept of *parenting.*"

The legal process works against cooperative co-parenting. That's why it's important to make every effort to try to talk directly to each other about what's best for the children or at least to try to negotiate with a competent mediator or lawyer who doesn't exploit your emotional vulnerability—and empty your pockets—at your children's expense (see also pp. 88–94). Divorce laws vary, but if some form of joint custody is available in your state it is usually the best route, because of the message it sends to your children and to the other parent. Presumably, you agree that it's essential for your children to have two parents. Then why shouldn't this understanding be reflected in your legal agreement?*

*According to data compiled by the Children's Rights Council, in *The Best Parent Is Both Parents: A Guide to Shared Parenting in the 21st Century,* "the legal concept of joint custody has been defined by state legislatures in terms that

At the same time, having joint custody doesn't mean you will automatically be a competent, nurturing, thoughtful co-parent. A legal designation on paper does not define the way you parent in practice. Some who co-parent successfully have joint custody; others have sole custody.

It's true that, "joint legal custody" means that each parent has equal responsibility and equal authority in children's lives; "joint physical custody" means that the child has two homes, although not necessarily equal time in each one. But, as family therapist and mediator Isolina Ricci, Ph.D., stresses, "Joint custody does not necessarily mean *shared* parenting [her term for co-parenting]." Ricci notes that even some joint physical custody plans can be quite "one-sided." A father, either because he is not available or not willing, might have 30 percent of the overnights and all of the "fun" activity time with the kids, while the mother is left with more of the day-to-day activities. Ricci explains, "Maybe he shares the major decision-making, but he may never take his child for a haircut."

As discussed in the previous chapter, mothers can also inhibit their ex-husbands' role by staking out parenting as their eminent domain. For many women, divorce marks the first time they begin to feel any separate sense of power and control. It is tragic when they exercise this newfound strength at their children's expense.

True co-parenting cannot be mandated. Studies that compare different types of custody indicate that when it is imposed, joint custody doesn't necessarily work any better than sole custody: it's

---

range from the vague and general to the specific and detailed." At this writing, forty-eight states and the District of Columbia have some form of joint custody option. In nineteen states—California, Connecticut, Florida, Idaho, Iowa, Kansas, Louisiana, Maine, Michigan, Minnesota, Mississippi, Missouri, Montana, Nevada, New Hampshire, New Mexico, Oklahoma, Oregon, and Utah—joint custody or shared parenting is the presumption or preference. Only one state, South Carolina, does not permit joint custody, and the North Dakota statute is silent on the subject. Because the various terms used by legislators (among them, joint legal custody, joint physical custody, shared parenting, joint parenting, co-custody, concurrent custody, shared custody, joint managing conservators) have different legal ramifications, it's important to research the laws in your state. See "Resources," page 319, for books that can help.

the *relationship* with a parent that makes a child feel wanted and welcome, not the allocation of hours, days, or weeks, not how big a child's room is, not how much fun the child has when she's with that parent. "It's more than just having you live there or asking how you're doing in school," says eighteen-year-old Orin Delaney, whose parents divorced when he was nine. "What matters most is your parents' involvement in the things that make you feel like they care about you."

Therefore, before you take an adversarial approach to custody, counting days and figuring out how much time with your children you're going to demand or give up, search your soul. Take a cold, hard look at yourself—your needs, your motives, your temperament, your interests, your time constraints. Do you have what it takes to be all that a co-parent has to be? Are you willing to provide structure and limits in your child's life, as well as comfort and good times? Are you willing to give your children everything they need, including the other parent?

You must also keep in mind that co-parenting doesn't work unless you keep both feet in your own house! Especially if you've been more of a hands-on parent than your ex-spouse, it's hard to resist the temptation to run the other parent's household. Not respecting your co-parent's boundary is the fastest route to perpetual conflict, especially if your ex is now living with a new significant other. You both deserve privacy and autonomy, and the kids deserve a chance to develop their own separate relationship with the other parent.

It's embarrassing to admit that it took me several years—and a number of sessions with a family therapist—to "get" this concept. In the beginning, I was eternally frustrated because I couldn't "control" Mark's parenting. Looking back, I asked the kids too much about life at Dad's and offered too many prescriptions, which, I now realize, was out of my bounds, as well as a not-so-subtle way of criticizing him!

You also may have to put aside some old ideas. For example, instead of worrying about whether you "have" your children, concentrate on what each of you brings to parenting (love, hands-on care, values). However you allocate parenting time, think in terms of the children *living* with both parents, not "visiting." Circumstances may not allow equal time, but the children need both of you, and you both offer them different gifts. And even if your child sees one of you considerably more than the other, neither should be considered the "custodial" parent or even the "primary" parent if you interpret it to mean *better*.* Isolina Ricci suggests using "first" and "second" parent, but an enlightened term means nothing if it reflects an unenlightened attitude.

Ask yourself if you are able—for your children's sake—to maintain a minimal level of cooperation with the other parent so that you can—with some negotiation—make joint decisions about major issues (education, religious training, and health) and have discussions about day-to-day concerns as well (homework, chores, rules, curfews)? "Both parents need to take care that each becomes and remains a *real* parent rather than one a disciplinarian and the other only a recreation director," stresses Isolina Ricci. You don't always have to agree (more about that in the next chapter), but a co-parent who is able to support the other parent is a good co-parent.

Focus on your parental *responsibilities,* not just your parental rights. You'll need to be honest about whether you, consciously or unconsciously, see yourself "getting" the children as the spoils of your marital war or "giving" them as a kind of consolation prize to the spouse you left behind. Ask yourself if you are demanding time with your children because you think it's best for them, because that may reduce the amount of money paid to your ex-spouse, or because it will make you look better in other people's eyes. Or perhaps co-parenting is a way to get the kids off your hands. Years later, some parents who battled over schedules admit that they really weren't fighting for time *with* the kids as much as for time *without* them.

Consider what you'll do *within* the time you spend with your children, not just how much time you'll have. Picture your life

---

*Legally, "primary parent" status is determined by a number of factors, among them, who prepares and plans meals; bathes, grooms, and dresses the child; purchases and cares for clothing; takes responsibility for medical care, including visits; makes the child's social plans; who makes day-care arrangements; puts the child to bed, sees her through nightmares, wakes her in the morning; disciplines, handles religious or cultural education, and teaches the child elementary skills. With cooperative co-parenting, both parents should participate in *all* of the above.

without your spouse and with your children. Will you be doing as much as, more, or less for and with the kids than you did when you were married? True co-parenting means dealing with the minutiae of everyday living—their homework and your after-work fatigue, making dinner and giving baths, establishing bed-time rituals and slogging through morning routines. It means paying as much attention to a child's mood, her fight with a best friend, or her disappointment about not getting picked for a team—her inner life—as noticing when it's time for a haircut, new sneakers, or a dental checkup—her outer life.

Ask yourself bluntly if you're willing or able to be a hands-on parent: taking your child to the movies—or to the dentist; making sure he practices his guitar—or surprising him with concert tickets; overseeing chores—or going camping; shooting hoops in the backyard—or cheering her from the sidelines; folding clothes—or shopping for new ones; making pancakes on a Sunday morning—or vacuuming the house; teaching him how to read a unit-pricing label—or letting him teach you how to use a computer; monitoring homework—or allowing her to play hooky . . . just so you can steal some extra time together.

Hundreds of these little parent/child moments add up to a lifetime of connection, as Morgan Grant, a father divorced five years ago, points out: "I wanted to really be there for my kids, not just as a weekend father. But I travel a lot, and because of my work schedule, I couldn't see them during the week for the first two years. So I tried to make sure that the weekends really counted. Now that I've changed jobs, they're at my house half the time. Recently, I was reminiscing with Dana, who is twelve, about those early years, and I was shocked. She didn't even mention things like vacations or amusement parks. She remembered the time when we took a ride to look at the beach after a winter snowstorm and the time she helped me repair a wagon."

Designing Your Parenting Plan

A parenting plan, which details parental responsibilities and rights, may be part of your overall separation agreement, in which case the terms are legally binding; or it can be a separate document. Your parenting plan should attend to:

- *Living Arrangements:* establishing regular times when children will stay with each parent at each house; where they'll be for school holidays and vacations.
- *Financial Contributions:* calculating responsibility for everything the children will need—school (including college, if possible), religious training, camp and summer trips, activities, clothing, books and school supplies, computer, sports, or musical equipment, dental and medical bills. If one of you is a long-distance parent, include the cost of phone calls and transportation.
- *Decision Making:* outlining the process whereby major decisions, as well as those covering day-to-day issues, will be made.
- *Contingencies:* designing a blueprint for day-to-day operations—for example, transporting the kids to and from school and from one parent to the other, making appointments, taking them shopping or to the dentist—as well as a promise to work together in the event of emergencies, sudden changes in finances, job situation (what happens if a parent has to relocate), health, or other areas. See appendix II for a typical parenting agreement.

The parenting plan you design at the time of your divorce should be viewed as a work-in-progress; you may have to modify or make it more specific over time. Parents often don't stick with the initial plan, but in the beginning it helps to concretize as much as possible. Remember, divorced or not, when you have kids nothing can be carved in stone! Arrangements will be modified as adults' lives and circumstances change—new jobs, new significant others, new homes—and as children grow and change. After three to five years, in fact, it's sometimes hard to recognize the original arrangement, which is why it's a good idea to build in an annual review.

Although it's impossible to describe every conceivable co-parenting variation, living arrangements generally fall into one of the following broad categories:

Home Base   Children live primarily with the first parent. They live with the second parent for specifically scheduled periods—weekends, alternating weekends, school vacations, summers. Approximately a quarter of my sample reported a home-base arrangement. This type of plan seems best to some parents because their children are, in their opinion, too young to make frequent transitions or too old—preteens and teenagers who are unnerved by commuting. Some parents may be forced into a home-base plan because they live too far away from each other or because one parent's work schedule is erratic. One mother commuted from California to Texas, where her sons lived with their father, because she thought that his lifestyle offered more stability. And sometimes, regardless of circumstances, some parents believe that a home-base plan is just *better*.

Bird-Nesting   The adults take turns living, for equal or unequal amounts of time, in the same house with the kids. This is a typically short-lived arrangement, because it's hard on the adults, especially when one partner becomes romantically involved, as was the case with Gabe Delaney and Sally Washington, the one set of co-parents in my sample who bird-nested for the first year. Their son, Orin, nine at the time, loved the arrangement. As Gabe explains, "Nothing changed for Orin—except which parent was in residence." Many couples bird-nest in second homes, as Mark and I did at our Fire Island beach house for several years, but even then, when ex-spouses' lives start to diverge dramatically, as they inevitably must, you usually don't want to share *any* residence.

Split Time   Legally, "split custody" means that each parent is "awarded" one child or certain children—a controversial and, one would hope, last-resort option. However, a few families in my survey evolved an *ex facto* split-custody arrangement over time for a number of reasons: The parents felt it was important to devote separate time to each child; the siblings didn't get along with one another; one of them didn't get along with a new spouse or with step-siblings; the kids got older, and different living arrangements worked better for each one. If these plans are to work well, parents should see to it that split siblings spend some time under the same roof—for example, they live at different parents' houses during the school week and together on the weekends.

Dual-Homes Plans* Children move back and forth between two residences, living with Mom in one house and with Dad in the other. In some families, the time is split fifty-fifty. Equal-time plans might feature alternating days, split weeks, or rotations of longer chunks of time—two-week periods, months, several months, even years, as in the case of one mother whose work took her (and her daughter) to Israel for a year. Or the split can be other than equal—say, sixty–forty or seventy–thirty. The children might spend three days and alternate weekends, two weekdays and one weekend day, one week night and alternating weekends, or two or three long weekends a month. Some experts believe that these plans enable children to develop meaningful relationships with both parents and therefore give them the best of both worlds. Nearly two-thirds of my sample opted for some variation of this theme.

Free Time This is an unstructured plan in which a parent drops in at will, or the children stay with the other parent whenever the kids or the parents choose. Depending on the family, the benefits and disadvantages can wash both ways. It can wreak havoc on schedules—or be a lifesaver when making last-minute plans. The children can feel that the other parent is *always* there for them— or that the parent is *never* there when they need him or her. Less than 8 percent of my sample had free-time plans. These arrangements seem to work best when both parents are relaxed about scheduling; when children are school age or older and therefore have the ability to keep an absent parent in mind; and, most important, when the other parent is strongly committed to the children and really makes an effort to be a presence in their

---

*I am using the definition of "dual residence" adopted by the Stanford Custody Project: Kids spend at least four overnights at the other parent's house within a two-week period.

lives—if only through long-distance phone calls. It is undoubt-edly better to attempt such flexibility only after children and parents have had the benefit of a more-structured plan. These loose arrangements are certainly not advisable in the initial stages of divorce when children are most fearful about losing one parent or when parents are trying to establish new routines or their own independence.

WHICH PLAN is best? There are no easy answers. Critics claim that in dual-home plans, whatever the ratio of time with each parent, life is more confusing, more complicated, and more stressful for kids with two homes; it's more difficult for them to accomplish the developmental tasks of growing up. These critics maintain that children do better with a home base. This may be a valid point for some children—and even for some parents. Some teenagers and young adults whom I've spoken with while writing this book (including my own son) have spent half their lifetimes commuting between two parents and give bad reviews to schedules that constantly uproot them.

Extrapolating from the research, however, it would seem that those kids' problems and complaints have little to do with living arrangements; they are more a function of parents' inability to cooperate and their insensitivity to the children's needs. Most experts agree that children's adjustment is determined by how well co-parents share the joint responsibility of raising their chil-dren. Based on this assumption, Eleanor Maccoby and Robert Mnookin, authors of the Stanford Custody Project, concluded that "residential arrangement is not related to co-parenting." Their findings coincide with an earlier (1986) study conducted by psychologist Deborah Luepnitz, which also found that *whom* chil-dren live with—mother, father, or both—was not related to how they fare.

Maccoby is presently compiling the results of a four-year fol-low-up study of the children who were six or older when their parents were interviewed for the Stanford Custody Project. "Our fifty kids in joint custody are really doing the best of all our kids—better than kids in sole custody spending all of their time with one parent. High contact with both parents, when the parents cooperate, does not produce loyalty conflicts."

Other studies have shown that children who live in joint physical custody have a sense of being loved by both parents and feel strongly attached to both as well. All the benefits notwithstanding, it is clear that the success of a two-home plan depends heavily on the maturity, stability, and flexibility of both parents. If one or both parents are unable to cooperate, having a home base may be better, because the amount of time and contact between parents can be minimized. Parents with erratic temperaments or difficult personal problems are not good candidates for shepherding their children between houses apart; but then one could argue that, unless they get professional help for themselves, they're not good candidates for *any* kind of parenting plan!

Maccoby stresses that a "downside" to dual-residence arrangements is that when one parent is unstable there's not much that the other parent can do. She cites several examples from her files: the policeman father of a three-year-old who leaves a loaded gun around; an alcoholic mother who drives under the influence; a father who gives a five-year-old boy a lift ticket and tells him to "Get lost!" because he wants to spend time with his girlfriend. These are clearly irresponsible parents. Still, Maccoby would be wary about endorsing any kind of arrangement that gives one parent "veto" power that bars the other parent's access. Besides, no parenting arrangement can mitigate the effects of having a severely dysfunctional parent. If your co-parent is alcoholic, physically or sexually abusive, or otherwise seriously unstable, urge him or her to get help.

The jury is still out; research offers no compelling evidence that any one plan works best for all families—and, because of the diversity of families who divorce, it is unlikely that research ever will. Studies clearly indicate, however, that the *structure* of a family doesn't determine the quality of parenting; people do. In all families, divorced or not, children need parents who are committed to their welfare, who support each other, and who keep their own personal problems and conflicts from interfering with their parenting responsibilities. One home or two, providing your children with two parents who love, care for, and support them is a goal worth setting, no matter what your family apart looks like.

Figuring Out What Your Child Needs

Dividing parenting time is an awesome trust. There are no formulas for designing an ideal parenting plan; even the experts don't agree. The final design rests with you and your ex-spouse. You are going to have to make the parenting plan work—and you have to be willing to modify the plan if or when it doesn't. Besides, you know your child better than anyone else. Begin by carefully considering your child's age and stage of development (also review "The Developmental Picture," pages 106–118). As stressed in chapter 4, children don't always fit a prescribed developmental mode; so be sure to read all the following sections, not just the one that describes your child's chronological age:

Infants and Toddlers (Birth to Age Three)   The most important consideration at this tender age is consistency of care. Who was the primary caretaker *before* the divorce? Infants and toddlers can be very upset by separations from whomever has been the primary parent. So if Mom has been more involved in the child's daily care, separations from her should be brief. Even if as few as four or five days go by, a very young child will assume she has "lost" her mother! Fathers, this is not a time to get into power struggles over your baby; a father who suddenly gets involved in bathing or feeding may have trouble with a child who perceives him as a stranger. Increase your participation gradually. The younger the child, the more slowly you should proceed.

At the same time, mothers have to recognize—and encourage—Dad's increasing participation. Inexperienced fathers are often skittish; they may even feel that their presence doesn't really matter. Cora Portinos recalls the night her ex-husband left, "It didn't even occur to Bob to kiss his daughter good-bye, because I had always been in charge. There was no real bond between them."

In the beginning, Cora was quietly annoyed at Bob's occasional visitor status. But when Bob showed up at Katie's second birthday party with a $200 electric car, she finally exploded. "I told him, 'Katie needs a real dad. I want you in her life but not to buy her things. You have to spend time with her and care about her, instead of trying to impress others by showing up with a large gift.' From that point on, Bob started taking care of Katie regularly. Before that, I think he was unsure if I would promote his involvement and, once I did, he really seemed to mature as a parent."

In families where both Mom *and* Dad fed, bathed, diapered, and spent significant amounts of time with a child prior to divorce, it's important for the child to maintain regular contact with both parents. And because a very young child is unable to keep a parent "in mind," no more than a day or two should pass without your seeing the child. If you adopt a two-home plan, also try to have the same blanket, the same type of crib, high chair, and toys, the same diet, bedtime, and play schedules.

Although friends criticized Helen Rogand for "letting" her ex-husband take care of their baby, she knew that Mitch had been a diapering Daddy with the older kids, and their youngest would not be an exception. Their sons were five, two and a half, and seven months old at the time; and the parents decided it was best to make the switch every two days. "I was sending frozen breast milk with them!" recalls Helen. "For our youngest, there never has been any other way to live than having parents in two homes!"

Of course, a child doesn't necessarily have to *live* with a father to see him. In home-base plans, Dad can stop by after work and even cover for Mom, as Eleanor Gimble found out. The mother of a five-year-old from a previous marriage, Eleanor got pregnant shortly before her second marriage ended. "Stan had two children from a previous marriage, nineteen and thirteen, and he was sick of being a Disneyland Dad. He told me he didn't want anything to do with our baby. I was hurt, but I decided I'd have it anyway. My only request was that he sign the baby's birth certificate."

Then, Eleanor, who had moved from Houston to Kansas City, was diagnosed with cervical cancer. She had a hysterectomy a week after the baby was born—and Stan had a change of heart about co-parenting. "The baby was five weeks old when Stan asked me to move back. He said he wanted to be the best Dad he could be. Now on Tuesdays and Thursdays he comes to my house and spends time with both girls [Eleanor's daughter from her previous marriage and their baby] so I can go back to college. He takes them every Sunday, too; sometimes we even do things together."

Experts are cautious about recommending two-home plans for young children. Dual-home arrangements are undoubtedly easier on very young kids when parents live extremely close to one another, when they share the same child care worker, and, of course, when the parents are willing, cooperative, flexible, and consistent.

Whatever your parenting plan, keep an eye out for signs of a very young child's distress—loss of appetite, excessive crying, withdrawal. Helen Rogand notes that her middle son, then two and a half, had the most trouble with the transitions (see pp. 180–183, "Comings and Goings"). "He'd cry when I'd leave him at his dad's and he'd cry when his dad left him with me!" To minimize the frequency of these shifts, Helen and Mitch eventually modified the arrangement from every two days to four days with her, three with him, which diminished her son's anxiety.

Preschoolers (Three to Five)   These kids are more resourceful than their younger peers and have more intellectual capacity to understand new parenting arrangements. But because, as they get older, kids' lives become more complex and demanding in any case, it's these children, not the very little ones, who seem to be most sensitive to parental discord. Two different studies bear this out. One, conducted at Judith Wallerstein's Center for Families in Transition, in Corte Madera, California, which focused on families whose children ranged in age from fourteen months to five years, found that the under-threes had fewer adjustment problems than the preschoolers! An earlier study, done by psychologist Shary Anne Nunan, also documented that four- to six-year-old children have more difficulty with divorce than younger children. The researcher notes, however, that "for these

children, the feelings of loss, sadness, and self-blame can be alleviated by continuing a primary relationship with both parents."

Clearly, co-parenting provides that kind of continuity, regardless of where the children live. Whatever the specific arrangement, consistency from home to home is still important at this age. Allowing for differences in parenting styles, try at least to coordinate bedtime, rules about TV watching, and diet, if possible. Wallerstein also stresses, "You can't have a child sleeping in the parent's bed at one home and in his own bed at the other."

Don't expect a preschooler to understand abstract concepts ("Mommy and Daddy will both take care of you"); they need to *hear* and *see* exactly what that means. Because these children have a limited grasp of time, as well as a rich fantasy life, their fears can get the best of them ("If I go to see Daddy, I'll never see Mommy again").

Preschoolers need lots of visual aids to keep plans straight. Huge wall calendars are essential, with color-coded days that symbolize when the child will be with or see each parent. One mother who split the week with her ex-husband went a step further: She gave her preschooler a color-coordinated lunch box so that he always knew which parent was picking him up. A red lunch box meant it was a "Mommy Day," and a blue lunch box, a "Daddy Day."

Counselors at the Center for Families in Transition developed "The Visiting Game" (I wish they had named it "The Going-to-the-Other-House Game"), a board game that allows young children to "practice" going from one parent to the other, with reminders along the way like "Remember your teddy bear." Create your own board game (use "Candyland" or another simple board game as a model); or play "Houses" (as opposed to "House"!), using cereal boxes to symbolize each parent's house and action figures for members of your family apart. By playing these games, children develop what Wallerstein calls a "cognitive map," which helps them understand and anticipate the transitions. "This quickly translates into real life and alleviates the fear that they won't see Mommy or Daddy again," Wallerstein explains.

Research indicates that half the children in this age group have the hardest time one year after their parents' separation. So keep an eye out for problems in the form of sleep disturbances, regression, whining, tantrums, inordinate fears, possessiveness, aggression toward other children. Such signs may mean that you have to get the child to talk more about his feelings—or that the parenting plan should be modified. Perhaps going back and forth between two houses is too much for the child *or* perhaps he's not seeing enough of one parent.

Donald Levin, then an intern at a Philadelphia hospital, separated from Michelle Varnet when their son, Etienne, was four. Michelle admits that Donald was the more confident parent; she never would have dreamed of *not* sharing parenting. Etienne spent three days at Donald's house and four at Michelle's, but within a year, Donald had to move to Washington to complete his residency. "Suddenly I became the primary parent. Donald came down every other weekend and stayed at a friend's house with Etienne. In between his dad's Philadelphia trips, Etienne was miserable. He cried a lot, and he was very sad. He was very attached to his father, and he needed him." Because it was so wrenching for him as well, when the year was up Donald moved back to Philadelphia to practice medicine and to be with his son.

Parents often must make sacrifices for their delicate preschoolers; many come up with very creative and complicated plans. Bernice Fava and her ex agreed to have joint physical custody of their two-and-a-half-year-old daughter, Anna, until she starts kindergarten, after which time they will still share decision making but Anna will live with her mom. "This way, we both see our daughter every day," explains Bernice. "I have Anna every morning until 12:30, and then I go to work from 1:30 to 10, Monday through Friday. He's self-employed, and he works at home, so every afternoon, Anna goes to her father's. Every other night she stays with me. The nights she is scheduled to be overnight with me, my ex brings her over, puts her to bed, and goes home when I come home."

School-agers (Five to Nine)   These kids understand more, are more realistic and more direct in expressing their anxieties, but

they share many of the same fears as younger children. Reassurance is particularly important. Remember the ad campaign that exhorted parents, "Did you hug your child today?" Keep it in mind; cuddling and expressions of love and caring are very important at this age.

In conceiving a parenting plan, remember that this is an age when it's particularly important for parents to be "chums" with their kids. Therefore, each parent should make an effort to spend both work *and* leisure time with the child. Richard Frater is grateful that his arrangement, which he and his ex-wife have maintained for ten years, enables him to spend weekday *and* weekend time with his kids during their school-age years. "At first we tried a more flexible schedule based primarily on our needs, but it was too hectic and confusing for the children. So we went to a fixed schedule. The kids still live with their mother from Tuesday afternoon to Saturday afternoon, and with me on Sundays and Mondays."

If your children live with you only on weekends, try to see them during the week, too—walk home together after school, grab a slice of pizza, shop for a new pair of sneakers, meet the child at the orthodontist. Weekdays can be hard for some parents, given the demands of work schedules, but putting forth this effort certainly makes for more secure children.

Some believe that this is the best age to initiate a two-home plan, because these kids are better able to understand time and cope with transitions; they won't fear losing a parent who drops them off at another parent's house. Also, by the time children are in school, formerly skittish fathers often feel more competent and relaxed as caregivers.

Adam Hartman was four when his parents split. For the first few years his father took him one night a week and on alternate weekends. Adam's mother, Doris Hartman, explains, "Originally my ex, who wasn't so comfortable as a father, stuck pretty rigidly to the schedule; he didn't want to take on any extra time, especially if it was to help me out." At age nine, Adam saw a movie about joint custody, and he realized he wanted more involvement with his father. "By then, Ben was more at ease in the parenting role. We first split the week and then alternated weeks."

I found, as have other researchers, that when school-agers are questioned about two-home arrangements, they're likely to respond with some variation of "It's good, 'cause I get to be with both parents." Several also commented that they "like it better than when my parents lived together, because they don't argue anymore." But listen closely; the words often don't always express the underlying feelings. These kids *are* relieved that their parents are no longer arguing, but they don't necessarily *like* the divorce! Encourage kids to allow the sadness and disappointment to surface; that's how they begin to heal and to see that their family still exists, although in a different form.

Kevin Paterson, who was eight when his parents divorced, remembers being "sad" and "confused" when his parents first split up—typical for his age. "My dad left for a while, and I didn't think he was going to come back. Then he did, and my mom moved out. She was living with my uncle." His mother, Loretta O'Brien, explains, "For a five-month period when we first separated, I moved out—because I felt guilty about wanting to end the marriage. I had lost my job, so I moved in with my brother. The kids would come over every Sunday."

But that's not how Kevin remembers it. "It was a pain," he insists. "It wasn't very consistent. It was whenever she called and got us." But then things changed, admits Kevin. Mom got her own apartment, and he and his sister, just shy of six, began to live a week at a time at each parent's home. Kevin, whose Dad was always very much involved in his upbringing, says, "I've gotten used to going back and forth," adding, as do many children in families apart, that he's "luckier" than friends who have lost a parent to divorce. "I like that I can be with both my parents." His advice to other kids whose parents get divorced? "Tell them that sometimes it works out."

Preteens (Nine to Twelve)   Keep the lines of communication open. Now is the time when kids first begin to pull away; they become more private and lead lives freer of parental intervention. These budding adolescents are also tremendously self-conscious about what people think. Some feel self-conscious about unconventional parenting arrangements (the definition of "unconven-

tional" varies from community to community); some wear their changed status as a badge of newfound independence ("Now I'm the man/woman of the family" or "My dad/mom needs my help"); and some try to hide what's going on in their families or pretend they "don't care."

These kids' bravado and pseudomaturity aren't any healthier than the younger kids' regression and dependency—all are warning signs. It's understandable that a child is sad or angry about the divorce, sometimes years after the fact. But feeling bad shouldn't be an excuse for a preteen's ignoring house rules, not doing chores, slacking off in school, or mouthing off to a parent.

Regular contact with the other parent, even if only by letter or phone, is always critical, but especially at this age because it helps to establish consistent rules and boundaries. Steve Posner lives in Idaho, and Joyce Newmann in Delaware; their twelve-year-old son, Brian, a child of divorce since he was two, lives with his mother during the school year and with his father during vacations and summer holidays. Steve calls Brian regularly, is aware of what's going on in school, and knows who his friends are and what he's interested in at any given moment. He also stays in close contact with Brian's mom. He says, "Lately, Brian has tried to play 'Divide and Conquer,' but Joyce and I are both very aware and immediately talk to each other. I suspect he thinks we're involved in a conspiracy!"

Adolescents (Twelve to Eighteen) Dealing with teenagers is a challenge in *any* home, because they specialize in exasperating parents, questioning their lifestyles, testing limits, and figuring out ways to shock and embarrass. Adolescents can be particularly rough on vulnerable divorced parents who often go through developmental changes not dissimilar to their kids'. The parents and kids—albeit in different styles—are trying to flee the nest at the same time! There may not be much you can actually *do,* but it helps to recognize that the turbulence that accompanies this transition can make for some mighty huge power struggles.

Suppose you want him to baby-sit for his younger sibling because you've got a date, but he loathes every moment of time he has to spend away from his peers. Or you want to go away for the weekend, but you're afraid that he may not be able to fend for himself. Recognize that it's hard for both of you: to deal with each other's changes (you as an unmarried man/woman, he as a young man), not to mention each other's sexuality. So talk about it. Explain to your teen the similarity in problems and goals. You will help him do his nest fleeing—even though at times it's uncomfortable for you to accept that he's growing up—and you need his cooperation—even though at times it will be "a drag" for him to be at home!

Although some kids voice a preference at an earlier age, adolescents are usually quite outspoken about living arrangements. In Eleanor Maccoby's follow-up study, which focused on children ten or older, 10.5 percent of the kids living in both parents' homes changed to home-based arrangements. Likewise, many teenagers I interviewed expressed sentiments similar to those of Adam Hartman: "I think there are only benefits to having two homes when you're little. But in high school it caused serious problems for me. I had an active social life. Clothing was a constant problem, because my school had a dress code, and I always had to carry clothes back and forth. Keeping track of where I was drove my friends crazy, and I'd always leave books in the wrong house. By my junior year, I just couldn't do it."

If your teenager objects to a dual-home plan, at least consider minimizing the traveling back and forth by lengthening the time with each parent. Most kids didn't want to tote—and most parents can't afford to duplicate—sports equipment, CD players, computers, and other valued and expensive and cumbersome possessions.

Parents also have to know their children—and understand their motives for preferring certain living arrangements. Helen and Mitch Rogand, whose sons are now eleven, thirteen, and sixteen, have tried a number of different family forms over the years. Because Helen's new house is forty-five minutes from Mitch's and closer to the boys' schools, they now live primarily with her. Weekend plans are usually "loose," often dictated by the boys' sports and social obligations. Sometimes the boys think— as do many kids who live in houses apart—that they can "escape" to their other parent's house. Helen explains, "This weekend one of the reasons my thirteen-year-old wants to go there is because he's grounded here. But the kids know that we discuss whatever is going on with them. Mitch will probably have Sean do extra chores this weekend—and I certainly will when he gets back!"

Sometimes teenagers switch from two-home arrangements to a home-base plan in order to spend more time with the same-sex parent—a move that several studies support and experts frequently endorse. But remember to take factors other than a parent's gender into consideration (see the following section). It's particularly important to think about which parent has more home time and is more capable of providing guidance and supervision. Research indicates that "parental monitoring" is increasingly important as children move into adolescence.

At any age, parents must walk a fine line between encouraging a child's input but not letting her think she has inappropriate power to call all the shots. Most younger children don't have the maturity to know what's best for them, but even teenagers, who have a better handle on their needs, prefer not to define or drive the family plan—no matter what they say.

Your Child's Resiliency and Other Considerations

Other relevant factors come into play whenever you design or modify a parenting plan. Note that "gender" is not one of them. Gender—a topic to which an entire chapter (9) of this book is devoted (see pp. 233–251)—may be a consideration in some instances, but studies indicating that girls tend to fare best with their mothers and boys with their fathers are *based on sole-custody situations*. More importantly, by definition, co-parents take pains to maximize the contact with *both* parents, which obviates problems that can arise when a child has little or no contact with the same-sex parent.

However, it is important to bear in mind . . .

Your Child's Resiliency   How does your child handle stress, transitions, unexpected changes? Does she have physical or emotional qualities or a learning difference that might render her more vulnerable to stress than other children? Is he given to tantrums or moodiness, nightmares or fears? For reasons that elude the experts, some children are simply less resilient than others.

Take Kenny, whose mother recalls, "I had to always keep him covered with a towel or blanket when I changed him; otherwise he screamed bloody murder. It was as if being uncovered made him feel too insecure." As a preschooler, Kenny had to sleep with a light on because monsters threatened to devour him. Although a rich fantasy life is typical of young children, the degree to which Kenny's fears immobilized him was not. "He had special rituals that he performed at bedtime, and he couldn't get to sleep unless he did."

Although serious problems won't engulf all children who are fearful, shy, easily angered, insecure, or uncomfortable with or confused by change, Kenny and kids like him are definitely not good candidates for arrangements that require constant emotional or physical transition. Living in two homes—packing and unpacking, dealing with different parenting styles, negotiating plans—can be particularly unnerving to a sensitive child.

Siblings   Younger children can often handle two-home parenting arrangements better when older siblings make the journey with them. Together, Jennifer and Jeremy were an alliance of compassion, shared experience, and consistency. They are still fiercely devoted to each other, and I'm certain that their relationship today was forged, at least in part, by their parents' adversity. I'm also convinced that Jeremy, by nature not a kid who should have been shuttled back and forth between parents so frequently, fared as well as he did partly because of his older sister's support.

A warning is in order, too: There's a fine line between healthy closeness between siblings and an unfair dependency of one on the other. Parents, pay close attention to supermature, capable kids who seem to take care of or watch out for everyone else in the family. They have their own experiencing, understanding, and growing to do, and they may unwittingly sabotage that process while nurturing their younger siblings.

Be aware that just as younger children resonate their parents' emotional state, they also tend to imitate older siblings' responses and behavior. They may suddenly act aggressive or seem depressed, even when they don't really understand what's going on. Fourteen-year-old Gretchen, who was going on six when Loretta O'Brien and Bill Paterson separated, doesn't remember much about the early years of her parents' breakup but she now realizes that she took her cues from Kevin, who was eight at the time. "I remember when they told us. My older brother, Kevin, was crying, so I started crying, too. But I didn't really understand what was going on."

Extended Family Members Children can lose more than a parent in divorce. Grandparents, aunts, uncles, cousins, and long-time friends may not have any direct impact on your parenting plan, but keep these relationships in mind. Jeff Davidson, who had been co-parenting with his wife for the first two years after their separation, complained when she decided to take their two sons, then seven and eight, from New York to Texas; he missed the boys bitterly, and so did their grandmother—his mom who lives in New York. At the same time, Jeff grants that the move "had some benefit to the kids because her parents, grandparents, and siblings could help with their rearing."

In some families, the availability of a trusted family member actually makes a particular parenting plan possible. Bernice Fava's mother—Anna's grandma—lives half an hour away from both co-parents. Bernice notes, "If my ex-husband is out of town or has appointments, he brings Anna to my mother's house." Bob Portinos's retired father—"Gramps" to little Katie—is also central to the Portinos's family apart. "Ever since kindergarten," explains Cora, "Bob's father has picked Katie up at the bus, and she stays at his house until I get home from work."

Adult Supervision In structuring a plan, some parents who work full-time have to consider each home's proximity to a familiar sitter or to a reputable day-care center. Naturally, it's better for young children to stay with a person or in a center they've already gotten to know. Unfortunately, in a few of the families I interviewed, either because of distance or discord, Mom opted for one type of day care and Dad another, which can be very hard on kids.

The best, although sometimes unaffordable, option is to hire an *au pair* or baby-sitter who works for *both* parents. Finding the right person can be tricky, though. It's not unusual for parents to hire and fire a string of sitters, or for parents to disagree. Dirk Fukuda and Pam Costanzos were perhaps more fortunate than other co-parents because they conducted the search *together.* Their sons—and their live-in baby-sitter—travel back and forth between the parents' houses every week.

Environment   Physical surroundings, as well as rules, responsibilities, and procedures, are often transformed for children when their parents' living arrangements change. Scrutinizing the new environment *from your child's point of view* will give you the best sense of the change she faces; and you will be better prepared to ease her into the new circumstances. Will the child leave a familiar apartment building or house, a neighborhood with lots of friends? Must she adapt to an unfamiliar urban, suburban, or rural environment? Will she have to share a room for the first time— with siblings or step-siblings? Will she have more chores? Will each parent, now single or, possibly, with a new partner, have different expectations?

Logistics   How far is one parent's home from the other? It's obvious that long car rides can be tiring for very young children, and if the parent has to drive alone, even dangerous. You can plan trips during nap time or with a baby-sitter or grandparent in tow, but most experts agree that an hour or more in a car is very stressful for younger kids. But traveling can be hard on older kids, too. It takes a big chunk out of time otherwise spent socializing, doing homework, or just relaxing. Remember, too, that new travel arrangements will affect the child's involvement in curricular and extracurricular activities as well as access to friends. Is one home closer to the child's school and friends? Will he have to commute to school for the first time—by school bus or public transportation?

"X" Factors   The "X" stands for what else is going on in the child's life besides his or her parents' divorce that might cause further stress. For example, if you've decided to separate and your child is about to enter first, fourth, or ninth grades—"transitional" grades requiring the greatest developmental leaps—factor in that added strain. Cory was two when his parents divorced. At first, he spent a week at a time with each parent. Now that he's in first grade, his mom, Martha Wainwright, explains, "He is with me every week and his father every other weekend. We felt he needed to be in one place during the week. He was making the big adjustment to a full day in school, and we didn't want him to feel pulled at home."

Puberty, first romance, bad teachers or other school problems, a prolonged illness, participation on a team, the death of a beloved grandparent—or even of a pet—all can be X factors. Or, it can be something in a parent's life that makes the child's existence more stressful—a new job or the loss of employment, illness, a new romance or a remarriage, the birth of a brother or sister. Just one X factor can cause even the best parenting plan to go awry; a combination of two or more can really tip the apple cart!

"It's very difficult in divorced situations or in stepfamilies to recognize whether problems are related to the divorce or to problems a particular child is having," observes Helen Rogand. If a child doesn't seem to be doing well with a particular arrangement, before you hasten to change a plan, think about whether the child's problem predated your separation, what red flags you might have missed because of your own "craziness" in the wake of the divorce, and what outside influences, including peer pressures, might be affecting the child. Also, don't forget to ask yourself, "Does this happen in families that aren't divorced?" Often, the answer may be "yes."

KEEP IN mind that when you design a co-parenting plan, everyone will need time to get used to the new regimen. Work as hard as you can to make your new residence a *home* for you and your kids. Be careful about your language. If you continually refer to your house as "my house" and the other parent's as "Mom's/ Dad's house," your children may begin to wonder where *their* house is! Instead, use the address to identify the two homes—in my case, for example, the kids lived with me at "Eleventh Street" and with Mark at "Horatio Street."

Don't expect immediate smooth sailing. Some counselors suggest a temporary two-month plan which can then be adjusted if necessary; but listening to the experiences of many co-parents, I think that may not be long enough. It depends on how old your children are (younger children may be more adaptable to a new regime than older kids), how many kids are involved (the more children, the more complex it may be), how complicated the logistics, the kids' relationship with each other and with each parent—and the degree of cooperation between the parents. You can always modify a plan that doesn't work, but only after you understand why it's not working—give it time.

Comings and Goings: If It's Thursday, This Must Be Horatio Street

Journeying back and forth from one parent to another can be inconvenient, cumbersome, and, for some kids, downright uncomfortable; it can intensify divided loyalties, feelings of loss, and fear of abandonment. And, of course, having a child come and go can be wrenching and disruptive for parents.

Transitions are tough for everyone, but you can alleviate some of the stress by paying close attention—first of all, to your child's "style" of departure and reentry and, second, to your own participation in it. Some children and parents get into fights when they know it's almost time to leave; others become clingy and sad. The trick is learning how to "read" your child. Wallerstein advises, "Watch your child. Every kid develops his own ways of exit and entry." What does *your* child say—or act out—at transition times? Does he get quiet? Does she act belligerent? Does he scamper around the house looking for articles of clothing, books, toys?

When your child is getting ready to leave, what's happening

inside you? Are you sad, resentful? How do those feelings affect your behavior? For example, do you let your child know that you support the other parent's role in his life (by saying, *with a smile,* "Daddy is coming to pick you up soon")? And rather than rushing to condemn the other parent, do you reassure the child when he or she is late or has to cancel at the last minute?

Rachel Grauman's marriage ended when her daughter was seven. She split weeks with her ex-husband in the beginning, but then she moved three hours away. Stacey now is with her dad every other weekend, all school vacations, and seven weeks in the summer. With both arrangements, Rachel has had to respect transition times. "A few hours before the exchange, Stacey and I would always have a little spat. In the beginning, there are all these little things that you're not used to. I didn't know how to read the signs."

Rachel has since learned to give some time to Stacey, now ten, and to attend to herself as they prepare for each weekend departure. "We both needed cool-down space. It takes a few hours to separate in your head before you actually separate," Rachel points out. Holidays—a time when all families operate on short fuses—are particularly sensitive times. "If you're having a Thanksgiving or Christmas dinner," she advises, "make sure you have a few hours after the event for calming down."

Sometimes kids feel sorry for the parent they leave behind, as Ciji Ware, author of *Sharing Parenthood After Divorce,* found out when her then four-year-old son seemed to get depressed on Sunday evenings when he left his dad's. "He's all alone when I leave," her son lamented through tears, "He doesn't have any fun if I'm not there." It's important to learn to reassure a child who's leaving, as did Ware's ex, that even though you miss him when he's not there, you're fine.

On their return, some kids need to be left alone; others like to be fussed over. Some want to retreat to the privacy of their own space in the household, be it their own room, or a corner of the living room where their "stuff" is stored; others will inspect the entire house or apartment, as if to make sure everything is as they remember it. Wallerstein notes that some kids will actually walk around touching things.

Ownership of space is important to children. Even one drawer of a parent's desk or dresser—and the feeling that the child has a right to it—can make an arriving child feel that he's coming home. "Don't do anything to their space in their absence," stresses Janine Roberts, a family therapist in Amherst, Massachusetts and co-author, with Evan Imber-Black, of *Rituals for Our Time*. Roberts, a co-parent who speaks from professional *and* personal experience, points out that if you rearrange furniture or clean out a child's room without her, you're unwittingly depriving the child of her domain.

Be aware of children's need to touch base. Try to time their homecoming so that you don't have to leave for work, school, or a date right after they arrive. "If possible," suggests Roberts, "get centered yourself *before* they come back, so that you can really be there for them." Even fifteen minutes of parental attention can make children feel welcome. Have a milk-and-cookies moment with a young child; or make it a more sophisticated snack—call it "tea"—if your kids are older. This is a good time to hear what they have to say—and also to let them know you have a life, too.

"Tell kids what happened to you when they weren't there," suggests Janine Roberts. "It's one way of saying, 'You're part of life here.' " At the same time, Roberts cautions not to "grill" the kids when they return—a pet peeve of many children I interviewed. Let the child decide when or whether she wants to talk about her time with the other parent; if she does, listen—without negative editorializing!

If you're a long-distance parent, comings and goings can be particularly hard; and the above principles are even more important. Be prepared for big physical and emotional changes in your child—and a wrenching feeling inside yourself—when there are gaping spaces between parent/child meetings. Miriam Galper Cohen, who became a long-distance parent when her then fourteen-year-old son moved to his dad's in Vermont, sums up her struggle in *Long-Distance Parenting:* Within the first day of a typical weekend stay, she admits, ". . . the thought creeps in that he'll be gone in two days. . . . It's difficult to open and close your heart within such a short time."

Another dilemma is that the long-distance parent usually gets all the fun time. "The summers were sort of a circus for Brian," admits Steve Posner. "It was all play, and he had my undivided attention." The inequity can be balanced somewhat by at least staying in touch and being aware of what's going on in your child's life. Send lots of letters, make tapes for each other, plan to watch the same TV show or ball game so you can compare reactions; and also share your news with him. Gary Shannon, who commutes four hours every third weekend to spend Thursday through Sunday with ten-year-old Matthew, keeps a calendar with his son. "It's like their diary," Gloria Shannon explains. "They write in everything they do, and then Gary marks off the next time he'll be in town."

Long distances or long absences are particularly hard on kids who are either too young to sustain an image of the absent parent or frightened that out of sight means out of mind. Isolina Ricci suggests keeping a "thinking box" in between dates—a collection of cards, buttons, shells from a beach trip, a book you think she might enjoy, or anything else that shows her that she is at least with you in spirit. Bear this in mind even if you're just a traveling parent. When Janine Roberts had to take a trip to China, she knew that she would be gone for a month. So she gave her then four-year-old daughter a picture book, which her ex-husband read to the little girl every night. "I used a spiral notebook and pasted in pictures that showed what I'd be doing every day." Not all ex-spouses might be quite so cooperative, but Roberts insists, "They ought to be. Remind them that this is in the child's best interest."

Making Transitions Easier

If your child is having trouble with transitions, review the X factors and look carefully at your own behavior. Parents *can* make it easier for kids: be clear with each other about pickup and drop-off times (19 percent in my survey cited scheduling mixups as a source of problems); be on time; don't negotiate differences in front of the kids; be respectful of each other's space, time, and interests; don't undermine the other's authority or planning.

Common sense and courtesy go a long way. If you know the other parent is taking the kid out to dinner, don't give her a snack an hour before she leaves! Even though your ex's house was once *your* home, too, don't barge in unannounced. Allow for differences in your respective hellos and good-byes. And don't criticize the other parent's style. Sandy McGee needed lots of hugs and kisses from little Julia when she said good-bye. "Meanwhile, my ex would be gunning the car—his way of saying, 'Enough, already!' "

You also might try experimenting with different days of the week to see which one makes transition times easier. Some families prefer Friday nights. Others think of Sundays as a sacred family day/evening. Doris Hartman notes, "Adam always spent Sunday with me, no matter what the schedule was." Bill Paterson and Loretta O'Brien found that by beginning a new week on Mondays, each parent had a Sunday. "That way you have the whole weekend together," points out Bill. "If you switch on Sunday night, it interferes with the weekend. Also, no one has to drop them off or pick them up. Monday afternoon after school, they just take the bus to the other parent's house."

If a child feels leaving is synonymous with *losing* the parent he leaves, he may balk about switching houses. This kind of resistance usually has nothing to do with life at the other house, although it's tempting to blame it on your co-parent! At the same time, Judith Wallerstein advises, "There's no reason to force a child to go—and certainly don't carry a child kicking and screaming," she says. Instead, consider the child's age and stage of development.

Psychologist Neil Kalter suggests that when parents split young children's time during the week, it's best to make the switch while kids are on neutral territory, like the child's day care or school. "It's not as sharp a split." Also, it can be helpful to prepare a young child for the transition by talking about what's going to happen at the house ("I know Daddy is going to take you to see your grandma"). So ask your co-parent what's on her agenda (and tell her why you are asking). Also call to tell her your plans. In time, this process will seem an ordinary part of your parenting.

Always encourage the child to talk about his feelings, but remember that you don't have to "cure" the child—and you certainly shouldn't assume that her pain was *caused* by the other parent. Ciji Ware sums it up: "If transition days are causing you problems, do some objective investigating to see if you can discover *what* is causing the difficulty, rather than *who.*"

Analyzing your child's comings and goings can also provide cues for the creation of transition rituals. They are wonderful ways to help kids feel secure. Before he leaves the anxious child may need an extra hug, story time, a neutral TV time; the angry child a soothing activity; the forgetful child a self-created packing checklist. Depending on your child's nature, you might want to have a snack, a family meeting, a game, cooking, or a "veg-out" period when no one is expected to talk or to do anything in particular. Noticing that her kids needed to "decompress" after having been at their father's house, Deborah had a "house rule" for the night the kids got back: They were not "allowed" to do chores or unpack. They "had" to call friends or watch TV. "The next morning, they woke up bright and cheerful and did what they were expected to do!"

Most kids also need some kind of "comfort bag" to shuttle back and forth with them. The objects change as the kids get older: a very young child might tote a snugly animal or a blanket, a school-ager a favorite book or toy, a preteen her "boom box" or favorite tapes. Parents sometimes duplicate security items to make each residence feel like "home." Sue Carver, whose daughter was three and a half at the time of the divorce, says that Dawn had the same "blankie" at each house. "We'd buy three or four of them at a time, just to make sure! She's twelve now, and I think it still helps calm her down when she's upset."

A number of parents report that their kids are similarly tenacious about comfort items. For instance, one mom whose son was eight at the time of the breakup, notes that for many years the boy toted his original crib blanket between his parents' homes. Mom put the blanket away when her son went off to college. One day, when he was home for Christmas break, she was surprised to find the soft and faded pint-size quilt spread out on his pillow again. He had just celebrated his twentieth birthday!

Always try to give your kids a little piece of yourself to travel with. Poems written on napkins, courtesy of the "Lunch Fairy," found their way into my kids' sandwich bags on days they went to Mark's house after school. Deborah Nachum created a "Travel Fairy," who left little surprises in her kids' backpacks and suitcases. "Once, when the kids were going on a plane trip with their father," she recalls, "the Travel Fairy stuffed TV dinners into their backpacks, made out of gummy fishes, candy peas and carrots, and candy corn. Their being able to laugh as they flew away more than made up for the extra sugar!"

"But Will We Still Be *a Family?*"

That's the question, whether voiced or unvoiced, that children are asking (themselves, if not out loud) as their parents are divorcing. I heard it over and over, from kids of all ages, when speaking with them about this book. In fact, after years of living in both places, one house may feel more like *home* to a child. Adam Hartman opted to live with his mother in high school, not his father, he says, because her home felt more like "family." He says, "My father had a smaller apartment, but that wasn't the only reason. I still felt my mother as the custodial parent. We ate meals together."

I heard similar comments from other kids. Given everyone's busy schedule, dinner is often the one time when members of a household get together. For these kids, especially, the *feeling* generated at a communal meal is evidence of security and—yes—normalcy. So think of other ways to produce "family dinner" feelings with your kids. Watch a good family TV show together (they *do* exist!); take hikes; go biking; have picnics; build something or do a joint research project. In short, *be* with them.

Start early to develop new traditions to suit your new family apart. Devise new ways of celebrating holidays and other special events (more on this in chapter 11), and create everyday rituals around meals, bedtimes, and the chaos of getting out in the morning. For example, Deborah Nachum, trying to lighten up the tedium of school-night dinners, introduced "Pig Night"! Every Wednesday, the kids could eat any way they liked, even without utensils . . . as long as they cleaned up the kitchen afterward. The kids looked forward to this special night and it gave Mom a chance to relax. Surprisingly, the kids even cleaned up without complaining!

Holidays may be a bit harder because they tend to evoke feelings of the past, especially in the early years of becoming a family apart. Since you are probably used to certain rituals, maintain workable aspects of the old but add a few new twists. Cook all the familiar goodies that your kids love but dress the table differently, invite new friends, or share the occasion with other families apart. At first, some kids and older members of the extended family may balk at a new practice. For instance, Fredda Herz Brown, a family therapist and author of *Reweaving the Family Tapestry,* recalls how shocked her father was to see *her* at the head of the seder table at Passover!

In time, new rituals will not only feel right, they will also help adults and children create new family feelings for their new family form. Certainly, a turning point in the Blau family apart was the year everyone was able to celebrate Thanksgiving *together!* I heard tales of similar holiday and milestone celebrations in other families (see chapter 11). To be sure, it takes work, courage, creativity, and cooperation between parents. But those who go the extra distance for their children say the rewards are immeasurable—for the kids and for them.

Obviously, some parents never get it right. One eighteen-year-old who lived in two parents' homes for more than a decade never felt entitled to the space in either one. He now thinks of his dorm room at college as "home." *Neither* parents' house "felt like a family," but that wasn't because of the divorce or the living arrangement. "My parents were always busy working. Mom was tired and grumpy when she came home, and Dad always came home late."

When he was growing up, this same young man never felt free to have friends at his house. "My mom encouraged me more. But I only brought friends home who knew my parents well." Things haven't changed. Recently, he asked his stepmother, a meticulous homemaker whom his dad married a few years after the divorce, if two friends could come for the weekend. "She told me to bring *one*. I'm sure she was afraid of the mess we'd make. But it's tough for me to form a life when I feel I can't even bring people back home. I still feel like I'm treading on foreign soil."

No matter how you divide parenting time, making room in your heart is the best way of letting a child know that you have room in your home. Another young veteran of divorce, reviewing his childhood from the perspective of twentysomething, sums it up nicely: "The most important thing is to give your kids the support they need. That's what a family is supposed to do."

—— 7 ——

THE BUSINESS OF CO-PARENTING

Key #6: Accept Each Other's Differences

He Says Potato, and She Says Pahtahto . . .

Barbara and Tony Palumbo are just about as dissimilar as two people can be. "I'm heavy metal, and he's classical. I'm a sixties flower child—a joiner. Tony's more introspective; he's not into socializing." Barbara adds, "We can talk—but we don't always agree."

Tony does agree with his ex-wife about one thing: "We definitely have different ideas about life." He explains, "I'm a vegetarian; she eats meat. I'm in the theater—an actor and a director. She's logical, more didactic. I don't believe in modern medicine, and she does."

Because of their different styles, Barbara admits that at first when she and Tony separated, she wanted sole custody of six-year-old Kim. "When two people are at odds, it's not very easy to talk over major decisions." Not surprisingly, Tony and Barbara locked horns over several important issues: Kim's schooling ("I place more importance on grades; he just says do your best"); discipline (Barbara thinks she's "the heavy"); and health (he's into holistic healing).

Still, these co-parents have managed to sidestep their obvious differences to keep the focus on what's best for their child. Both attribute this to personal growth. The more confident they felt in their new, separate lives, the better Barbara and Tony could listen to each other's thoughts about Kim without feeling threatened.

"I don't know how they ever got married—they're so different!" says their daughter, now nineteen. Kim has always been aware of her parents' disparate views on life, "but I never thought of it as being a difficulty for me. They never really put me in the middle." Kim, who has scant but clear memories of her parents' marriage, insists, "Aside from the fighting I heard when I was younger, they've been pretty good. I know they put their differences on the side for my sake."

Successful co-parents like the Palumbos are able to develop a *businesslike* relationship in which the main enterprise is raising their children. They conduct their affairs equitably and with respect for the other's contribution to the final product. With each one controlling a different division of the company, they must keep one another informed of policy decisions and, at times, strategize and make decisions together. Each partner brings independence to the relationship, confidence in parenting, and trust in the other's ability and commitment.

Think "Business Partner"

The best way to accept your ex-spouse's differences is to think "business partner" whenever you interact with him or her. Isolina Ricci first described this approach to parenting after divorce in *Mom's House, Dad's House,* which was derived from her work with fifteen hundred parents. Years later, having counseled hundreds more, Ricci says, "This approach stands the test of time."

Imagine yourself launching a new venture. You might be the more conservative one, tighter with money, slower to acclimate to change, and more deliberate in your decision-making process. Or you might be the more liberal partner, a person who has expansive (and expensive) ideas, quick to try new methods and to explore new territory.

Either way, when you meet with your partner to discuss employee policy—everything from work hours to job descriptions to benefits—you would listen to her suggestions. You wouldn't necessarily think of a business partner as a best friend or feel that you have a place in his life outside the office. You wouldn't be shocked if the two of you see the same situations from distinct, even opposing, viewpoints. And you not only would accept a business associate's differences, you would respect those differences and recognize that they can enhance the partnership. So what have you to gain if you insult or summarily dismiss your co-parent's point of view?

Further, you wouldn't interrupt, ridicule, criticize, or discount your business partner before hearing him out. Allow your co-parent the same courtesy. You wouldn't try to second-guess your business partner's motives or analyze how her childhood or her past relationships figure into her approach to the company. So don't play "shrink" or bring irrelevant history into decision-making sessions with your co-parent.

"Sure!" you say. "That looks good on paper. But I was *married* to him/her. I know what I'm up against." So did the co-parents interviewed for this book, but they managed to change their attitude—which, in turn, enhanced their ability to co-parent.

To be sure, this is not an easy assignment, because people frequently divorce over the very differences that they now must learn to accept. But consider the alternative: If you're not willing to modify how you respond to the other parent's views—if you can't treat him or her with the respect and deference that you would accord a business partner—conflict over your different parenting styles will probably escalate over time, causing the co-parenting relationship to deteriorate—and your children to suffer.

The success of a co-parenting venture is measured by its product: healthy children. With hard work and time, many co-parents are able to get past the rough spots: 79 percent responded "always" or "almost always" to the statement "Even when my ex and I disagree on a personal level, I am able to put aside our differences to deal with the children." These co-parents have been able to restructure their relationships to avoid fruitless power struggles. You can, too. Following are the successful strategies most often cited by cooperative co-parents. Use them in tandem with the conflict-management strategies in chapter 3 (pp. 71–100) and the tasks presented in chapter 5 (pp. 130–154) to help you change your attitude about your ex and develop a more productive—more businesslike—co-parenting relation-ship:

"I keep my own feelings out of it as much as possible." Annie King, mother of five-year-old Willy, freely admits that some days she'd definitely prefer to have "ex" Wes King completely out of her life. "But I can still be civil—I don't necessarily have to like him—and I can do what is necessary to make decisions for Willy's sake." Annie credits a woman's support group for divorced and separated parents with her growing ability to keep from "dumping" her feelings in counterproductive ways. "Now when Wes calls me up and starts chewing me out—which he does sometimes when he's had too much to drink—I try to stop myself from becoming too emotional," says Annie.

"I say to myself, I know where he's coming from: it's his anger or possibly the alcohol talking. I tell him, 'Look, I don't have to listen to this anymore.' Most of the time, I can just hang up the phone and forget about it. If I do get angry or upset, I'll call a friend and vent. I certainly won't take it out on Willy."

"I remember I'm not married to her anymore." Paul Carver explains how he stops himself from flying into a rage when Sue, his habitually late ex-wife, doesn't arrive on time to pick up Dawn. He realizes that he's still bound to Sue, but by a mutual commitment to a joint project—parenting their daughter—not by their previous marital ties. This enables him to put their differences in perspective. When a business partner does the "same old thing," it may annoy you, but you probably don't take it personally. Therefore, rather than automatically going into overdrive when your ex-spouse pulls something that feels infuriatingly familiar, take a deep breath and be happy that you don't have to deal with this particular trait every day!

"I needed her help; she needed mine." By definition, it takes two to co-parent. Carl Bosco and Gail Connors found this out when a crisis—their son's sudden paralysis—forced them together after four years of acrimony, "She realized that if the shit hit the fan, I'd be there," says Carl. Interestingly, when he talks about their marriage, Carl complains that he never felt needed; Gail complains that she never felt that Carl was willing to commit. Today, all that is beside the point; in place of their old push-pull mode

of relating to each other, Gail and Carl have evolved to a more *distant* association—"a mutual using society," in Carl's words.

"I wanted to have a good divorce."   Helen Rogand was determined to make her divorce "work." Helen remarks, "I wanted it not to be like everyone else's divorce. I wanted to be the one who stayed friendly, who didn't have to slug it out with attorneys—*to rise above.* I wanted our family to be different." Helen appreciates that Mitch "apparently had the same attitude," because he respected her need to adjust to their new relationship. "I remember one time during that first year, our oldest was playing soccer. Mitch and I were on the field, sitting together watching the game, and his girlfriend was waiting in the truck." This also helped Helen remember what she once saw in Mitch and why she had had three kids with him. "What I see in a lot of divorces is an inability to believe that the other person ever had any good feelings about you—so you have to cut off. I don't think either of us was willing to do that."

"I don't leave things to chance."   Yvette Hoving points out, "You wouldn't run a business without goals and guidelines. Neither should you try co-parenting by mind reading!" In families apart, the adults must be clear about their expectations, specific about their plans for the children, and conscientious about keeping track of schedules. Communication is key (see chapter 8, "The Parental Hotline").

"I hired someone to take up the slack."   You don't expect a business associate to do everything you can't do, or to be good at everything; have similarly realistic expectations for your co-parent. Even with their good intentions, Helen Rogand was annoyed in the early days, because Mitch would arrive late or change plans at the last minute (a pet peeve of 28 percent of my respondents). Her solution: Have a baby-sitter on call. "I didn't want to make my plans around his timetable or bank on his reliability."

Parents rarely sabotage each other's plans on purpose; more often, busy schedules or illness result in last-minute changes. So it's best to have an alternative plan that takes into account that the other parent may be delayed or even have to cancel. Besides, if you want another parent to work on changing bad habits that

work against co-parenting, like lateness or forgetfulness, harangu-
ing him won't help, but backing off might. Seemingly less interested parents often become more responsive when they know
they're appreciated.

"I accept that in some areas, we just can't come to an agreement." At
least half of the parents interviewed in my study indicated that
they expected differences between them always to exist, but that
they have learned to handle them better. Asked to cite specific
trouble spots, 26 percent mentioned "different standards" in
terms of personal hygiene and housekeeping, kids' clothing, manners, nutrition; nearly a third cited "discipline"; 18 percent were
at odds when it came to crisis management, with the men generally claiming that the women "overreact." Some wanted more
structure, others less. Some had different ideas about religion,
others about health. These parents won't necessarily change the
way they run their "division" of the new family apart, but they
have stopped railing against their partner's style of management.

"I learned how to negotiate." Over the years, Arlene Steinberg,
who describes herself as "laissez faire," and Peter Levine, who
likes a more structured life, have used a mediator and a variety of
therapists to get over the rough spots. Equally important, Arlene
educated herself. "Early on, I realized I'd better learn how to
negotiate—otherwise, I was going to get bulldozed, because
Peter is very good at it!" Among other tools, Arlene read *Getting
to Yes,* a very short but very helpful book by Roger Fisher and
William Ury of the Harvard Negotiation Project; then she really
worked hard to apply the principles. "We're still very different,
but now I can negotiate better than I ever could when I was
married!"

Problem-Solving Principles: How Michelle and Donald Got to Yes

In *Getting to Yes,* the authors stress separating the person from the
problem. That means you put emotions aside, you don't make

assumptions, and you don't blame. Equally important, you focus on interests, not positions. You don't try to sway the other parent, because if you each take a position and try to argue a particular "side," no one wins in the end—least of all your kids. You can't obliterate differences or pretend they don't exist. But if you keep an open mind and work *with* your co-parent, your differences can actually enrich your children's options.

Take the case of Michelle Varnet and Donald Levin. When their son, Etienne, was in eighth grade, they were faced with an awesome decision that bedevils many urban parents: where to send their child to high school. Etienne, a good student, had gotten into Vanderbilt,* one of a handful of prestigious public schools in Philadelphia, but Michelle thought the classes were too big. She wanted her son to go to the International School, a multicultural private high school, which Etienne didn't like. Neither did Donald; he was torn between Vanderbilt and Cushing, one of several other private schools where Etienne had been accepted. "The three of us had many discussions and at first I thought, 'How are we ever going to figure this out?'" Donald admits.

Michelle and Donald were as different from each other as two co-parents could be—their backgrounds, their interests, their religions, even their countries of origin. Michelle had moved from her native France to marry Donald, and nine years later, when they divorced, they were already traveling on different tracks. Donald, launching a medical career, had been putting in extremely long hours which had left Michelle to make a life of her own. "I must say we were quite creative about our separate lives," says Donald. Once Etienne was born, he was their only bond, so there was no question that the parents would share custody. Etienne was four when the marriage ended.

"We had some anger, but there was a lot of trust between us," says Donald. "Etienne's interest was always paramount to both of us." Despite their differences, the parents developed a solid co-parenting relationship—they celebrated birthdays together, attended school functions, kept abreast of Etienne's activities at

*School names have been changed.

each other's houses. But Donald stresses, "We're not friends. We don't socialize or spend time together unless it has to do with our son."

Past successes notwithstanding, choosing a child's high school *is* an awesome decision, as is deciding the best course of medical treatment, figuring out what to do when a child is having behavioral problems, or dealing with any of the major dilemmas that confront not only co-parents but *all* parents. It's just harder when you're divorced. Generally, you have to choose one of three approaches to a disagreement: *share it*—figure out how to handle the predicament together; *divide it*—when homework was a problem, Mark helped with science and social studies and I took over English and math; or *delay it*—put off a solution until the issue is absolutely pressing.

Michelle and Donald knew they could neither delay determining where Etienne would go to school nor divide this kind of problem, so they worked together to solve it. Their process illustrates several key principles of problem solving:

Look at the bigger picture. "Co-parenting goes beyond sharing time with the other parent. It's accepting that there are two of you who have equal input. And it's about relinquishing control," Michelle points out. "To me, the school decision was very symbolic of what it's like to make a decision with an ex." Michelle notes that it was most helpful for her to understand that this decision was part of an even bigger picture. It was a test of how well their family apart could function. A sense of trust, confidence, and respect, both immediate and future, were on the line. "I tried very hard to function honestly with myself and with them, rather than have regrets later on." Both parents had always wanted to be good role models for Etienne whose part in making the decision, says Donald, was the culmination of years of teaching him to think for himself.

Get objective input. Early in the process, Michelle and Donald consulted a family therapist whom they had seen in the past. "We had been locked into tense, useless discussions for a few weeks, and we needed an outsider to help us break through," says Michelle. In addition, they talked to other parents, and Etienne talked to kids his age at the various schools. "It was a joint research project," explains Donald. "I spent hours on the phone and so did Michelle!" These efforts helped the parents distance themselves from their own interests, and it cooled down their discussions. Each became a reporter, not a convincer.

By the way, *objective* input is just that: free of emotional overlays and unsolicited "advice." Members of your family or your friends—especially divorced friends still licking their own wounds—might be partial to your "side," but their counsel can cleave an even wider gap between you and your ex and make you both lose sight of your common goal.

Know where you're coming from—and keep an open mind. "I realized if I wanted our discussions to go anywhere, I really had to look at my own motivation, to see whether it fit with what my son really wanted," explains Michelle. "I'm French. I wanted him to cultivate his bicultural background, but when I realized that wasn't *his* interest, I made every effort to look into the options." Michelle told Donald and Etienne why she wanted the International School but, she assured them, "I'm not going to exclude anything—wherever you want me to go look, I'll go."

Listen to where the other parent is coming from. Often, when two people disagree, they become polarized. Family therapists and conflict-resolution experts suggest that the dissenters actually reverse roles, each one trying to express the other's point of view. Michelle and Donald didn't have to go that far, because she was receptive—and willing to listen. Michelle recalls, "When Donald realized that I was able to get past my own investment, he became more open, too." Donald agrees. "Michelle did an amazing turn-around. I give her an enormous amount of credit for opening up her mind and considering other options."

Be respectful of the other parent's private life. Michelle lived alone at the time, but Donald had a steady girlfriend. Whenever Michelle had to call him at home, she always asked, "Is this a good time for you to talk?" They arranged meetings on mutually acceptable turf when it was convenient for both parties. After all, you wouldn't barge in on or call a business partner after work hours!

Work on one difficult issue at a time and stay in the present. Michelle and Donald were very careful about staying on the subject at hand—the school decision. Past infractions were never thrown up as ammunition or "proof" that the other parent didn't really have Etienne's best interest at heart. They didn't bring in old gripes, make sweeping generalizations, or become accusatory.

State the problem as a mutual concern. Michelle and Donald brainstormed together, considering a number of possible solutions. They talked over the pros and cons of each school, where Etienne's friends were going, what traveling would be like if he went to this school or that, and the expense (even though Donald had agreed to pay). Neither accused the other of trying to "color" Etienne's decision. And both parents realized that there wasn't a "right" answer. By working together, they believed that their son's best interest would guide their thinking and would enable them to make the best choice for him.

Be patient. "It was a lot of work—an incredible process," Michelle reports. "It would be very hard if we didn't respect each other." Most of us don't know much about creative problem-solving. A good primer on negotiation, like *Getting to Yes* or Dudley Weeks's *Eight Essential Steps to Conflict Resolution,* will help, but mastering the craft of negotiation takes lots of practice. No matter how "skilled" you are, tempers will occasionally flare, and you may even lapse into old, ineffective modes of arguing. Give yourself (and your ex-spouse) a break when that happens; learn from the lapse.

Know that decisions can always be reversed or modified. Because each one's final choice was not the other's preference, in the end, Michelle and Donald went along with Etienne's first choice, Cushing, which was neither parent's favorite but acceptable nevertheless. All three agreed to rethink the decision the following year if it didn't seem to be working out.

Trying a particular course of action always should be viewed as a good first step. It's okay to feel a bit leery about the resolution of an issue—as long as each parent is heard and responded to with respect and neither has been bullied into taking an untenable position. Agree to wait a specific amount of time to see what happens before discussing the issue again. If one or both of you think that the first solution didn't work, take time to see why and then try again. For example, if your child isn't getting homework done, don't tie the problem into one house or the other or make it someone's "fault." Just search for possible solutions. Brainstorm and come up with a few ideas. You could try one solution one month—for example, to bar TV completely during school nights. Then next month, try another—to set aside a prescribed time and place for homework. Or you could each try different approaches and see what seems to work better. The end solution may be a creative mixture of both parents' ideas or an understanding of what works best in each parent's house.

The "M" Word

Because Donald was able and willing to foot the bill for Etienne's private-school tuition, the co-parents didn't have to deal with what is potentially the most explosive postdivorce issue: money. Money often highlights parents' differences; it can bring out the worst in ex-spouses, particularly those who argued about how to spend money during their marriage ("You were always a skinflint/spendthrift!"). In fact, over a third of the parents I surveyed cited "Who pays for what" as a source of ongoing conflict. That's on the low side, because my sample is composed of parents who are *trying* to work together; other studies indicate that as many as half of all divorced couples argue about money.

There is no "right" way to divide postdivorce expenses. In some agreements, one parent pays for all the kids' expenses and gives spousal support as well. Often in joint-custody agreements, kids' expenses are split, either down the middle or by a formula that factors in each parent's ability to pay. Some parents arrive at a formula by calling in lawyers and accountants and studying each other's tax returns; some act in "good faith." But regardless of how ironclad the terms of a legal agreement, the hostility over money doesn't usually end when you sign on the dotted line. Typically, tensions rise and problems are precipitated . . .

When co-parents don't live up to their end of the bargain. Research indicates that in half of all mother-custody situations, noncustodial fathers pay less than the agreed amount; in 25 percent of the cases, they pay nothing. Joint-custody parents are much more likely to pay their allotted share (and they rarely end up back in court), but checks may arrive late or sporadically. If the initial agreement was vague, disputes can also occur when one parent *claims* that the other was supposed to pay for a particular item but welshed on the deal. Withheld money can lead to withheld time—and vice versa. Clearly, neither is a positive scenario for children.

When the original agreement is contested. This sometimes happens when not enough money was budgeted in the first place or when one spouse's earning capacity has changed. "Right after the divorce, he got a new job with a tremendous salary increase. Our agreement was based on his old salary," explains one disgruntled mother who confided that she was "thinking about" taking her ex back to court; this move is seldom a good option for the children, although many parents justify it the way she does: "I don't think my son should have to suffer."

When one co-parent resents what the other one buys. A common scenario is when a Disneyland Mom or Dad lavishes gifts on the kids, and the everyday parent (more often, the mother) is resentful. She feels that Dad will "spoil" the children and that if she fails to match his buying power, the kids won't love her as much.

When co-parents have to share an unplanned expense. Although it's best to try to foresee every need and anticipate every contingency, that's not always possible. Many divorce agreements, for example, don't include college tuition. Arlene Steinberg and Peter Levine, whose original parenting agreement called for contributions based on each parent's income, still find—eleven years later—that most of their negotiations center on who's going to pay for expenses like winter jackets, lessons, summer camp, and, most recently, college.

ONE REASON disputes over money are almost inevitable is that when most couples split up there simply isn't enough money to duplicate the previous standard of living; setting up a second household costs at least 30 percent of the first. However, money is inextricably entwined with your children's welfare. It's not worth arguing over every penny when you consider the price your children will pay.

Kids shouldn't have to ponder adult concerns; they certainly shouldn't be preoccupied with lawyers and accountants or whether the electric bill is going to be paid. Their fears about money and the effects of their parents' arguments over financial matters take a tremendous toll. Some kids believe that a parent who withholds money doesn't love them, especially if they over- hear an angry parent saying, "If you cared more about your children, you'd make sure they were provided for."

Nor should kids have to act as collection agents for their parents, but, sadly, many feel they have to defend or scold one parent or the other when money is demanded or withheld. "I don't understand why he doesn't see what we're going through," laments a sixteen-year-old whose father has recently begun to send checks late. "I wish my father could see what happens here because we don't have the money. If my Dad knew that it really mattered to us, wouldn't he be willing to give my mom a little more money a month? Mom told me his law- yer is a real sleazeball. He treats her as if she's a criminal. That gets me mad, too."

When children perceive that one parent is "deprived" or angry, they sometimes feel guilty for anything they are given. "I knew it made my Mom furious, so I started hiding what Dad bought me," admits a twelve-year-old girl. "And if we did something really fun, I'd be afraid to talk about it, because she'd probably say, 'Oh, he has money for *that*, but not for the things we really need!' "

Some kids also have to make up for the shortfall themselves, especially when it comes to college tuition. Only 10 percent of the parents in Judith Wallerstein's study were contributing to their children's college tuition; most of my survey parents said it was a real "sore spot" for them, too. In the meantime, it is their kids who feel the pinch.

"I had to make incredible sacrifices just to go to a private college. I had to give up all sports in my senior year, so that I could take a job," says one boy who, like many children of divorce, was caught in the middle of his parents' financial war. According to this young man, his father has "tons of money," but when it came to coughing up for college, Dad dug in his heels and refused to pay more than his ex-wife.

Conversations about money usually lead directly to each co-parent's Achilles' heel: women often fear destitution; men fear being taken advantage of. Both have to make peace with these issues if they are to make peace with each other.

In our culture, you are what you "have"; money often symbol-izes self-esteem. So if one person earns more than the other, money can also be the ultimate form of leverage. "When one parent has three and half times more income than the other parent, there's bound to be some competition involved," Annie King insists. As with many divorced couples, the concept of "fairness" shudders and cracks when she and her ex discuss finances. "Even the few times when I've asked Wes to take little Willy for a haircut—I mean, they go to the same barber—he refuses. He tells me, 'That's what I give you child support for!' "

Typically, mothers also become bargaining agents for their children—another dangerous pitfall. Arlene Steinberg's daughter asked her if she could take piano lessons. "If Peter thinks the lessons are a good idea, we'll split the cost; if not, he won't pay his half," explains Arlene.

Arlene's dilemma resonates in many families apart. Whether it's because a child needs braces or wants an expensive pair of sneakers that all the other kids are wearing, it's usually Mom who asks Dad for the money. No wonder parents argue! A better approach is for parents to discuss their child's needs and wants with each other and with the child. That way, Mom doesn't have to justify her motives or her judgment, because Dad can check out the situation and the cost for himself. Even if parents can't agree because their values are different, they can at least negotiate the issue in a way that puts their child's interest first.

In the future, there may be less of a disparity in divorced father's and mother's incomes. Women who have careers and substantial incomes prior to divorce may not have to worry about depending on their ex-husbands for economic survival; some may even earn more. For now, however, they are more the exception than the rule; most women are likely to experience a dramatic drop in income after divorce. And the parent with more money—the father—ultimately has more power; and some men abuse that power. One mother says her ex-husband made her come to his house to pick up the child-support check. That probably isn't typical, but many women would identify with the feelings it evoked: "I call it my weekly groveling."

What's a mother to do? "The sooner a woman can get financially independent, the better off she is," maintains Patricia Greshner-Nedry, who speaks from experience and now runs peer support groups for divorced parents. Going back to school and starting a career helped her see her ex in a new light—as the father of her children, not a husband who "left" her—and, just as essential, to see herself as an independent woman. She adds, "It's important for women to contribute."

When computing how much support a woman needs, it's important for fathers to remember that Mom's time is money. If both parents work, the cost of taking care of the kids has to be factored into the equation. When co-parents prefer parent care over day care, an equitable solution is to compute what it's worth to have one parent work less. "I cut back on my hours so that I could be with our daughter," one mother explains. "Doug felt better about giving *me* more money than giving it to a sitter or a day-care center."

Unfortunately, men sometimes don't see the equation quite that way, points out Greshner-Nedry. Some men especially resent the idea of having to pay alimony (spousal support) to their ex-wives in addition to contributing to children's expenses. In their minds, it's all the same thing—money out of their pockets.

Greshner-Nedry says that men need to understand that, especially in the beginning, financial support enables a woman to get job training or to go back to school. Even men who are willing to pay are skeptical. "She's not taking any steps to change her situation," complained one man about his ex-wife. "I feel like she's going to live off me for the rest of my life."

Another man bristled, "My ex-wife spent a long period of time deciding what she wanted to do, and she had no income. She went from being a social worker into the business world, and that was her choice. I didn't feel that *I* had to finance that."

Greshner-Nedry responds, "Again, it's that whole thing of

renegotiating. My ex-husband and I decided that when I got my degree I wouldn't get any more spousal support, and that was reasonable. That's the important word, *reasonable*—that's what the courts look for." She adds, "I always tell men, 'Your financial generosity at this point enables her to get financially independent sooner, and that will never come back to haunt you. But taking the other tactic very well may.' "

It's also important for women who earn less than their husbands to curb their resentment. Your husband doesn't "owe" you. The lingering anger will do nothing to improve your standard of living; it will only poison your children. It used to bother me that Mark could afford to give our children things I couldn't. But I have come to realize that my children—most children—don't measure love in dollars. Equally important, instead of being consumed with what I couldn't do, I focused on I what I *could* do. And in finally having the guts to stand on my own, even though at times I was terrified, I gave my children something even more valuable than money—a good role model.

"You're Only Human" and Other Truisms about Co-Parenting

With most divorced couples, differences in parenting styles and sensitivities about money can persist for many years, sometimes forever! Despite them, most co-parents learn over time to cooperate. But, in the meantime, regardless of both partners' good intentions or practice in negotiation skills, there are bound to be a few skirmishes along the way and new challenges to face; they simply go with the territory. The following co-parenting axioms may help you dodge the shrapnel—and keep the whole situation in its proper perspective:

Co-parenting machines usually break down at some point.

But that doesn't make either of you "bad." Divorced parents can unwittingly fall into what family therapist and divorce mediator Isolina Ricci calls "all or nothing traps": do it right or don't do it at all. Because parents have so few positive models for interaction after divorce—with each other and with their children—many tend to go to extremes when they run into a snag that threatens to escalate out of control. One wrong word, one misplaced sock, one time late picking up the child and one parent is ready to blame the other and even to change the parenting plan. What is really needed, says Ricci, is guidance and education.

For example, a mother is totally exasperated because so many articles of clothing seem to be "disappearing" at her ex-husband's house. She says to herself, "He's so goddamn irresponsible—and they're becoming just like him. Life would be so much easier if they didn't see him at all." She starts believing her ex allows the kids to run wild, and the next thing you know, she's calling her lawyer. In reality, Mom doesn't need to criticize Dad or cut him out of the picture altogether. This family apart just has to recognize that mishaps are inevitable. And they need to learn how to create better systems for keeping things straight.

Kids get confused, they tend to be forgetful and distracted, and they're often irresponsible. That's not necessarily because one of you isn't a good parent; that's because *they're kids!* So before you get enraged, get creative. Figure out ways to make life simpler, more organized, and less stressful—for yourself and for your kids. Especially if you're new at co-parenting, you may need a fair amount of structure and organization.

"You need to have systems for *everything,*" says Patricia Greshner-Nedry, who went so far as to color-coordinate her kids' clothing when they were younger. "I kept all the red and blue clothing at my house; everything else, down to the socks, went to my ex-husband's house. Sorting laundry, it was very easy to figure out what they had to take back to their father's!" Grandparents benefited from this scheme, too. "Naturally, when they visited the kids, they liked to see them wearing whatever clothing they had given them. This made it simple. My parents just made sure anything they bought was red or blue!"

Co-parenting won't stop your kids from being sad about the divorce. Most children don't want their parents to split up.

Emotional repercussions can surface years later, particularly if they are young when you first separate. The danger is that you'll then blame the new behavior on the other parent. One day, your child may appear to be sadder than usual, start having trouble in school, or become more aggressive at home or with friends. Perhaps he *is* having trouble adjusting to new living arrangements or perhaps the other parent is not as attentive to his needs as you are. Equally possible, in developmental terms, the child finally may be "ready" to allow the reality of your divorce to sink in.

"Forest was five when we divorced," says his mother, Yvette Hoving, "but his grief didn't begin until he was seven. He had been baby-sitting for a dog, and the dog died. Somehow that must have triggered it, and he cried his eyes out. At five, he was too young to conceptualize what it meant when we said, 'Daddy's not going to live here.' At seven, he had the thoughts and the words."

It's important to pay attention to signs of distress in your child, but don't jump to any conclusions that it's because there's something wrong with the parenting plan or that this is something that needs "fixing." At first glance, it would seem inconceivable that Forest Hoving, who lived primarily at his mom's, could be pining for his dad. Bart Hoving stopped off at his ex-wife's apartment five or six nights a week and often stayed through dinner. But Yvette Hoving explains, "Forest was sad about the divorce in general. Even now, at fourteen, he verbalizes, 'I'll never know what it's like to have two parents.' "

Divorce makes kids sad and angry; no parenting plan and no degree of cooperation between co-parents can sidestep that reality. If you're unsure about whether a child's behavior reflects on something you or the other parent is doing, check with a professional who has experience with divorced families. You may discover that there's nothing either of you can *do*—except to love the child, let him vent the feelings, and let him *be*.

Children act different with each co-parent. Somehow, when children are disrespectful or unruly, such behavior always seems to coincide with their coming back from being with the other parent—or, at least, that's when you *notice* it. Again, don't assume that your ex's standards are lax or that he or she is somehow "poisoning" the child against you. You may need to look at what happens during transition times (see pp. 180–188). Or, just as likely, the kid's behavior has nothing to do with *either* of you!

The same child often acts completely different with each parent. This is a common phenomenon and, when you think about it, completely understandable. Don't *you* act different around different people? Children in nondivorced homes know how to "play" their parents; in families apart, kids are superpros!

"My father was more of a disciplinarian, but I was always better behaved around my mother," admits Adam Hartman, adding, "Maybe I was testing him." In a similar vein, Lewis Fukuda, twelve, confesses, "I know I can swear at my dad's house and I can watch cartoons there. My mom's not strict—but she has cows about different things." Like Adam, Lew admits that he tailors his behavior to suit each house.

Co-parents usually have different parenting styles. And that's fine. With the exception of providing a fair degree of consistency for very young children, a "united front" about everyday issues is unrealistic. Children *can* accommodate different expectations and standards of behavior. They do it in school, at the playground, at a grandparent's house, in church or synagogue. In fact, some experts think it's beneficial that they do so; it makes them more adaptable and resilient. They simply learn what's expected of them in both parents' houses. Children often use parents' differences to divide and conquer, so you may get complaints ("Dad doesn't make us do chores"), but your rules are your rules.

Some researchers disagree. Eleanor Maccoby, the driving force behind the Stanford Custody Project, suggests that it's better for divorced parents to coordinate rules, diet, and bedtime in each home and to have a consistent time and place for homework. At the same time, Maccoby acknowledges that among the parents in her study, discussion about such matters diminished over time and that only about a quarter of the families were able to achieve a consistent level of cooperation.

Personally, I believe that the degree of coordination comes down to individual choice, mediated by the child's age (the younger the child, the more you should try to coordinate) and by your co-parental relationship (some people will be fortunate if they can coordinate only the BIG items). Get real: Each of you may have vastly different ideas about how children should behave, what they should eat, how they should dress, what time they should go to bed, whether or not they should have chores, or how and when they do their homework. It's unrealistic to think that you can iron out those everyday differences—even with the skill of a Harvard negotiator.

More important, trying to coordinate everything could put more stress on the co-parenting partnership which, in turn, often leads to more conflict. As family therapist Ron Taffel puts it, "You have to prioritize. Parents' conflict is what hurts kids, not the fact that the kids go to sleep a half hour later in one house or eat more sugar when they're there. Kids tell me all the time that they can deal with the separateness, as long as their parents don't argue."

Luckily for Gregory Macnamara and Ellen Rasmussen, a divorce mediator set them straight early on. "She said we were both intelligent and fairly responsible parents," recalls Greg, "and the only way this would work is if each of us does our thing and doesn't try to legislate what the other one does."

Instead of trying to exert your authority, cut the other parent a little slack. So what if the socks don't match or if the kids eat spaghetti every night because that's the only meal the other parent knows how to cook? None of us is so perfect a parent that we don't have occasional lapses or take a short cut here and there. So save your problem-solving skills for the BIG items!

And if you're really wise, you'll also refrain from commenting, which also tends to generate conflict. Take TV, for example—a bone of contention between many co-parents. Christopher Derby, separated for eight years and the father of three children, 20, 17, and 11, says his ex-wife, Myrna, thinks too much TV is the reason their youngest is slipping in school. Chris, who (in his mind) provides a more regulated, structured home environment, doesn't agree. "I think it's a matter of order and discipline. TV isn't the issue, and taking it away altogether would just punish him inappropriately." Still, Chris keeps his opinion to himself, admitting that at times it's hard. "Besides," he owns, "I can't be sure that I'm right or she's wrong. I don't live there, so I don't know what Billy is like with her, so a lot of times I just dodge an issue instead of confronting it!"

In your kids' eyes, neither of you is the "better" parent.

Whenever the kids got sick, Mark bought chicken soup; I make it from scratch. And although I would have liked to think that my way was better, I came to see that Jennifer and Jeremy got well either way! Years after the fact, I can admit that Mark is as wonderful and caring a parent as I am—but he does it differently. How often I hear co-parenting mothers talk about how much "closer" the children feel to them, because they're so "good" at nurturing, listening to problems, taking care of kids when they're sick.

Some women aren't aware of their bias. After five years of co-parenting in a dual-home arrangement with Jay Lippman, Patricia Davenport wanted to move from the heart of Chicago to Evanston, a nearby suburb, but her agreement stipulated that she needed her ex's approval. Jay was willing—his second wife worked in Evanston, anyway—but he didn't agree about *when* the move should take place. "It's the middle of the school year. I think it would be better for the kids to finish out at their old school, staying with me on Monday through Friday, and with you every weekend," he told her.

Despite her ex-husband's objections and, it would seem, despite potential adjustment problems for the kids, Patricia pulled the kids, ten, eight, and six at the time, out of their private school in Chicago and enrolled them in a public school in Evanston. She explains, "I thought they would be even more disadvantaged, hurt, and disrupted by suddenly living at Jay's all that time when my apartment was more their home emotionally." All things considered, perhaps Patricia did act in her children's best interests—or perhaps her ego got in the way. An admission Patricia adds later in the interview is telling: "Despite joint custody, I'm the primary parent, the one they depend on . . . I'm just closer to them. I couldn't bear the thought of their continuing their school lives in Chicago and my not being a part of it."

Parents who think they're "better" than their ex-spouses tend to shortchange their kids. And it's not just women. Now that so many more men are assuming parenting roles, some of them are guilty of the same misguided thinking. "I'm more nurturing than most mothers," insists Henry Gunther, whose description of his family apart also reveals his prejudice: "I have *primary* residence/ *possession,* and her *access* is . . . [emphasis is mine]." Henry, who is active in a fathers' rights group in Texas, is still battling over custody with his ex-wife—three years after his marriage ended. Perhaps his ex-wife is as "off the wall" as he claims—or perhaps his need to be "primary" obscures his vision. In any case, the person suffering most from the ongoing litigation is their six-year-old son.

The problem with viewing yourself as the better parent is that your children's welfare may be compromised by your (conscious or unconscious) desire to *win.* Moreover, if you think that your style, your rules, your practices are superior to the other parent's, every decision is turned into a subtle (or outright) power play. So whenever your children are with you or do something your "way," there's a good chance that they will feel disloyal to the other parent.

In contrast, when you step back and truly allow the other parent to contribute, your kids won't feel the tension. What is more, you may be in for a delightful surprise. One woman, who describes her ex as more of a "play father" when they were married, admits, "It amused me trying to picture him with three young kids. He never changed diapers or gave baths—he'd just take them places." Her ex-husband rose to the challenge and became a very proficient hands-on dad. "And when I have the weekend to myself, it's heaven!"

Such benefits notwithstanding, as co-parenting partners, both of you need to do what business partners do: *Keep your eye on the bottom line.* "Accept the best of what each of you has to give," suggests Helen Rogand. "Even when we disagree on stuff with the kids, we can appreciate each other's strengths. Everyone benefits when everyone is involved."

— 8 —

THE PARENTAL HOTLINE

Key #7: Communicate about (and with) the Children

An Executive Committee

"It was the first time Nicholas couldn't play one house against another," says Elena Costos, recalling an event that marked a new plateau for her family apart. The cast of characters included her ex-husband, Jim Miller, their two children, Nicholas and Lanie, Elena's second husband, Neil, and Jim's second wife, Bonnie. "Nicholas pulled something outrageous. He lied about where he was after school, and Neil caught him.

"Neil called Jim, and they agreed on appropriate consequences. Neil told Nicholas what the punishment was, but since Nicholas was going to be with Jim that weekend, Jim enforced it."

For the first few years, even though she and Jim co-parented, Elena admits that they weren't very good at discussing the kids, who were four and three at the time of the divorce. Jim would pick them up every Tuesday and alternate Thursdays for the weekends ("He never missed a day"), but Jim and Elena had little contact and less conversation. They argued over time; Jim withheld money. Elena remembers that Nicholas, the "more fragile child," was "displaying symptoms from the time we separated." But it was not until third grade, when he began slacking off in school, that his parents, with the help of a family therapist, began to understand how their poor communication was affecting their son's emotional health.

"I remember that first session in the family therapist's office," says Jim. "We are all lawyers—Elena and Neil, Bonnie and I—opinionated and used to managing our own cases. The therapist picked up on that immediately and told us, 'I don't want to see Nicholas—I want to see *you four!*' " The therapist explained that both of the kids were getting lost in the adults' shuffle; the only way to ameliorate the situation was to work as a team. Although Jim and Elena's battles over custody had left a residue of resentment, the therapist recognized that these parents and stepparents had the children's best interests at heart. Elena notes, "He made us form an executive committee."

"We spent the next several sessions airing some complaints but mostly learning how to communicate," recounts Jim. "This guy knew he had four egos to deal with, so he simply said, 'You *have* to talk. You have to get together and work out the rules, because every week there will be incidents at each house—and you have to let each other know what happens.' "

Both couples felt relieved. "We started acting like four adults. It was like paradise for us all to finally be talking," says Jim. "Bonnie and Elena chatted endlessly," he adds, noting that he and Neil also kept in close touch. "That first time I carried out Neil's punishment, it affirmed his discipline and gave Nicholas a sense of consistency. It worked like a charm and had an immediate effect on Nicholas. Within two weeks, he began doing better in school!"

Elena adds, "Now if we say 'no TV,' they enforce it at their house. These kids have four adults breathing down their necks—they're not left alone!"

It's not hard to figure out why this executive committee was so successful. *They communicated—consciously and cooperatively!* When Nicholas realized that his parents and stepparents talked to one another, he knew he couldn't wriggle through their parenting net. Kids are less likely to try to manipulate—indeed, they can't—if they know that their parents (and stepparents) are in touch with each other. Even if a kid *says* he hates it when "my parents talk behind my back," as one eleven-year-old boy complained, communication between parents (in nondivorced homes or in families apart) tells kids that parents are aware of who they are—on weekday or weekends, angelic behavior or devilish pranks—and that they care.

"It used to bug me that Dad knew things about me that I didn't tell him—and I knew Mom told him," recalls an eighteen-year-old boy whose parents separated when he was eleven. "I know now I didn't like it then because when I tried to tell Dad that Mom let me do something, he knew it wasn't true. But it was probably better for me, because I knew I couldn't fool either of them." The boy recalls a fifth-grade friend whose parents got divorced around the same time. "Her parents had bad fights—she went back and forth, living with her mom and dad, and she'd hear it all. They never talked to each other, except to yell and complain. I saw what a divorce could have been like."

Communication is key in *any* relationship, but it is vital when you're co-parenting. Chapter 4 dealt with the importance of listening to your children, helping them understand what divorce means, and keeping up the dialogue. Here we reinforce that theme and also stress how vital it is to maintain communication with the other parent. Difficult as it may sound, conversations with your ex should have a cooperative, caring, and supportive structure that keeps the lines of communication open—between both parents' houses, between parent and child, and between your family apart and the outside world.

Parents' Communication = Children's Protection

Whether you are on your own, living with another adult, or remarried, you and your co-parent (and his or her significant other) can form what stepfamily experts John and Emily Visher call a "parenting coalition." Designed to provide a safety net under your kids; it's comprised of all the adults—parents *and* stepparents—who are involved in the kids' lives. Like any executive committee, it's where the buck stops. This doesn't mean that you have to have exactly the same rules in your different houses or even the same relationships with your children—after all, you are two distinct people. And, as discussed in the previous chapter, it's unrealistic to expect that ex-spouses will always agree on everyday matters. However, the adults should at least keep each other informed—about kids' activities and attitudes, their behaviors and feelings—so that each parent knows what's happening in the kids' lives, even when they're with the other parent, at the other house.

Divorce researcher Judith Wallerstein notes that while attorneys and the courts focus on "big" issues, like education, religious training, and moral influence, "joint custody succeeds or fails on the bedrock of 'little' issues." In short, the children in your family apart will fare infinitely better when you at least communicate about their daily habits, their schoolwork, and their friends.

"Communication is so important," says Bill Paterson, whose children, now fifteen and seventeen, have lived a week at a time with him and his ex-wife, Loretta O'Brien, for the past ten years. He and Loretta plan a weekly conference call to keep each other posted. "The kids have another life with the other parent. I hear one view from them and the adult view from Loretta. Both perspectives are important."

If you can communicate with your ex about everyday matters, then when a BIG issue arises, you are more likely to be able to tackle it as advocates and allies. And your children will feel protected.

"Our children brag about having two parents who love them," says Bertha Samuel, divorced since 1988 when Jill was eight and Patrick four. Bertha remembers feeling betrayed and angry when Arlen left her for another woman. But, at the same time, she didn't want her kids to grow up the way she had—without a father. "So I chose to get on with my life and let my children be whatever they would be with their father."

She admits, "It was really hard in the beginning. I still loved him, and he wanted to be with this woman. I swallowed a lot." Bertha joined a women's group, sought the help of a counselor, and, in twelve-step programs, started dealing with the leftover pain of her childhood. There she found other women going through similar trials. "I had people I could talk to instead of dumping on the kids or taking out my anger on Arlen."

Her efforts have paid off on numerous occasions. Recently, when Jill's school notified the co-parents that their daughter would be placed in a prealgebra class instead of algebra, her mom thought it odd. "She had scored pretty well in her seventh-grade placement test, and this was a kid who tended to do as well as the other kids in her class. Arlen's new wife is a high-school math teacher, and she agreed with Bertha's assessment. "So, all three of us went to school and spoke with the counselor!" And Jill was moved to the algebra class!

Another recent incident proved the power of parental communication: Bertha found matches and lighters in eight-year-old Patrick's jeans pocket when she did the laundry. "I talked to him about how dangerous it was. Then I found another one that I knew was from his dad's house. When Arlen came over, I gave him the lighter and told him what had been going on. He promised he'd talk to him, too."

A week later, Arlen told Bertha he had talked to Pat but didn't share the details of that father/son conversation, which was all right with Bertha. "All I know is that the problem stopped, and that's what counts."

Some parents don't realize how important it is to keep the lines of communication open. When participants in my survey were asked to rate their response to the statement "I communicate with my ex about what happens when our children are with me," 45 percent said "always" or "almost always," but 51 percent said "sometimes" or "usually," and 4 percent "rarely." The thought of keeping in touch may be particularly hard if you're trying to bounce back from an acrimonious divorce. The last thing you want to think about is *communicating* with someone whom you feel is out to get you! But if you want to protect your children from the emotional fallout and help them thrive, *you have no choice.* Clinical psychologist Marla Isaacs recalls one fairly angry divorcing couple: "They didn't have a lot of communication, but when it was important, they talked. Their child knew he wouldn't get lost between the cracks."

Try to let your desire to protect your child's welfare guide your behavior. Betty Merchant, a newly divorced family therapist, was upset because her ex, Eric Pittman, was canceling dates with nine-year-old Abby to spend more time with the married woman he was seeing; his illicit affair began to take precedence over his parenting. "It was infuriating—there was so much deceit. He acted as if he was above it all." But because of her own work with divorcing clients, Betty knew that as much as *she* wanted revenge ("I wanted to call the woman's husband"), the real issue was advocating Abby's right and need to have time with her father.

"She didn't understand why her daddy kept breaking their dates. Finally, I confronted him by saying that it was disrespectful for him to keep lying to her and to pretend that his not seeing her didn't matter. I told him I would cover for him for just so long. I had done everything I could not to malign him, but eventually she would figure things out, and he would lose her."

Betty, who consulted a colleague—another family therapist—to help her over the rough spots, didn't rail at Eric or threaten him (although she would have liked to!); she simply tried to make him see the impact of his behavior on his daughter. "Over time, he did change. I think part of that was because the relationship ran its initial romantic course, and part of it was because he didn't want to lose Abby."

Keeping Your Co-parent Informed: It's *Your* Responsibility

No matter how tough it seems, you must do whatever you have to do to keep your co-parent informed. Start by cultivating your best self; when you feel good inside, you're less likely to be threatened or haunted by the past or tempted to withhold information from the other parent. Work off the steam; confide in trusted friends; get professional counseling. Use the time when you're away from the kids to heal and to center yourself. Even though you may feel ragged now, be assured that study after study (including my own) confirm the curative power of time for personal growth and the favorable effect of good communication—for everyone. If you're not there yet, you'll get there—if you keep in mind that it's *your* responsibility to . . .

Set aside time for co-parenting conferences. Co-parents should not use pickup or drop-off times for communicating important information. You can't have meaningful conversations over kids' heads or in the chaos of transitions. Plan a specific time, and, ideally, involve stepparents or new partners, as the Costos/Miller team did. If everyone can't (or won't) attend, at the very least each co-parent should let her or his significant other know what was discussed (more about remarriage and parenting coalitions in chapter 10). Some co-parents who speak at least once a week on the phone or in person may not need a formal structure for these conferences. Other parents need to schedule a specified time to talk—a weekly meeting or a phone call. Conferences are best held when the kids are not within earshot. Some co-parents prefer talking from work, where they are naturally in a more businesslike mode and conversations are less likely to escalate. Also, if you're in a new relationship, talking to your ex from work is less likely to stir up your partner's jealousy!

Write if you can't talk. It may be time-consuming and tedious, as many parents report, but in the beginning, writing may be your only alternative. "A lot of times parents can't do more than write notes to each other," observes family therapist Ron Taffel. He remembers one couple whose six-year-old son was having tantrums; the parents were too angry to talk. "I suggested that they write something along the lines of 'This is what Andrew did while he was with us.' Once the kid realized that the other parent knew what was going on, he immediately settled down."

Don't ask children to deliver notes—any more than you would ask them to deliver oral messages. To make the whole process easier, you might consider creating a form letter that both of you can use. Leave space to write entries under such subheads as "Activities," "Problems," "New Things Learned/Attempted," "Plans We Made," "Scheduled Appointments/Events," "Questions for My Co-parent."

Keep track of issues and items that you want to discuss. Don't call your ex-spouse every day with questions and reminders; and don't rely on your memory. Have a pad ready, use yellow stickies, talk into a tape recorder, and make note every time you think of something that your co-parent needs to know. "Every week I make a list of all the things I want to discuss with Loretta," says Bill Paterson.

He explains that this is his week with the kids, and he reads from his current list: "Checking into gymnastic program for Gretchen; went to dentist—Kevin's braces off; awards program at school tonight, although I'm sure Loretta will get a letter from school and Gretchen will probably tell her, too. Went to a meeting on college planning—Loretta was on vacation; otherwise, she would have been there. And I want to tell her about a mid-quarter grade of Kevin's that I had to sign for; it dipped a little lower than usual."

Post and distribute a schedule.   Young kids need to see—in bold relief—where they'll be and who'll be with them. As they get older the size of the schedule might shrink, but its importance doesn't. Depending on the nature of your parenting plan, every month or so, discuss the schedule; be as specific and detailed as your long-range planning allows. Include holiday plans, school days off, and any other departures from the normal routine. Make sure everyone's home and work telephone numbers are on the schedule. If a parent is taking a vacation, where can he or she be contacted? Finally, make two copies of the schedule and send one to the other parent.

Notify—and remind—the other parent about appointments and events: school conferences, doctor's and dentist's appointments, games, meets, recitals, PTA meetings. If you know about appointments and events in advance, include those dates on the schedule. Don't assume that the other parent already knows—and don't depend on the kids to relay this information. If you're on the receiving end, and you already know about an event or appointment, be gracious—and grateful—that you're getting the information firsthand. By the way, if reminding your ex feels like an onerous task, remember that it's for your child's sake. Even though outsiders at a Little League game may look cross-eyed at a foursome of parents and stepparents cheering on a single child, it makes the kid feel like a million bucks!

Let your co-parent know who will be attending children's events.   Joint functions can be uncomfortable for some co-parents, a breeze for others. More than two-thirds of the parents in my survey said they can "always" or "almost always" attend events and celebrations together (more on this in chapter 11). Still, it pays to err on the side of sensitivity. Let the other parent know whether you'll be alone, with friends, or with a new significant other. If you're uneasy about seeing your replacement (or you're afraid your ex will be), it's better to talk about it beforehand. You might plan to sit together, to sit separately, or perhaps, because the tension would affect the kids, to decide that it's better that each of you attend alone.

Discuss changes of plans in advance—and directly with your co-parent. If you're going out of town, make sure that your co-parent knows where to reach you. If you can't pick up or drop off a child as originally agreed, give the other parent as much notice as possible. At the same time, if you're on the receiving end of a last-minute change, give the other parent a little slack—especially if it's not a chronic situation.

Changes in the schedule are often cited by co-parents—and children—as a source of conflict. "My mom had agreed to drop my sister and I off at Dad's office in the city," says Heather Dresdin, sixteen. "But there was a mix-up; he thought we'd be there at 3:30. I called him at 4:10, and he flipped out, because he and his wife had an appointment. Then when I told Mom he was angry, *she* flipped out!" What's wrong with this picture? Nancy Blake should have called ex-husband, Tod Dresdin, herself, rather than put her daughter in the middle. Instead, the ax fell on the kids' heads. "We ended up staying with Mom that night, and Dad picked us up on Saturday morning," recalls Heather. "As soon as we got in the car, he started giving us the third degree in a very hostile tone, asking us why the plans got so mixed up."

If you need to have a plan clarified or deliver a reminder or a request, do it directly—not through the kids. Children who are asked to carry messages end up feeling disloyal to one parent and resenting the other. Direct contact between co-parents also cuts down on he-said-she-said communication which kids absolutely abhor. "It was unfair—to put me in the middle of it. They drove me crazy," says a twenty-year-old boy whose parents used him as an information conduit. "I'd cringe whenever I'd hear, 'Ask your mother . . .' or 'Tell your father . . .' It always led to an argument between them, and somehow I always thought it was my fault."

Discuss contingency plans.   What happens in case one of the kids gets sick at school? When one of you has to travel? When it's a snow day? When school is closed but it's not a work holiday? When a hired day-care provider doesn't show up? The more you contemplate these possibilities, the less thrown you will be when they occur—and they will! It's good to try to plan ahead as much as possible. Make a yearly list of what's coming up so that you can anticipate discussions about camp, a new school, a parent's wedding.

Be reasonable about extra time.   When the other parent asks to alter the schedule to spend extra time with the child—say his mother is coming to town or he just got free tickets to the circus—give in graciously. You can't feel cheated when you let the child's needs and welfare dictate your decision. "The first few years we fought over every minute as if it were gold," admits Elena Costos. "Now I realize that by letting the kids go, and by allowing them to develop a relationship with Jim, I've gotten closer to them."

Keep files on your children and share them.   Every school year, I labeled two manilla file folders "Jennifer" and "Jeremy." In them, I kept every bit of correspondence and information related to the kids, schedules, calendars, phone numbers, reports—you name it. As they got older, one folder per child wasn't enough! Mark kept similar files at his office, and it was reassuring to know that when one misplaced something—as one of us invariably did—the other would have it. Mark and I always made sure that both our names were listed with the kids' schools, and we requested duplicates of everything (more on this in "Your Children's World" at the end of this chapter), but whenever a school calendar, a report, or a newsletter arrived, we'd call to see if the other had received it, too . . . just to make sure. I always considered myself lucky that Mark had easy access to a copy machine!

Think before you speak.   Review the communication and negotiation skills you learned in this book (pp. 71–100 and 130–154) and, most important, remember that the children's well-being is your *mutual concern*. Don't start sentences with recriminations ("I've told you this a thousand times . . ."), sweeping generalizations ("You never pay attention . . ."), not-so-subtle digs ("You obviously don't care if your child gets enough rest"), or indictments ("Janie stays up too late at your house"). Instead, simply state the problem ("I've been noticing rings under Janie's eyes") and ask your co-parent to be part of the solution: "I'm concerned that she's not getting enough sleep, or perhaps something else is wrong. What do you think *we* can do?"

You may need to take a few days, even weeks, if necessary, to figure out how to broach a touchy subject and to think through what you want the discussion to accomplish. Recently, Betty Merchant found herself in this position when Abby announced that she didn't want to go out West with her daddy this summer. "She didn't want to be away from me for a whole week." Betty, still angry at Eric for the months he neglected Abby in favor of his married lover, knew enough not to blurt out what she really wanted to say: "If you had been a little more dependable, maybe she would feel more comfortable going away with you!"

"That would just get him angry at *both* of us!" Because summer is several months away, Betty is giving herself time to rehearse a calmer approach and to figure out the best way to talk to him. "I know how he's gong to react if I'm not careful. But I want him to see that instead of thinking that it's ridiculous for Abby to be anxious or to get mad at her for her fears, he has to help her feel more secure." Given Betty's commonsense strategy, there's a greater chance that these co-parents will be able work *together* to make their daughter feel comfortable about the trip.

Do what you do best.   In any effective committee, each executive knows his strengths and weaknesses, likes and dislikes. For example, one of you is more likely than the other to assume the responsibility actually to design and produce a schedule or a form letter. If it's you, instead of resenting your ex for not doing it, just do it. If it's not you, let the other parent know that you appreciate the effort.

You may also *care* more about an issue than the other parent and therefore might categorize something as a "problem" which your co-parent doesn't even see. For example, a number of co-parents complained about grooming. Invariably, one parent cares more about how the kid looks than the other. If you're the one, put yourself in charge of grooming! Instead of griping "You never comb this child's hair," comb her hair yourself after the other parent leaves. Even better, teach her how to brush her own hair.

This principle applies to your emotional assets, too. You may be better at explaining things or empathizing; your co-parent isn't deficient—only different. Eventually, your kids will know where to go to get their needs met; with two parents, their chances improve greatly.

Consider what happened when Patrick Samuel, then seven, tearfully called his mother from a pay phone to let her know that he had gotten lost on the way from school to his dad's house. Bertha immediately called her co-parent, Arlen, to let him know. She recalls, "I also knew that Arlen would get there and laugh. So I got in my car and drove down there to give Pat hugs and dry his tears. Sure enough, a few minutes later Arlen pulls up on his moped, carrying an extra helmet—and laughs. It was his kind of macho thing to do, but I know that my ex always stuffs his feelings. At least I got there first to tell Pat that it was okay to be scared—and then he rode off with his Dad."

Support and respect the other parent's role and authority.   Imagine how wounded little Patrick would have felt if his mother had chastised his father for being such an insensitive boob or, worse, if she had refused to let him ride home on his dad's moped because Arlen had laughed at his son's misfortune. It's not always easy to give space to someone whose judgment and sensitivity you question, but it's important to put this issue in perspective: few parents are downright incompetent; few are utterly incapable of caring for or caring about their children. Your co-parent may not be an "ideal" father or mother, but that doesn't make him or her "bad." Not so incidentally, often one parent's attitude actually *improves* when he or she feels supported by the other.

Consider the alternative: When you undermine the other parent's authority, the children suffer, not the adult. They sense that they have been left in the care of someone who's uncaring or incapable, someone the other parent doesn't trust. Children feel torn and battered when one parent denigrates or harasses the other; and if they've heard they're "just like" Mom or Dad, imagine what goes through their minds when they are told what a terrible person that parent is!

Setting the Tone for Kids: How to Spot Communication Problems

Indeed, the messages you give your children about the other parent can mean the difference between a stable adulthood and one fraught with emotional problems, fear of intimacy, and an eternal need to "make peace" in all other relationships. But you can protect your kids by watching what you say and empower them by listening to what they say.

Remember, too, that what you *do* is as important as the words you use, so *show* your support of the other parent. Encourage your child to communicate good news and accomplishments ("Why don't you call your father? He'd be so happy to hear about that"). Or, suggest calling the other parent when help is needed ("Dad/Mom is really good at math. Maybe he/she can help you with that problem"). And let your child know that you can work *with* your co-parent ("I don't know how we can afford to let you go on this school trip, but maybe if your Dad and I put our heads together we can come up with a solution").

Allow your child to talk freely about what she did with the other parent; let her know it's okay to enjoy herself when she's not with you. Judith Wallerstein reports that some older children and young adults who have seen their fathers regularly report lingering feelings of guilt around their mothers. If you're still angry at your ex or jealous about time not spent with you, a child intuitively knows that it's not a good idea to repeat aspects of her "other life." As one twenty-two-year-old put it, "Children are very perceptive. We see things and understand things our parents don't give us credit for."

In chapter 4, I stressed this point, but it bears repeating: *Keep them talking; keep listening; and keep them feeling part of the process.* If you don't have dinner together regularly or other quiet talk-times, you may want to schedule regular family meetings with your kids—to problem-solve, to plan vacations and other fun events, and to discuss what your family apart is doing right (see pages 273–275 for more about family meetings). Reliable, continuing dialogue with your kids generates immediate and lasting benefits.

All parents need to be good communicators, but the challenge is heightened in divorce because messages travel across households—sometimes even when they're not supposed to! In each of the following difficult situations, the key is direct, open, and clear communication:

When Kids Complain

When a child complains about life in general—his teachers are unfair, memorizing history dates is hard, she has to wait too long for a learner's permit, the new house is creaky—it's always a good idea to ask yourself, whether this a typical, run-of-the-mill kid-gripe or part of your child's adjustment to the divorce or to your new family form. Some children are more direct than others. They will complain that the divorce is "not fair," or grouse about traveling back and forth between parents. Remember, sadness, anger, and resistance often go with the territory. Acknowledge the emotions, and allow children to experience them. Don't try to talk them out of a feeling.

The most common complaints usually center on "the schedule." It's not a bad idea to ask your child what he or she would do to make it better and then incorporate as many of those suggestions as possible. Abby Merchant, who missed her mom and her new puppy when she was at her dad's house, came up with a clever modification that suited everyone. Betty explains, "Every Wednesday, he picks her up at dinnertime. She sleeps there, but then she comes back the next morning before school. She likes her routine here, and Eric and I saw no reason to change that."

Many parents are astonished when kids come up with such creative solutions. But remember, sometimes children's wanting to change a schedule is a test—to see if they're listened to or if the other parent really "wants" them. And sometimes it's because the schedule isn't meeting their needs. In either case, don't let them think that they have the final say—they don't really want it anyway.

When Plans Change

If you have to change the schedule, try not to do it at the last minute. Tell the kids why, and, if they are angry or sad about it, hear their feelings. Children learn very quickly what they can or cannot say to a parent. Their anger won't hurt you, but unexpressed feelings can harm them.

When the other parent doesn't show up on time or calls a half hour before the prearranged pickup to say she can't make it, you will have your own reaction—in fact, you may want to send out a hit man! But focus on your child's feelings instead. If she needs to vent anger, sadness, disappointment, let her—without editorializing.

When Kids Are Fearful

Review your child's developmental needs (pp. 106–118 and 166–175). Is fearfulness a natural part of a "stage" he's going through? Is something happening at school? Talk to your co-parent and find out if he acts frightened at the other house. Encourage the child to talk about his fears. Use a displacement technique (see pp. 110–111)—puppets, drawings, a book about a child who's fearful—to help get the conversation flowing. A little compassion and warmth go a long way toward easing anxiety. Hugs, kisses, holding hands as you walk down the street, a loving greeting when he comes in the door: these are the little moments of connection that make a kid feel secure.

Children can also become apprehensive if schedules are chronically inconsistent and if they feel they can't depend on their parents. If your child has become clingy or fearful, reassess your parenting plan and the degree of cooperation, communication, and constancy between you and your co-parent. Does your child always know what the schedule is? Where to reach you and the other parent? Has one parent gone away recently without leaving a telephone number or other means of contact? Nothing is more heartbreaking than a child—of any age—who can't find a parent. Deborah Nachum agonized one weekend as she watched teenage Davy make scores of phone calls to locate his dad. "Davy's grandmother was very sick, and no one knew where to reach him. Davy finally tracked his father down by calling his business partner. I admired my son's resourcefulness!"

When Kids Come Back from the "Other" House Bearing Tales

"Daddy says you're not spending the money he gives you on me." "Mommy says all you care about is your new girlfriend."

Such statements—out of the mouths of babes—can launch an all-out war. Your response should always be some variation of "I'll talk to Mommy/Daddy directly about that." Most important, try to understand *why* your child is carrying tales. Might the child be testing you to see if you really will allow her to have a relationship with the other parent, or with a new adult in the other parent's life? During the first and second years after parents separate, children also try to re-create what Isolina Ricci calls "that old family feeling." Parents' arguments are familiar and engaging and therefore more comfortable than this new family form. Some children would sooner instigate a fight between their parents than learn to accept the new order.

When Kids Lie   Some kids are ace connivers, especially when they sense that they can get between two parents who are less than close to each other. "Dad/Mom said I could," is a common children's ploy to get what they want, even in nondivorced homes. Remember the stock answer: "I'll talk to Dad/Mom about it." Letting kids know that you compare notes with the other parent is one way to nip tale-telling in the bud. If the lie reveals a major discrepancy that affects the child's welfare—for example, Dad thinks he's been going to an after-school program, and he has been talking to Mom about hanging out at the mall—immediately check out the story with your co-parent ("I'm troubled because Johnny mentioned that he was at the mall this afternoon, and I thought that you told me he would be at soccer practice"). Even if it's a first-time offense, pay attention. Twisting the truth or outright lying is usually a warning signal of needs unmet or even serious emotional problems.

When Kids Are Confused   It's inevitable: there will be legitimate mix-ups, mishaps, and miscommunications between parent and child and between parent and parent, which, in turn, affect the child. Maybe Mom and Dad are giving the kid different signals or they're not communicating with each other. Or maybe a plan that looked good on paper isn't working out that well in real life. Stop; slow down the action; give your children an opportunity to tell you what *they* think is wrong. If their confusion is chronic, you might want to consider instituting family meetings (see pp. 273–275).

When Kids Complain about the Other Parent   Staying out of the cross fire between your child and the other parent is a real challenge, because her complaints may validate your own feelings about your ex-spouse! Perhaps your child is parroting things she's heard you say. Might the complaints be her way of defending you, of taking sides? Although a whopping 95 percent of the co-parents in my survey claimed, "I don't ask the children to side— either overtly or covertly—with me against my ex," their children's comments in interviews tell another story: they some-times feel pulled between two people they love.

Support your child's process—let her vent the feelings, but don't cheer her on. Kids prefer to have their own anger—not yours! "I don't like talking to my mom about my dad," says sixteen-year-old Heather Dresdin, "because she ridicules him, and that bothers me. If I'm annoyed at him, she just jumps on the bandwagon."

A better alternative is to wriggle out of the middle and suggest that she take the gripe directly where it belongs ("Why don't you call Daddy and tell him that he hurt your feelings?"). Otherwise, you run the risk of inadvertently teaching your child to avoid appropriate expression of hurt or anger to the appropriate person.

Sometimes, of course, kids won't admit—or don't realize— that their feelings are related to the other parent. "The night his father got remarried, Etienne totally denied that he had any bad feelings," recalls Michelle Varnet, "but he was in a terrible mood when he came home. He told me he was unhappy with me, because I wouldn't let him take the TV into his room. He had a perfect day except *I* ruined it." Michelle tried to talk to her son. "But I couldn't reach him, so I finally called his father." The co-parents decided it would be best for Donald to speak to Etienne himself, which he did.

It is possible for a co-parent to intercede in parent/child battles in positive ways, but only when communication is open and above board. Tina Gorman recalls having a terrible fight with fifteen-year-old Duane, who had been in a rage. "When I told Tom about it, he played mediator. We all met for lunch, by which time Duane and I had calmed down considerably. I was amazed when Tom said to Duane, 'If my temper hadn't been so terrible, maybe your mother and I would still be together.'" Tom says, "Duane had never displayed that temper with me, but I saw that Tina needed help. I was like a referee and a support, and it made me feel good to be there for both of them."

When Kids Get into Trouble at the Other House

When the other parent has levied some kind of punishment—grounding, extra chores, revoked privileges—it's always a good idea to find out why. However, remember that not all infractions are of equal weight; a kid might be grounded because he didn't clean up his room when asked, or because he was caught smoking pot. The first is a house-specific offense, the second a serious legal, ethical, and familial violation. Unless there's a high degree of contact and cooperation, house-specific issues should stay house specific; it's pretty hard to have a kid "do time" with you when you didn't define the offense or determine the consequence. However, you can at least acknowledge a child's misdeed ("I understand that Mom grounded you because you didn't come home right after school") and be supportive of the other parent. If you believe the punishment fits the crime, say so; if not, stay out of it!

However, concerns over smoking pot or lying (for example, the child says she's going to one friend's house in order to attend an unsupervised party at another's) are matters that *both* parents should know about and act jointly on. Mark and I always held "summit meetings" on such occasions. First, *we* talked. If one of us felt more strongly than the other about a particular infraction, which sometimes happened, by talking it out and keeping our focus on the child, we were able to avoid becoming polarized. Then we had a conference with the child in question and presented a fairly united take on what was involved.

When you're making "house rules," it's essential to set limits and let kids know that you mean what you say; so make sure you can follow through. Many parents, divorced or not, are lax about making punishment stick; then they go overboard and "ground" a kid for a month. Kids know when you're bluffing or ambivalent or confused, especially children of divorce. In fact, many of them made comments similar to this fourteen year-old boy, "I don't really take my parents seriously when they ground me. They never carry it out. Besides, when I'm punished at my dad's, I know I'll be going to my mom's!"

When Kids Say They Don't Want to Go to the Other Parent's House
Whatever you do, don't let children think that they can make the decision not to go. But be a detective. Look at what's happening in the kid's life and in both houses. Consider time and healing; maybe the child simply hasn't gotten used to the idea of having two homes. Perhaps you have to look at how the child is making the transition (see "Comings and Goings," page 180). Maybe she feels disloyal or worried about leaving one parent and going to the other. Maybe she resents what appears to be—or is—competition in the form of a new partner. Maybe she feels closer to one parent than the other.

Guess at what might be the problem—say, a new stepmother—and try to discuss the child's feelings, perhaps by opening with "Lots of kids your age stop wanting to go to their dad's house if there's someone new in his life. Do you ever feel that way?" If the child seems resistant to talking about it directly, try role-playing, use action figures, draw pictures, or read a book about stepfamilies. Your solution should meet the child's needs but, at the same time, ensure that she develops a relationship with the other parent—as Abby Pittman did by staying at her dad's house and stopping off at Mom's house to check things out before she went to school.

When teenagers balk at traveling it's usually because their social life and extracurricular obligations conflict with parents' weekend plans. Still, it's vital for kids to maintain ongoing contact with parents and with the extended family. Isolina Ricci advises parents of teenagers to "clear up for themselves and for their teenagers what part of the time together is negotiable and what is not." For example, kids shouldn't be allowed to miss family rituals—like trips and special excursions, birthdays, and holiday celebrations.

Ron Taffel warns, "You have to steel yourself for their threats and arguments." Kids will tell you they hate their cousins on the other side or that Grandma is a lousy cook, but, says Taffel, these connections are important to maintain. "They'll come up with four or five reasonable excuses, but even as kids get to be pre-teens and teens, if you manage to insist, they go. These events are anchors that keep kids feeling as if they're held in the world."

When a child doesn't want to go to the other parent's house, monitor your own reaction, too. Are you secretly glad, triumphant? Do you indirectly contribute to the child's attitude? And if you're on the receiving end (the one the child doesn't want to see), are you giving the child what he needs when he's at your house? Might you be secretly relieved, feeling free of the responsibility? Perhaps you even want to retaliate, directly or indirectly, and tell the other parent—or even the child—that you don't want him, either.

It helps to know that sometimes other parents have felt the same way. Work overload, new relationships, and the stresses of daily living can sometime make caring for children seem overwhelming. Recognize and deal with the feelings; otherwise, they will seriously impair your relationship with your child.

When Kids Are Jealous   They could feel threatened by the new direction your life is taking: a new job that takes you away from home for longer hours, different activities or interests, or a new person in either of your lives—someone you're dating, a live-in lover, a new partner. You are an adult and have the right to develop a new life without your kids' approval. But be sensitive. Most experts suggest giving the children a chance to adjust to their parents' divorce before introducing too many new things, especially new people, into their lives (more about second-time-around love in chapter 10, "Going with the Flow").

Juggle your plans to make special time alone with the child, to talk and to really listen. New directions, particularly new relationships, signal an end to a child's reconciliation fantasy, so make sure that it's clear to the child that Mom and Dad wouldn't be living together even if you hadn't moved to a new house or if the new people in your lives were suddenly out of the picture. The best antidote to a child's jealousy may be extra reassurance. But jealousy may also be a child's way of showing allegiance to the parent who isn't dating. So if a child seems upset about the other parent's social life, ask yourself: Are you jealous, too? Could your child be mimicking and thereby supporting you? Are you afraid that the child likes Dad's new girlfriend and is being taken in by her? If you secretly fear losing the child, he might unconsciously pick up those feelings.

When Kids Exhibit Emotional Extremes   Extreme sadness, anger, and wild mood swings should always be seen as red flags; the child and your family apart may require professional help. We're not talking about an occasional tantrum, a bad day, or breaking a rule every now and then. This is par for the course in any home. We're talking about a child who is, by his behavior, asking for help: who is sullen or melancholy day after day after day, who cries or flies into a rage with little or no provocation, whose eating or sleep patterns change drastically, who refuses to listen to his parents, who locks himself in his room or stops wanting to be with friends and do the things he normally does. The problem may have nothing to do with the divorce *per se*—but with the way you and your co-parent are behaving. Your child may be angry or sad and unable to express the feelings; he may feel torn; he may feel frightened and insecure; he may be acting out one parent's rage against the other. Begin by looking in the mirror, then seek professional advice if necessary. When parents continue to fight and when they can't communicate or coordinate on behalf of their kids, their children become the casualties of divorce.

Your Children's World

Kids have to interact with day-care providers, teachers, counselors, camp directors, friends, friends' parents, neighbors, doctors, dentists, school nurses, coaches, music teachers, group leaders, part-time employers. The older the kid, the longer the list and the wider his universe. But the outside world is still not tuned in to divorced families in which both parents participate in the child's life. Sadly, some still construe this as "abnormal." So warn your kids that not everyone will be sensitive to the situation or their feelings.

Don't put your child in the position of having to tell outsiders about your divorce or your parenting arrangements. Head these problems off at the pass, by running interference. Contact every institution and person who deals with your child and explain your circumstances and your parenting arrangement. Expect anything. Regardless of the proliferation of divorced families and more couples opting for shared parenting arrangements, many co-parents report that schools and other institutions are often resist-ant, and may even scoff at the notion of co-parenting in general.

You have to let people know that both parents are active in and committed to the child's welfare, and that you would like this to be reflected in any dealings related to your child. Make sure that everyone and every place—from school to community cen-ters—list both parents in the directory, are willing to send corre-spondence, reports, forms, and calendars to both parents, and know to contact both parents in case of emergency. Be persistent.

Do the same with members of the extended family, neighbors, and children's friends' parents. Make sure they also have both parents' numbers and that they understand that the child has two homes and that both parents are to be contacted in case of an emergency or just to make plans. Expect some people to react strangely, to think you're "odd," because you are able to sit next to an ex-spouse at a piano recital or because your child has two Thanksgiving dinners. The important thing is that your children know that you're both there—in the family and in the outside world—keeping each other posted and up-to-date. Then even the strange looks and the "stupid questions" (as one kid put it) about their family apart won't matter so much!

— 9 —

THE MIX-'N'-MATCH PARENT

Key #8: Step Outside Traditional Gender Roles

Attention! This Is Only a Test . . .

Marriages fall apart for many reasons, but traditional *gender* roles—how one is socialized to behave as "man" or "woman"—are at the core of many relationship problems. Sociologist Deborah Tannen points out in *You Just Don't Understand,* that effective communication is often so difficult because men and women seem to come from different cultures. They speak different languages—what Tannen calls "rapport talk" for women and "report talk" for men—because they are shaped by such different societal experiences and expectations.

Listen to couples' complaints about what "went wrong" in their marriages, and you're likely to hear echoes of chore wars and other he-said-she-said battles. She's people oriented, he's action oriented; she's a connector, he's a competitor; she works overtime to keep the relationship going, he works overtime to escape her demands.

Did gender issues trip up your marriage? To find out, check which of following gripes fit your experience:

I complained because my partner . . .

1. . . . didn't show emotions.   ____
2. . . . cried whenever I got angry.   ____
3. . . . wasn't communicative.   ____
4. . . . always wanted me to talk more.   ____

---

5. . . . thought of himself/herself as a "helper" where the kids were concerned.   ____

6. . . . criticized the way I fed, diapered, bathed, or disciplined the kids.   ____

7. . . . never stayed home from work to nurse a sick child.   ____

8. . . . played the martyr when the kids were sick.   ____

9. . . . didn't think my work was as critical as hers/his. ____

10. . . . refused to be understanding when I had a business meeting or trip on a weekend.   ____

11. . . . never appreciated how much I sacrificed my career in order to be a good parent.   ____

12. . . . resented me for not cutting back my work hours after our children were born.   ____

You've probably figured out that women typically check the odd numbers and men the even numbers. Many of us were guided by the values of the forties, the fifties, even the early sixties, which dictated that Dad brings home the bacon and Mom cooks it. So don't be surprised if your marital gripes ran true to your gender.

However, by the time you became a parent, you may have discovered that the old roles no longer offered the security they had promised. The happily-ever-after dreams of your marriage may have been soured by the rhetoric of the women's movement or sobered by the financial reality of needing two incomes in order to make ends meet. And, like many couples, you found yourself—and your marriage—floundering on the rocky shores of change and upheaval as gender stereotypes have been broken down. Increasingly, in fact, with more mothers in the workforce than ever before and with fathers taking a more active role in parenting, traditional gender assumptions have been turned inside out and upside down.

Nowhere has the battle of the sexes been more obvious than in the drama of divorce. Among the most consequential realizations that emerged from both gender and divorce research is that although fathers and mothers play different roles in the development of their children, *both are equally important.* This finding has led many states to encourage joint custody; moreover, many divorced fathers have challenged the traditional assumption that women are "naturally" better parents. And, some divorced mothers, realizing how difficult it is to juggle home and work responsibilities, welcome the change; if you're reading this book, you're probably one of them!

Although fathers taking on more diverse parenting responsibilities and mothers encouraging their efforts certainly represent a departure from tradition, co-parenting requires an even greater stretch. This chapter looks at the value of being what I call a "mix-'n'-match" parent—moving beyond the gender stereotypes toward new, freer, more practical roles for today's mothers and fathers.

Why Flexibility Is Important

Children need two parents, each of whom is competent *and* empathic, independent *and* intimate, able to be competitive *and* to connect. Moreover, our times—our lives and our economics—have changed, requiring much greater flexibility. It is not enough for a man to be a "good provider" who avoids his emotions, or for a woman to be a "nurturer" who does not know how to support herself. Parents who are able to step out of traditional gender roles—in nondivorced families and in families apart—can be better parents by providing the best role models for their children in the nineties and into the twenty-first century.

Research suggests that those who are not locked into traditional gender roles can survive better in the world and in their relationships. One study, conducted by Donald Baucom, professor of psychology at the University of North Carolina at Chapel Hill, asked couples to rate themselves in terms of these roles—how "typically" female and male they act. The findings indicate that the more "androgenous" each partner's capacity, the healthier, more adaptable, and more resilient their relationship. These men and women give themselves high scores on *both* "masculine" and "feminine" scales. That is, they each see themselves as assertive, ambitious, and self-confident—traditionally masculine qualities—*and* as emotionally attuned, interested in interpersonal relationships, and sensitive to other people's rights and needs—traditionally feminine qualities.

When men and women possess attributes commonly linked to both genders, their flexibility is greater in all relationships. He doesn't have to be the sole provider; she earns and manages money, too. She doesn't have to be the only hands-on parent; he, too, is tuned in to the kids' physical and emotional needs. Even if such a couple divides some responsibilities along traditional lines, their decision is purposeful and personal, not dictated by society.

After divorce, androgyny—balancing traditional male and female roles—is equally vital. "Parents locked into either side of very gender-specific skills are in trouble," says Ron Taffel. "Co-parents need to widen their definition of what they think women and men can do." Taffel says women need to be able to mete out discipline, fix a bike, and become knowledgeable about things they might historically not be interested in, like sports and computer games. Men should be able to manage a household, to listen to and talk about feelings, or braid a daughter's hair. As one mother puts it, "I never think of the gender role of a task. I just do what is necessary." And a father comments, "When my son is with me, I attempt to provide for all of his needs."

Even if a parent has a new partner, the biological parent has to be in charge of his or her kids. If he leaves the nurturing to a new stepmom, or if she puts a new stepdad in charge of discipline—children will quickly become resentful about the new adult in their life (more about recoupling and remarriage in the next chapter).

Many of the participants in my survey have discovered the virtues of androgyny. When asked to rate themselves on the statement, "I am able to step out of 'traditional' gender roles when necessary," three out of four responded "always" or "almost always" (40 percent and 35 percent, respectively), 18 percent answered "usually," and only 7 percent checked off "sometimes" or "rarely."

Their comments are more revealing. Some say that they were never locked into traditional roles. Even in their marriages, the men cooked, did housework, took care of the children, and saw to their kids' emotional needs; women worked outside the home and did "guy stuff," as one mother puts it. "There was never any question about this. I was always more adept with a hammer and he likes to cook better then I do," notes one. Often, parents who express these views were born in the late fifties or during the sixties. One explains, "I'm thirty-four, he's thirty-nine. We were strongly influenced by the times."

However, some parents indicate that a nontraditional division of responsibilities represents an essential change, ushered in by divorce: "Because I have not remarried, it has been necessary for me to play a variety of roles," says one mother, echoing other women and men who discovered the need to broaden their repertoire of skills. "I *have* to be independent now, as it's just me and my daughter," notes another. "I have no alternative," a single father says bluntly.

These parents are proud of their growth and accomplishments in so-called nontraditional spheres. You'll note through this chapter that however else they describe their progress, almost every man mentions his struggle for mastery over cooking, a symbol of nurturing that most mothers take for granted. One father notes, "My cooking isn't bad, I'm a great emoter, encourager, and cheerleader. And my daughter comes to me for advice and support about sex, romance, and even gynecological matters."

Women, on the other hand, mention independence most frequently, which marks their ability to be "good providers," something most fathers take for granted. Says one mother, "I am financially independent from my ex. I run a business, and I work hard. I feel I am a feminist and able to step out of gender roles. However, I fix bikes only in an emergency!"

Stereotypes versus Co-parenting Realities

While my study revealed a surprising number of parents who had overcome gender stereotypes, prior to doing my own survey, the research on gender differences had led me to believe otherwise. Most studies seem to reflect, if not support, the notion that the old stereotypes are intact. Observational studies, in which video-tapes of couples' interactions are analyzed, have reported distinct differences between men and women in their styles of communication and their approach to intimacy. Some researchers have even documented that men and women have different *physiological* responses to conflict; compared to their wives, husbands literally *feel* the tension of a marital spat more acutely; they sweat, their pulse rate escalates, and they shift uncomfortably in their chairs.

Given the physiological and psychological differences, as well as the influence of traditional gender norms—rewards and punishments accorded men and women in society—it's easy to see why marriage is often a his/her phenomenon. And it's understandable that when describing their marriage, it seems as if the woman and man experienced completely different relationships!

An equally impressive body of research points to "his" and "her" divorce. Studies focusing on postdivorce parenting practices—degree of involvement, styles of discipline, long-term adjustment—show that men and women often react to and interact with their kids in different ways. However, before you buy into these studies and, worse, allow them to limit your possibilities, *caveat emptor.*

Particularly when research is reported in the media, it should be read with a discerning eye. Consider, for example, the findings of Eleanor Maccoby's 1991 study on adolescents in joint custody (a follow-up of the Stanford Custody Project), which were reported by two highly reputable newspapers. Given each newspaper's treatment of the subject, however, it was hard to tell this was the same study, especially from the headlines. The *New York Times* reported the study, along with several others, in an article entitled "Children of Divorce: Steps to Help Can Hurt," while the *Wall Street Journal* titled its article with a far less pessimistic "Joint Custody's Success Depends on the Parents."

The *Wall Street Journal* began its account by saying, "Joint custody arrangements aren't always as bad as they've been painted, a Stanford University project finds." Explaining that the study found an almost equal proportion of conflicting and cooperating joint-custody parents, the article reported that while parents' conflict can harm children, when parents cooperate, joint-custody teenagers do as well as those living in sole-custody situations.

In contrast, the *New York Times,* after citing a number of other studies that allegedly point to the dire effects of joint custody, doesn't mention parents who cooperate, or that they comprised half the sample. Instead, the article talks about the problems of teens caught in the middle of their parents' battles, mentioning only part of the researchers' conclusion, "that dual-residence arrangements were harmful when there was a lot of conflict between divorced parents."

Neither newspaper actually *misrepresents* the research findings. However, by framing the articles differently, and, in the case of the *New York Times* account, by reporting only the statistics that weaken the case for joint custody, each leaves the reader with far-different impressions. This is not an isolated example. Several eminent researchers in the field deplore the fact that so many prominent articles in the lay press have denounced both joint custody and mediation. In some, the reporters don't bother to cite evidence and, where statistics are mentioned, their interpretation of the findings is frequently misleading or inaccurate.

Even when empirical findings are presented without bias, they may not tell us what occurs in *individual* divorces nor do they elucidate the ways some *individual* parents are able to rise above the generalizations about gender. It's also important to consider the source of the data. Many divorce statistics are from studies done on small, select populations—samples of white, middle-class families. Some findings are based upon highly-specific samples—for example, children who are already in trouble because the parents' acrimonious relationship predates their divorce or families thrown into the family-court system because the parents are battling over custody. They don't necessarily represent "typical" divorced families—because divorced families are incredibly diverse—and they can't possibly reflect *your* family's potential.

Most important, *divorce studies usually report life in sole-custody families* where Mom is the primary caretaker nearly 90 percent of the time. The gender picture changes when we look at co-parenting families. In the Toronto Shared Parenting Project, which compared shared- and sole-custody parents, the authors note that *virtually no gender differences were evident in co-parents' responses,* whereas among sole-custody respondents, "men and women consistently differed."

Granted, my sample is also skewed, in that I purposely sought out divorced parents who already had decided to cooperate and to do the hard work necessary to make their family apart work. These are parents who were, for the most part, able to agree on custody. None went through court-connected mediation, a process designed for parents who usually can't rise above their own self-interests until someone talks some sense into them (even then, some can't).

My respondents' behavior and their choices were not mandated by a judge. Knowing the importance of keeping both parents in their children's lives, these parents were instead guided by sound judgment and concern for their children—and they designed parenting plans accordingly. Thus, it's not surprising that so many parents in my study, particularly fathers, are atypical when compared to "typical" qualities reported in divorce literature and research.

In fact, the picture often changes when parents voluntarily decide to co-parent. Each partner is more likely to cooperate—the man by paying child support, the woman by encouraging fathers' participation. Many co-parents in my survey also sought counseling at the time of their divorce and found that when both parties are educated about the importance of working together, the turnaround is often astounding. Men and women are more able to release themselves from the tight constrictions of their former gender roles.

Fathers who formerly didn't have much hands-on involvement with the kids discover that nurturing their kids also nurtures something deep inside them. And their ex-wives are often pleasantly surprised, if not shocked, at their ability to go beyond rigid role definitions. "If he had been more like that when we were married," one woman told me, "maybe we wouldn't have gotten divorced!" Several mothers in my survey realized that by cutting their ex-husbands a little slack, giving them time to adjust to the new routine and to the idea of hands-on fathering, these men became increasingly devoted to the kids.

When Sarah Jones and Garth Howell were divorcing, their older son, Danny, then seven, wanted to live with his father, "My first impulse was to drop all that respect and unconditional love stuff, take him for myself, and run . . . regardless of his feelings or his father's," admits Sarah. "Thankfully, I didn't follow that impulse."

Much to her friends' and neighbors' surprise, Sarah "allowed" Danny, who was quite attached to Garth, to live with his father during the week; Dean, age one, stayed with her. By staggering the boys' alternate weekends at the other parent's house, Sarah and Garth have arranged for the brothers to live together on the weekends. "I feel joint custody keeps both parents on an even keel and prevents one from wielding power over the other," she says. "Garth and I are no longer ex-wife and ex-husband—we are MOM and DAD—first and foremost. We are Danny and Dean's parents!"

The ability to nurture and discipline your children is not a gender-linked phenomenon. *Quality of parenting transcends gender.* Competence as a parent is related to one's emotional stability and maturity. And children are put at risk when a parent exhibits uncontrolled anger or debilitating depression—qualities found in both men *and* women. Judith Wallerstein confirms, "Intact people do better in *all* relationships."

Therefore, when both parents are committed to their children's well-being and determined to maintain communication and cooperation toward that end, traditional gender lines tend to fade, brightened by healthier, more hopeful realities. If you are already sharing responsibility for the kids or at least trying to figure out how, be reassured: there's a good chance that you and your ex-spouse will outshine the stereotypes.

How to Stay Out of the "Stereotraps"

Certainly, many "stereotraps" that parents fall into are knee-jerk reactions to decades of conditioning through outdated, unworkable societal norms. Some people still look askance at daddies

who do day care, mothers who tote briefcases. Times are changing, but people's lives seem to be shifting faster than the institutions that serve them. In the meantime, we can set some *new*
societal norms for ourselves and for our families apart. Following
are several notable guidelines to keep you out of the "stereotraps"
and in the Androgenous Zone:

Opt for joint custody, or at least share parenting responsibilities.   As the
Toronto Shared Parenting Project indicates, the seeming differences between men and women are often a function of *custody*
arrangements, not gender. "I have several woman friends who are
noncustodial parents, and we have more in common than not,"
maintains Jasper Mulroy, the noncustodial father of a five-year-
old daughter. "The hardest thing is that you're putting in a
lot—money *and* energy—and you have very little say. You don't
even have much time with the child, and that time isn't necessarily the time that you want. Recently, for example, I wanted my
daughter to see the spring thaw at the river's edge, which comes
only once a year, but I couldn't share that with her."

Fathers who want more involvement with their children are
often angry that "the system" reinforces the stereotypes. Jasper
points out, "I fought hard for women's rights, but when it came
to custody, I was treated 'like a man'—incapable of raising a small
daughter. I think that my resentment over that creates more
animosity than shared custody would."

Noncustodial fathers have one societal cross to bear—that
they aren't "naturally" good or meaningful parents—and noncustodial mothers have another—the stigma of having "given up"
their children. Both situations cause a great deal of pain, which
is counterproductive to good parenting. Therefore, regardless of
how custody is legally designated or where the children actually
live, agree to co-parent, which signals to each parent, to the
children, and to the world, that you're both going to be there for
your kids. Your family's life will be better for it.

Don't pit time with children against dollars and cents.   Disgruntled
divorcing (immature and irresponsible) parents tend to use the
bargaining tools society gave them: women use kids, and men use
money. This is a dangerous gender trap that can seriously compromise your children's future.

Mothers: late or even nonexistent child support or alimony payments do not justify your barring him from the kids. Every roadblock you erect translates into kids' sadness, hostility, and guilt, as well as potentially serious problems in school and in adult relationships. Your kids won't love him more because he buys extravagant presents or takes them on exciting trips, but as they get older, they may resent you for cutting him out of their life.

Fathers: don't let your ex-wife's anger about money be a reason to decrease your emotional responsibility to your kids. "I stayed away at first, because I didn't think I was much of a father if I couldn't at least take my kids out for the weekend. I was always so broke," says a noncustodial father attending a workshop about money and divorce. For the past year, he has had to work at two jobs to keep up with child-support payments. Early on, he explains, the fact that he was slow in paying or only made partial payments angered his wife. She threatened him: no money, no children. The situation pained and embarrassed him. "I wanted to be there in both time and money ways for my kids, but I felt like a failure." Concerned and depressed, he sought the help of a counselor at a local family center, who brought his wife into the process. "She finally realized I was doing the best I could and that it was hurting the kids for me to stay away."

Develop your own identity. One of the best ways of avoiding gender traps is to be yourself. When I asked Jennifer if her father and I fell into more or less "typical" roles after the divorce, I was somewhat shocked to hear that, in her opinion, we did! But then she explained further, "Well, at first you did, but you've each gotten better—Dad has taken on more Mom things, and you've taken on more Dad things. I think it had to do with you guys being more comfortable with the divorce and with each other." And, I would add, *with ourselves.*

As I worked on becoming a whole person—one who could be both nurturing in my relationship *and* accomplished in the world—I began to feel better about myself and, in turn, was able to develop a better postdivorce relationship with Mark—and, not so incidentally, be a better parent. I'm certain the same was true for Mark. The more confident he felt in the "Mom" domain, the less threatened he was by differences in our parenting styles.

My experience is borne out by research and professional observation. A study conducted by the National Center for Women and Retirement Research, which looked at women who exited long-term marriages, indicates that when women search out their identities and broaden their definitions of themselves—as being more than mothers and housewives—it not only speeds the healing process, it improves their relationships with their children. Although men were not included in that survey, psychologist Christopher L. Hayes, who launched the study, suspects that to be better parents most men have to do similar work on their identities. "They have to take a broader view of what being 'a man' is—and incorporate the positive qualities of the opposite sex, such as nurturing, verbalizing, and participating in everyday child rearing responsibilities. This is especially important for fostering a sense of intimacy among their sons."

If you don't have a clearly defined sense of who you are and what you want out of life, look at what might be standing in the way of that self-knowledge. Perhaps the gender lens you've been using is narrowing your vision. Make two lists—one that counts the ways you already transcend the stereotypes, another that shows the areas that need work. Applaud yourself for the first list and work on changing the second.

Stretch your repertoire of skills.   Try new things, expand your limits—you'll be surprised at what you can do. It's essential for women to become independent, to learn how to manage money, and to reeducate themselves through schooling, counseling, or a challenging new job. Network, do "guy stuff" around the house. And for men, it's vital to learn to be emotionally accessible and expressive, to nurture the kids and be comfortable spending time with them. Learn to master "woman's work"—become a domestic engineer! Develop your own social network, and establish rituals and new traditions for yourself and your kids.

Co-parenting itself will help you discover new personal assets. "I was brought up traditionally. The woman cooks, cleans, takes care of the children," says Tony Palumbo. "But you soften around the edges as a co-parent. I now use more of my intuitive self, and once I thought that was totally Barbara's domain. If we push ourselves, we grow in amazing ways." Tony, now remarried, adds, "Without even being asked, I do eighty percent of the laundry, ninety-nine percent of the food shopping, seventy to eighty percent of the cooking!"

Be gentle with yourself, too; co-parents often feel they "need practice" in their new domains, so they hang in until they get it right. Gary Shannon's attitude is representative: "It has taken awhile to get the knack of cooking certain things. My timing is lousy! Still, I am very practical and do what it takes to get things done." But Richard Frater, father of a fourteen-year-old girl and twelve-year-old boy, proclaims, "I refuse to buy tampons for my daughter!" And Amy Fried comments, "I'm not a great pop mechanic, but I try!" Michelle Varnet says, "I can't get involved in sports with Etienne, but I can take on other traditional male roles." Freda Miles, who responds that she is "almost always" able to step out of traditional gender roles, explains, "What stops me is anxiety and incompetence, not a sense of what I should or shouldn't do." Interestingly, her ex-husband, who also responded "almost always," adds, "Philosophically, always; in practice, I do not sew and have a limited cooking repertoire!"

Give your ex-spouse a break when he or she starts acting true to gender type. The first time Jeremy got sick when he was at his dad's house, Mark thought it might be better to send him back to me. I don't recall precisely what I said, but I remember thinking that Mark was trying to get out of his "turn." Silently, I gloated, *he's really not as good a parent as I am.* Mark (and I) unwittingly fell into the stereotrap that says, "A man can't minister to a sick child." The real issue was Mark's learning how to father in a way that he never had in the past, not because he wasn't capable of doing it, but because it had been my territory. As it turned out, Jeremy stayed and Mark fared quite well. Knowing what I know now, I wish I had been more generous and understanding—and less cynical about Mark's intentions. Learn from my mistake.

If you're a mother, support your ex-husband's effort to nurture and to master the typical "Mom" things—like cooking. Help him understand your daughter's concerns, especially during adolescence. Make sure he knows about school events and other meetings, even though he may be one of the few men there. Support other fathers who show up as well. Many fathers report feeling isolated in their new roles; they say that the reassuring approval of kindly (female) friends and neighbors keeps them going.

If you're a father, let your ex-wife know what kinds of "guy things" your son enjoys. Maybe football isn't her cup of tea, but if she's willing to learn what a first down is, encourage her. Help her understand your son; adolescent boys, in particular, are a trial and a mystery to many mothers! Applaud the steps she takes to support herself; and, when possible, help her financially until she can stand on her own. Stuart Mercurio advises fathers, "Don't get caught up in your pride thing about money—do it for the kids."

Think before you talk in stereotypes. Men and women tend to lapse into verbal shorthand about each other, often relying on gender stereotypes to prove a point. "Oh, he never talks about his feelings, which is just so typical of men" or "Isn't it just like a woman—all she wants to talk about is the relationship." Understandably, old generalizations can incite rage in a man or a woman who is trying to do things differently. So try not to think of your co-parent as "man" or "woman" but as a person and an ally in the tough business of child rearing. Jeff McGuinn theorizes, "My ex-wife didn't really trust me with our son at first because I am a man. I know I didn't spend as much time with him before the divorce, but that's because I worked a lot. Besides, she did everything, so I wasn't needed."

Don't compete. Being a competent co-parent doesn't have to translate into one-upping your ex-spouse. Several fathers' comments are revealing: "I cook/clean better than most women," "I think I am more nurturing than most mothers," "My house is cleaner and the laundry gets done better over here." At the same time, you don't have to go to the opposite extreme and obliterate your own gender identity. "I was a good mom during my week," says Gabe Delaney, whose description of himself as a "good mom" exemplifies the difficulty so many men have in owning their nurturing selves. Being a "good *father*" is enough, so take pride in your growth, as Bill Paterson does: "I share duties now. I make fifty percent of the meals and I perform various household chores. Most important, I'm the best father I can be."

Appreciate the unique contribution each of you makes to your child's development. Fathers and mothers are different people. "Only her father can be her father," observes Joanna Hepburn, a mother who indicates that she can "always" step out of gender roles when necessary; her now twenty-two-year-old daughter sees her long-distance dad once or twice a year. Tina Gorman says she's grateful that her son Duane "has a loving father in his life—it's so important." Tom Gorman adds, "There's certain stuff that dads like to do with a son. Every year, since he was four or five, Duane has come fishing with my buddies and me the first weekend of the season. This year, the trip conflicted with his senior prom, so he drove up by himself on Sunday morning. I was glad to see that it means as much to him as it does me."

It's not that mothers can't take their sons fishing—any more than fathers can't take their daughters shopping or teach them how to cook. A parent's qualities have less to with gender than with *who they are as human beings.* Mary Lou Welsh, who separated when her son was eight, points out, "Each individual, whether male or female, has his or her own unique talents, needs, and responsibilities."

One parent may have a special interest, aptitude, or hobby that she alone shares with the child. Besides, no one can do everything and be all things to a child. Cara Rasmussen, who is quite "nontraditional" in most respects, remarks, "I'm no ballplayer, and Neil is an athletic child—he loves basketball. I have no interest in that, but David does. He plays with him, takes care of practice. If it were all up to me, I'd feel overburdened trying to do everything."

Not so incidentally, having two parents who are different from each other enriches the child's life. Twelve-year-old Dawn Carver, who has, for the past eight years, lived at her dad's house on Tuesday and Thursday nights and one weekend night, explains, "It's a whole different lifestyle from a lot of your friends, because you're constantly on the go. But at least I get to see *both* my parents. I get different things from both of them. And a lot of my friends whose parents got divorced when they were little can't even remember their dads."

Remember that good parenting knows no gender. You don't "know best" because you're a woman; you aren't incapable of learning how to be a good homemaker because you're a man. Don't be discouraged by the widely held belief that single mothers *can't* discipline their kids and single fathers *don't* discipline their kids. Mom *or* Dad is capable of being what the experts call an "authoritative" parent—one who combines firm limits with affection. I prefer to use the term *balanced,* which connotes psychological equilibrium as well as a style of parenting; indeed, in order to sustain this blend of limits and love, you have to be on an even keel emotionally!

Your parenting-role models—your own mother and father—may get in the way of your becoming a balanced parent. Without realizing it, you may have adopted their style of parenting or fought really hard to be exactly the opposite. Either way, you probably tend to swing to parenting extremes, being rigidly strict or softly permissive; studies have shown that neither is effective. In a strict household, children may abide by the rules (if they don't rebel entirely), but their intellectual growth, creativity, and ability to reason may be inhibited. In permissive households, children may feel loved, if not indulged, but internally they are at sea, because they lack structure and discipline; they may never learn how to play by the rules and may be confused when faced with too many choices.

In contrast, balanced parents set firm limits for kids, and they listen to children's input; they explain the reasons for their rules, and they propose logical consequences when kids don't abide by them. Balanced parents are nurturing, affectionate, and attentive to children's needs, but they are still able to impose discipline when necessary. While rigid parents fear change and permissive parents are thrown into chaos by it, balanced parents plan for transitions, discuss them, and help children develop a reservoir of skills that will enable them to cope. Finally, because balanced parents are stable and emotionally grounded, they recognize the difference between themselves and their children. They don't burden kids with adult responsibilities, and they don't decide what they want their kids to be. Rather, they look at who their kids are, allow them to make age-appropriate choices, and they nurture their children's interests and talents.

Don't blame ineffective parenting on divorce or on gender. Mothers and fathers have equal potential for becoming balanced parents. However, if you're a mother and you say things like

"Wait until your father gets home," you're caught in a stereotrap that makes you believe mothers can't discipline their kids. If you're a father, and you say, "I'll have to ask your mother about what kind of dress you should wear," you're caught in a stereotrap that makes you believe that fathers can't become aware of the latest and greatest fashions (if they're not already) or learn what kind of attire is appropriate. Those kind of remarks signal that you may have to change your thinking and your view of yourself.

As you become more aware of the blatant and subtle ways in which you're gender bound, you'll slowly free yourself of those self-limiting behaviors. You *can* change. Reading books about gender can help you understand the stereotraps and how to help your kids avoid them. But also read up on child development, explore different parenting strategies, investigate a course—anything that will help you put into practice the skills of good parenting. (See Resources, p. 321, for specific suggestions in both areas.)

Don't step back into the old roles if you remarry. Even when married couples have "egalitarian" intentions, when their first child is born, they tend to revert to type, especially when it comes to parenting and household chores. "She does more than she thought she would, and he does less than he said he would," says psychologist Carolyn Pape Cowan who, with psychologist Philip A. Cowan, oversee the Becoming a Family project at the University of California, Berkeley.

Apparently, the same thing happens with single parents who remarry. Several parents' comments indicate that the presence of two adults makes some androgenous parents assume—or revert to—traditional roles. "It's not really necessary with my current wife around," admits Gregory Macnamara. Even Arlene Steinberg and Peter Levine, who say they transcended the stereotypes in their marriage to each other, see differences in their second marriages. Arlene notes: "Since both of us have remarried, we have slipped into somewhat more traditional gender roles." And Peter comments, "I have always cooked and I can sew and shop for groceries, but in my current marriage we have split up the work along pretty traditional sex role lines."

It may seem "easier" for each of you to stick with what feels most comfortable, but children are infinitely better off with mix-'n'-match parents. Furthermore, your remarriage will have a better chance of surviving if you learn to be more flexible in all of your relationships while continuing to give your child what he or she needs—a balance of discipline and nurturing—instead of relegating either responsibility to a stepparent.

Inspire your kids to step out of traditional gender roles.   Gender conditioning is a subtle, invisible process. Changing the way kids think and act goes far beyond having sons do the dishes and daughters help you assemble the jungle gym.

Mom, don't think of your daughter as a girlfriend, and don't call your son "my little man" and expect him to be your "rock." They both need your affection, trust, and discipline; they both need to know how to take risks and how to cry. A son *or* a daughter can become overly attached to their mother and find it hard to separate, especially if Mom acts as if she can't take care of herself. But be especially aware of the danger of leaning on your daughter, who already may be more conditioned than her brother to take care of (and take responsibility for) your well-being. Teach her that she doesn't have to be everyone's mentor or savior, that she has to attend to her needs as well. At the same time, be aware of unconsciously pushing your son away because he reminds you of your ex. And don't take personally his need—and sometimes his painful longing—for a father. Especially as a boy moves into the school-age years, both because of his developmental need to separate and society's (unfortunately) still-sanctioned mandate that he not become a "mamma's boy," your son may tend to shy away from being "too close" to you.

Dads, do whatever you can to nurture your relationship with your son *and* daughter. They need you to demonstrate that a man is capable of being both independent *and* loving. Research shows that a boy's overall adjustment is linked to the father-and-son relationship, and that your daughter's long-term emotional health is dependent on you, too. If your adolescent daughter's budding sexuality makes you (or her) feel uncomfortable, when you take her out to dinner, invite friends to come along so the dinner doesn't feel like a date. To avoid leaning on your daughter, take responsibility for your own emotions. And learn to master "mom stuff," so you're less likely to put her in charge of the homefront. Equally important, help your son learn how to talk about and express his emotions; unless boys are given "permission" and example, they will suffer the same limited access to feelings that has plagued generations of men before them.

Parents of either gender would do well to remember that the bonds children develop with you serve as a model for adult intimacy; the lessons they learn from you will resonate throughout their adult life. By stepping out of traditional gender roles, we can open new vistas for our children—and prepare them for life in the twenty-first century.

Children's perspective definitely changes when they have mix-'n'-match parents. "Being an attorney, I already am out of a traditional gender role," says Cara Rasmussen, who notes that her son Neil, seven, thinks being an attorney is "woman's work"; his dad, a sales rep, works at home. Cara recalls, "Our whole marriage was a role reversal. David took care of Neil as a baby; he'd bring him to nursery school. And I remember one time, Neil remarked, 'There's a daddy bunny with his babies.' Until fairly recently he thought all daddies stayed at home with the children!"

— 10 —

GOING WITH THE FLOW

Key #9: Anticipate and Accept Change

The Inevitability of Change

Several years had passed since I last spoke with Nancy Blake and her ex-husband, Todd Dresdin; then I received her note: "This may not be what you're looking for," she wrote, "but my civilized, friendly relationship with my ex-husband took a very bad turn about a year and a half ago."

I remembered them well. Divorced for five years at the time of their first interview, Nancy and Todd had joint custody of their daughters, Heather and Kelly, then thirteen and nine. Despite incredibly different personalities, these co-parents seemed able to laugh off their own and each other's idiosyncracies; their ability to cooperate was both surprising and admirable.

It was hard to believe that the Nancy who wrote this note was the same optimistic woman who three short years before had described her co-parenting relationship in glowing terms when I interviewed her for the *New York* article "Divorce Family Style." Todd, even though remarried by then, had concurred: "Although we may not always agree, we can communicate, put our cards on the table. We listen, and we try to sensitize each other to the issues."

Four years later, he was unavailable for further comment, and she was so tired of butting heads with him over their daughters, that she was considering an appeal for sole custody.

The bitter turn in their co-parenting relationship underscores the importance of anticipating and accepting change. For Nancy and Todd, the precipitating event was an argument that ensued a few months after Nancy remarried. One evening, after an unscheduled weekend outing with their youngest, Kelly, now twelve, Todd brought her back several hours late without having called Nancy to inform her of the delay. "That night everything just came to a head."

In retrospect, change had been taking its toll on this family apart for some time before the blowup, but neither parent had heeded the early warning signs. Todd had come perilously close to a second divorce shortly before his new wife got pregnant, and Nancy felt then that the discord in his marriage affected their co-parenting relationship. The co-parents began arguing more frequently, and his checks began arriving late. At the same time, the girls and their emerging teenage problems centering on schoolwork, dating, and sex put new, additional strain on the co-parents. Predictably, they began disagreeing about how to approach such issues.

Nancy acknowledges that her own second marriage played a part in the new dynamics, too. "Before that, even though Todd had someone else, he probably thought he could just reenter my life at any time. Suddenly, it wasn't his choice."

Many divorced parents talk about "crashing" several months, sometimes years later, when the reality of their divorce—and the finality of it all—sinks in. It's the first time everyone really integrates what's happened to the family. Often, as was the case with Todd and Nancy, the moment coincides with change—remarriage, adolescence, a new baby.

Isolina Ricci calls these critical points "flashbacks," because suddenly you're facing familiar behaviors and disagreements that characterized earlier periods of the divorce. She notes that flashback events can occur all at once, one at a time, come and go relatively quickly, or last over the course of several years. The very foundation of your new life begins to quake—just when everything had seemed to be settling! It's almost like drawing a Chance card in "Monopoly" that instructs, "Move your piece back to the beginning of the game."

The hallmark of development is change; it's what *life* is all about, not just life after divorce. We're all aware of *child* development; we expect and accept that our kids will go through significant growth periods—toddlers stumbling through the "terrible twos" or teenagers bumbling through adolescent anxieties. We are confident that everyone will emerge safe and sound, with enhanced physical, emotional, and/or social capabilities. Likewise, we realize that we, as *adults,* go through similar life-cycle transitions—for example, the much-publicized "midlife crisis." What is less familiar perhaps is *family development.* Yet all three are the result of reacting and adapting to exterior and interior change.

Family development is more complex; it is systemic, involving the whole family and each of its members. Normal family life-cycle events can precipitate family development—a first child is born, the family moves, the children go to school, enter adolescence, and leave home, one or both members of the couple retires. In addition, crises requiring everyone to pull together to meet new needs, such as serious illness and death, or, in the case of families apart, divorce and remarriage, can trigger family transformation. And so can an individual's development which causes him or her to change and, in turn, affects the whole system.

No family is immune to these developmental phenomena, but in families apart, the overall impact can be downright dizzying. In addition to the main course—divorce—a family apart is served additional entrees from any one (or more) of three "change columns"—the parents', the kids', the family's. Like a Chinese restaurant menu, the list of possibilities is endlessly interchangeable!

Imagine a combination platter made from (a few of) the possibilities: a new baby; different living arrangements; a child is diagnosed with a learning disability or other special needs; dating (parents' or kids'); a child or parent is hospitalized or dies; a revision of parenting time; a child drops out of school; a parent's more demanding job; remarriage and stepchildren; the death of a grandparent; a co-parent changes his or her sexual orientation; a familiar child-care worker leaves; finances change (for better or for worse); remarriage "blends" two families and an only child becomes a half-sibling or a step-sibling, a youngest becomes the middle child; a second divorce.

Competent families apart expect and accept change, recognize it as a challenge, and do whatever is necessary for each member to get through the transition. In short, they go with the flow. How you handle these inevitable periods of growth and transition—which often *feel* more like chaos and pain—makes the difference between getting back on an even keel or backsliding, like Nancy and Todd.

This chapter looks at how the biggest "wave" of all—new loves and remarriage (a step taken by about two-thirds of all divorced parents)—can affect your co-parenting relationship and your kids' adjustment. Fortunately, there are general guidelines as well, principles that can help you get through just about any kind of change and make it easier for your family apart to go with the flow.

The Second Time Around: Love Is . . . More Complicated!

Co-parenting with an ex-spouse is difficult enough, but it can seem Byzantine when you have a new partner looking over your shoulder. Talk about complications! A fifth of the parents attributed a change in the co-parenting relationship to their remarriage and a quarter to their ex's remarriage. Psychologist Emily Visher maintains, "It's often harder to let a stepparent into your life than it is to co-parent." That makes sense. After all, if that special someone in your life doesn't approve of co-parenting, thinks it's "unnatural," or resents the steady presence of a former spouse in your life or your co-parent doesn't want to share the family domain with your new partner—or if *you* are insensitive to your new partner's need to be part of the family, watch out for the fireworks. Your co-parenting relationship might break down, your new relationship might falter—or you might feel eternally stuck in a bitter triangle—and neither relationship will prosper. Ultimately, everyone loses. No wonder six out of ten second marriages end in divorce.

While this was probably not the only reason their marriage didn't make it, Mark's second wife resented our ties, even when they were just dating. She couldn't abide the constant contact, the many teachers', doctors', and therapists' appointments we attended together, or the money he spent on the kids, especially when they were with *me*. Perhaps some of the tension might have been eased if Mark and I had realized the importance of forming a parenting coalition across households. Writing this book made me realize just how typical her reaction was. When asked to indicate "what issues, events, or situations cause(d) problems when you and your ex share parenting responsibilities," of the twenty-six choices listed, nearly four out of ten parents in my survey checked "stepparent or live-in lover"—more than any other single item.

Interestingly, studies confirm that a second marriage fares better when co-parents have a noncombative relationship. Therefore, new partners owe it to themselves to promote harmony between co-parents rather than thwart it, but this wisdom is lost on some people.

"When Bert, my second husband, and I first got together, my relationship with my ex caused a lot of fighting between us," recalls Loretta O'Brien, "because Bill and I talked so often and had so much contact about the kids." To deal with the conflict, Loretta tried to explain to her new husband how important the co-parenting relationship was to her and the kids. She also tried to accommodate *his* feelings by talking to her ex when she was at work instead of at home. "Bert had a very hard time, because he was struggling with his ex, but I held my ground. Everything finally started to change when Bill got serious with Dale."

Unfortunately, after years of flawless operation, a new partner can really throw a wrench into the co-parenting machinery. "Even twenty-five years later!" confirms Deborah Nachum. Sur-

prisingly, she is referring to her relationship with her first husband, whom she privately referred to as "Michael the Good,"
because he had always gone the extra mile for their kids and their
relationship (unlike her second husband, "Harvey the Bad," who
showed up only when he had to). A regular fixture during the
holidays even when she was married to Harvey, years later Michael continued to play Santa to the younger children (Harvey's
kids) . . . long after Deborah had divorced their father!

Enter Michael's new girlfriend. Deborah and Michael tried to
conduct business as usual. "Michael told me that on the way back
from Thanksgiving dinner at my house, she harangued him for
the entire six-hour drive home. She thinks our relationship is
unnatural!" The situation went from bad to worse. By the next
year, it was clear that Deborah wouldn't be spending Christmas
with Michael the Good, forcing their kids to choose.

"I can't believe it!" Deborah exclaims. "We've always been
able to work things out, but now he's too scared. And I thought
nothing could ever shake the foundation that we've built. At least
the kids are older, but it's still sad." Her kids agree; her older
daughter, now in her late twenties, laments, "After all these years,
I realize that this must be what a *real* divorce feels like!"

Just as a new love interest can endanger the stability of a
family apart, the presence of a former spouse can threaten the
future of a new adult relationship. After a somewhat rocky beginning, Jasper Mulroy co-parented with his ex-wife, Susanna,
for ten years. Their son, Troy, was two when his parents divorced. "Susanna and I sat by each other at our son's recitals.
I'd often stop for tea or even dinner or a board game at child-
exchange times. Sometimes we took our son to a movie together. I wanted to go on 'Donahue' as a model divorced
couple," says Jasper.

Troy was twelve when his dad married Helene, who had two
kids of her own, thirteen and eleven; then Jasper and his new wife
had a child, Daphne. Jasper believes that Susanna is, in part,
responsible for the failure of his second marriage. "All Hell broke
loose, because following Daphne's birth, I started to consciously
separate myself from Susanna in order to be closer to my new

wife. Susanna felt a little put out of her role. She wasn't Number One Wife anymore."

The good news is that the changes brought by a new-love interest do not have to be *negative*. Far from it, according to the Toronto Shared Parenting Project, which reports: "In most cases, the involvement of former spouses in a new intimate relationship was seen as having a positive effect (76 percent) on their shared-parenting arrangement." Just as Loretta O'Brien tried to help her new husband, Bert, accept her co-parenting role, my hunch is that co-parents probably also work harder to make new spouses understand how important the connection with their former spouse is—both for their kids and for the future of their second marriage.

Part and parcel of "working harder" is having the sensitivity to understand your new partner's point of view as well. Emily Visher, who became a stepparent more than thirty years ago, is still surprised by the pain she experienced during the early years of her remarriage. "As a society, we don't know what to do when you get an extra parenting person. At first, many people could not understand *why* I even wanted to be involved with my stepchildren. I was having to deal with the fact of *who was I* in this new family?" Visher stresses, "New partners often feel left out. That's why it can be vital for the success of the new marriage to form a parenting coalition. We coined that phrase precisely because it means *more than two*."

But when the co-parents themselves don't have the clarity, a wise new partner can often help them see through the haze. Elena Costos credits Jim's wife, Bonnie, for causing a major turnaround in the co-parenting relationship. During the angry years after the divorce, when the resentments on each side continued to build, Elena finally decided to sue Jim for nonpayment. "At that point," she recalls, "Bonnie called and said, 'This is getting ridiculous. Jim will meet you at such-and-such a time and place. He wants to give you a check, and he'll tell you what's wrong.'

"That was the first time we ever really discussed anything, the first time we listened to each other," Elena admits. "Bonnie was very smart; she didn't do what most stepmothers do. She didn't resent the money or the first wife—she took a mature, responsible position." Elena maintains, "The second wife is pivotal—she can be a troublemaker or a peacemaker."

Research shows that a new wife's cooperation is even more essential than a new husband's—because stepmothers are typically thrust into the nurturing role by biological fathers and because women also tend to *seek* more of the hands-on parenting than do stepfathers. However, a man's cooperation is certainly meaningful. "Terry is an extraordinary human in terms of how he's been able to come into this situation and not feel threatened," says Sally Washington of her second husband. "He used to joke that I'd talk to Gabe more than him. But somehow Terry understood: Gabe and I just had more business to discuss."

Obviously, when the adults act maturely, put the children's needs first, and keep the inevitability of family change in perspective, it's better for all concerned. You also have to give the system time to adjust. These families apart come to remarriage with a houseful of baggage—kids and a former spouse for starters. Depending on the psychological makeup of the adults and children and the number of other stresses that push against the family, it can take several years for everyone to co-exist productively. In the meantime, it's important for you to include your new partner. If your new and former spouses can't be in the same room, at least inform and consult your partner on matters relating to the children. Being in the role of parental advisor will help avoid his or her feeling powerless or unnecessary. At the same time, encourage your new partner to *be* part of the family.

Reflecting on her dad's long-term three relationships over the past fifteen years, Jennifer gave me an insight that can help ease the way for new partners. Thinking about the women in Mark's life, Jen says, "It's definitely important for a parent to spend time with his kids—separately—but I think the new wife or live-in relationship should also to try to get to know the kids *on her own* and find out what's going on in their lives. I never realized it, until one of my friends commented, but Harriet [name changed] didn't even come out of her room when I had kids over. That made me realize how little she had to do with us."

In the best situations, co-parents keep the focus on the kids and help their respective partners understand the importance of harmony across the two households; the adults form a parenting coalition, in which the new spouse and former spouse begin to see each other as allies and resources; and the new partner develops his or her own separate relationship with the kids. Otherwise, new partners, being left out, may sabotage the co-parenting relationship and, as Emily Visher points out, "The couple may gel, but not the *family*." But even in badly deteriorated situations, just *one* voice of sanity can help get everyone back on course. Sometimes the "voice" is that of a loving relative, a teacher, a therapist, a mediator—anyone who can help the adults listen to their children and to each other and help all parties articulate their needs.

Through Kids' Eyes: The Family Forest

Even serious dating can make a child feel resentful. Several of the young adults I interviewed complained that parents "pushed them aside" or "paid less attention" whenever someone new captured their parent's attention. Some parents try to avoid the complications. For a long time after Tina Gorman divorced Tom, she was very cautious. "When I was dating, I never let any man get close. If Duane didn't get along with them, they were gone. We had a sort of you-and-me-against-the-world attitude." New relationships ended before they had a chance to become more serious and change the family dynamics.

No one is suggesting that divorced parents take an eternal vow of celibacy. On the other hand, discretion *is* a good idea; most experts advise parents not to introduce children to everyone they date, nor to have everyone they have sex with sleep over. But the danger of not having *any* adult social life is that parent and child can become too dependent on each other. And, then, when Ms. or Mr. Right does come alone, and the parent becomes seriously involved, the child is probably going to resent having to share Mom or Dad with a virtual stranger.

Brian Posner was not quite three when his parents, Steve Posner and Joyce Newmann, separated—and, because of their work lives, ended up living in different parts of the country, a thousand miles apart. Still, they had joint custody of Brian and co-parented via long distance, with Steve taking Brian for two months every summer and on Christmas and spring breaks. "He had me all to himself for four years," says Steve.

Then, the family portrait added new faces. Steve remarried; a year later Joyce did. Within three years, Brian had three young half-siblings! Adding insult to injury, Brian's uncle's wife also gave birth to his first child, which meant that Brian, long the only grandson, had to share the spotlight. Joyce says, "All we could do was tell him it's okay to be angry, but this was a reality he had to accept."

Kids' anger comes in many shapes and sizes; it's often expressed as recalcitrance or even serious acting out. One parent reports that, at ten, her daughter stole money; another says that her son, fourteen, shaved the back of his head à la punk. Parents have to step back see what's happening through their kids' eyes. What did the money or that hideous haircut look like, and mean, to those kids? In both cases, their parents recently had remarried. The marriage opened a new door for the adults, but to the children, it must have felt as if another door were closing forever.

In a child's eyes, seeing a parent get married contradicts the natural sequence of family life. Even children who are extremely fond of a parent's new partner-turned-spouse probably agree with the sentiments of Etienne Levin, fourteen, who, as "best man," gave the toast at his father's wedding. "I had to stand at the front of the room—it was weird for me. It was out of order, like it should be the other way around."

Remarriage can also feel overwhelming to children because it can bring a new crop of people into their life. Besides being linked to two parents' extended family networks, one (or both) of their parents then bring a whole new tribe and all *their* extended relationships into the picture! As Emily Visher points out, "The family tree starts to look like a family *forest.*"

The following illustration is an example of how dramatically a family apart can change; the relationships indicated in capital letters are described from the vantage point of Sandy and Kerry, whose parents, Ellen and Greg Macnamara, divorced in 1983. Ellen then married David Rasmussen, becoming stepmother to Neil, David's son, who lived at his mother's house on alternate weeks. Greg married Alice, who had three kids from her previous marriage, and they went to their father's house every other weekend. Greg and Alice also had a baby of their own. It's interesting to note that even though our language has no terms to describe some of the "branches" in a family forest—like a stepbrother's grandmother—Sandy and Kerry are nevertheless "related" to Neil's grandma.

THE MACNAMARA/RASMUSSEN FAMILY FOREST

	Neil, 12 stepbrother	Kerry, 11/Sandy, 10 sisters	Mark, 3 half-brother	Carl, 16/Andy, 12 Gail, 8 step-siblings		
Cara's boyfriend	Cara David's ex-wife	David stepdad	Ellen mom	Greg dad	Alice stepmom	Steve Alice's ex-husband
	1 aunt 2 cousins	3 step-aunts 2 step-cousins 14 step-cousins	2 aunts 1 uncle 14 cousins	1 aunt 1 cousin	1 step-aunt 3 step-cousins	
	C's mom Neil's grandma	D's parents step-grandparents	parents deceased	G's mom grandma	A's mom & stepdad step-grandparents	
					A's grandmother step-greatgrandma	

KEY: −C− COHABITING   =M= MARRIED   −/D/− DIVORCED

Looking at the Macnamara/Rasmussen clan, it's easy to see how children can feel entwined by the various branches of a family forest. In addition to dealing with new adults, they can be thrown together with brothers or sisters who have different backgrounds or a new baby they never asked for. It can be particularly difficult if a step-sibling upsets a child's position in the family— an only child suddenly becomes one of two (or more) kids, an older or youngest sibling moves to the middle. And when all the kids are very close in age, especially if they're the same sex, it tends to encourage unfair and dangerous comparisons, not to mention fighting between the adults. "Inside" children who live there more of the time might have needs that conflict with "outside" children who come less often and (sadly) feel more like "visitors." That's why it's so worthwhile, regardless of how much time kids actually spend in your home, to make every effort to give them space of their own and, more important, a sense of belonging. New kinds of everyday rituals—at meals, bedtime, and house-switching times—can help your kids feel more comfortable.

Sometimes friction between siblings and step- or half-siblings or between siblings and a particular stepparent motivates co-parents to modify living arrangements. Because Sandy Macnamara didn't get along as well with her stepfather (David), co-parents Ellen and Greg decided that it would be best for her to reside mostly with her father (Greg) and stepmother (Alice). Kerry, who often locked horns with her stepmother, would live with her mother (Ellen) and her stepfather; the girls would be together every weekend. Meanwhile, Cara, David's ex, was having a personal crisis, so David offered to have Neil spend more time with them, going to his mom's only on alternate weekends, instead of every other week.

It took six months to work out the kinks, says Ellen, who in a follow-up note included a diagram to explain the complex new arrangement (see below). "Whenever Sandy was here for the weekend, and I'd have to drive her back to Greg's house, that was pretty awful, because we'd both be crying." Ellen is now quite pleased with the arrangement and, it seems, so are all the kids. She explains, "Sandy and I were joined at the hip, and this is making her more independent. Also, my relationship with Kerry is delightfully strengthened, and it's like Neil is a different child—no arguing, no back talk! One day, he admitted, 'I'm happier living in one house; I feel better.' "

Ellen's Diagram of the Rasmussen Household's Shedule

Weekend 1	Weekend 2	Weekend 3	Weekend 4
Sandy Kerry Neil	Kerry Neil	no kids	only Kerry

Co-parents can't be mind readers—they need to keep checking in with their kids and with each other. Nor do they have a crystal ball that will tell them the outcome of every change they make, the by-products of every decision. Often, the best you can do is look at the personalities involved and at the logistics of the situation, and be honest about everyone's limits.

Conventional wisdom among stepfamily experts suggests that a good rule of thumb (which works in many but not all cases) is to allow a year of adjustment time per year of the child's life—for instance, if a child is five at the time of the remarriage, it will take five years for everyone to adjust to new family members and the new regime.

One reason problems so often arise in second marriages and stepfamilies is that most parents don't adequately prepare themselves for the experience. A 1989 study, conducted by psychologists Lawrence Ganon and Marilyn Coleman, examined how remarried adults—100 men and 105 women—had readied themselves for the experience. The most common method of preparation (59 percent) was *living together* which, the researchers conclude, rarely helps deal with stepparent/child relationships, parent/child relationships, or the adjustment of the family as a whole once the remarriage takes place. They speculate that for many couples entering into new relationships, there is "innocence at what to expect."

Factor a co-parenting relationship into this equation, and the need for preparation and constant communication among the adults is even more crucial. Moreover, remarriage can be even more stressful for some children than their parents' divorce because it symbolizes both the finality of the original loss, more change, and, in many kids' minds, even more loss.

So if you're contemplating remarriage or even co-habitation with a new significant other, though no obvious problems exist, don't leave your fate to chance. The Ganon/Coleman study suggests that it's important to talk to parents who have been through it; join a support group; consider a few sessions with a good stepfamily counselor. Society still accords precious little support to stepfamilies, so the burden of making your second marriage work while maintaining a solid parenting relationship that includes your ex-spouse falls squarely on *your* shoulders. So read as much as you can on the subject. One chapter of a book, let alone a portion of a chapter, could not do justice to this complex subject.

Keeping Your Head above Water: Guiding Principles

"How can you possibly write a chapter on this?" asks an editor of a major magazine, herself a divorced and remarried mother. "Besides remarriage, there are a zillion different things that can happen after divorce, depending on the family."

In one respect, she's correct. Even if a parent never remarries, every family apart is shaken by change at some point after the dust settles. And each family's composition is different; so when a circumstance or event, like remarriage or the birth of a new sibling, *looks* the same, no two families experience it the same way. The unique personalities of their members, as well as other mitigating factors in the lives of the children and adults, determine how they react to and cope with change.

Allowing for these individual differences, however, certain common themes ran through the stories of those who were able to ride the waves without, as surfers would say, "wiping out"! The following guiding principles can help you and your kids keep your heads above water and go with the flow during periods of stress:

Respect the power of change. Asked to respond to the statement, "I respect the power of change in our family life, and I try to anticipate the effect of big changes (remarriage), or transitions (going to a new school)," 71 percent of the parents in my sample answered "always" or "almost always." A few actually made annual lists of impending change; most at least took the time to contemplate the effects and to try to prepare their children for them. "The ones who make it learn to respect yellow lights instead of waiting for red ones," agrees family therapist Ron Taffel. "They begin to gear up for them and start going over necessary discussions before the event actually happens or circumstances change."

Keep the principles of family development in mind—and remember that what happens to you also affects your children. For example, you may not think much about breaking up with someone you've been dating for a while—after all, it's not a *divorce;* you don't share children. But to a child, especially a very young child, six months or a year can feel like a long time. Even older children can be quite confused when a parent's special someone drops out of his or her life.

Forest Hoving, eleven, was very upset when his father broke up with a woman he had been dating for five years. "Forest had gone out to her house every weekend. She had kids his age, and he made friends there. When his father and she split up, it affected Forest greatly," claims his mother, Yvette. "Now he's afraid that whenever David, my new husband, and I have an argument, we might break up too."

Also expect that as your children develop, their perspective will change. Be prepared for the fact that it can be unnerving when kids start to ask for more details about why you divorced, which many do when they are old enough to start to process it differently (review "Telling the Children," pages 118–122, and "Happily—or Sadly Ever After," pages 128–129). And, as discussed in chapter 7, when kids are young at the time of the divorce, they also can have a delayed emotional reaction—or a different reaction—to their circumstances. They'll understand more and see their parents, the divorce, the new people in their life differently than they once did, which sometimes takes parents by surprise. Elena Costos notes that when her daughter, Lanie, hit puberty, the little girl who was once "utterly enamored" of her stepmother, did an about-face: "In the last three or four years, she complains about her temper and says Bonnie's hypocritical." Undoubtedly, Lanie's agenda has changed and perhaps Bonnie's has, too.

Admit that a problem exists.   "I think I was so hell-bent on making sure that all of the changes in Zoey's life—her dad's remarriage, his new child, and then my remarriage—would have a minimal effect, that I didn't see clearly what was happening," admits Tina Porter. She realizes that she was blocking the effect her remarriage would have on her daughter until Zoey, then ten, was caught stealing—her cry for help. Sadly, Tina's behavior is all too common; parents *want* their kids to be okay, so they unconsciously deny the impact of change until major problems emerge that they can't ignore. Psychologist Neil Kalter pinpoints several reasons for parents' denial: their own distress over the divorce, preoccupation with the ex-spouse, guilt over causing the child pain. "It takes courage and perseverance for parents to remove these blinders and look squarely at their children."

Listen to your kids; *they* usually have no trouble identifying problems that you might prefer to disavow. "My parents don't realize what they do by arguing, and then they try to deny that it affects us," observes a wise-beyond-her-twelve-years Kelly Dresdin. "It's really bad, because me and my sister get stuck in the middle of it."

Her sixteen-year-old sister, Heather, adds, "If I could wave a magic wand, I'd want them to both see how much it hurts us when they talk about each other. I'd want my mom to see that my dad is really not such a bad guy. And I'd want my stepmother not to hate my mom so much."

Figure out the real source of distress or upheaval. Look at covert messages that may be disguised by overt events, which is sometimes difficult because of the myriad of possibilities in each of those "change" columns—the parents' changes, the kids', and the family's. For example, a child's fears may camouflage feelings of sadness and loss. Amy Fried's ten-year-old son became almost phobic—fearing the dark, hearing voices in their new house. For Amy, moving out of the rented home and buying a house that was truly hers marked a new beginning, a chance, as she put it, "to create a new home for her family." Her fourteen-year-old daughter easily accepted the change, which occurred two years after the parents' separation. But to her son, Amy now realizes, "it was the final nail in the coffin of his parents' marriage."

When children act out or suddenly seem different—angry, grouchy, timid, aggressive, resentful—it may be that circumstances finally have forced them to realize "It's *really* over!" However, parents also have to be careful not to attribute *all* behavior problems or difficulties in school to family change. Tina Porter realizes that divorce issues obscured Zoey's learning disability. "She was always getting into trouble, and every time something happened, even teachers and counselors would say, 'That's because you got divorced,' 'That's because her father remarried,' or 'That's because she's jealous of the new baby.' I now see that's why her LD wasn't diagnosed until she was older."

Sometimes a family member's distress may be induced by something that, in your mind, is unfounded, even silly. However *you* see the issue, remember that the other person's perception needs to be heard, respected, and attended to. For example, a child is jealous of your new job. Is it because he's afraid there's not enough time (which he feels as love) to go around? Your ex-spouse is angry that you're moving. Is he afraid that means you no longer want to co-parent?

Increase structure and consistency. Structure is essential during periods of stress. If the source of the problem is the adults, due to their unresolved conflict or a new circumstance in either of their lives that affects the co-parenting relationship, be more "businesslike" in your interactions (review chapter 7). Stick to schedules, pay attention to time and agreements, keep up distance, but be courteous. If the difficulty involves the children, make sure you're being a "balanced" parent (chapter 9), setting appropriate limits and, at the same time, assuring children of your love. In short, you have to show kids you're at the helm, when they feel most out of control.

Monitor communication even more carefully. As more and more seeds are planted in the family forest, the potential for miscommunication increases. It can be like a game of "Telephone"—he tells her and she tells him and then he tells her until the message is unrecognizable! Review the principles of clear communication in chapter 8. Even if you've been "good" up to now, you may be thrown the first time you see your ex with someone new or when you hear that a wedding is in the offing. So watch what you say.

Also be aware that when two people are under stress, they often "triangulate," or draw a third person into their dispute: co-parents vying for their child's love; a child and a new stepmother competing for a parent's attention; or a co-parent and a new partner staking out their claims to the other parent. Any type of "triangle" results in a no-win situation that shifts the focus from the real underlying emotional issues into a dangerous two-against-one alliance. Someone is always forced to take sides, and someone always feels left out.

Acknowledging the existence of a triangle (and your possible role in it) often helps to break the pattern. For example, if the triangle is composed of two co-parents and a child, *your* behavior may help explain why the child needs to wedge herself in the middle. Are you and your co-parent arguing a lot, sending messages through the child? Either can unwittingly draw her into a triangle. You can also use a displacement technique (see page 112) to help children understand what's happening. Say the problem is with you, your child, and a new stepparent. Talk directly to your partner, but, with the child, read books about stepfamilies, role-play, or make up a story about how a little boy who wants to keep his dad all to himself complains or even tells lies about his new stepmother. Don't label the child a "troublemaker." If you look carefully, you will probably find a kid who is begging for attention and doesn't know how to ask for time alone or more direct communication with his parent.

Don't be hasty. Give children and yourself time and space to adjust—whenever possible, *before* actual changes take place. If you foresee a professional promotion meaning longer hours and different child-care arrangements, consider the ramifications, talk about them. If you're child is going to a new school in the fall, take the walk or ride to and from home with her over the summer. If you're planning to cohabit or get married, give kids time to get acclimated to the idea. And, for whatever reason, if you decide that it's necessary to revise your parenting plan, proceed with caution and take everyone's different perspective into account. Will the new plan require children to make more transitions or to spend more time in a less-familiar place—for instance, a new home and neighborhood? Take care in presenting this kind of information to kids; understand its impact.

By the way, if you're still in the postdivorce doldrums and you feel that you'll never even date again, let alone marry, *don't* make any bold promises to your kids. You don't know what the future holds, and kids believe—and remember—when parents say things like "I'll never get married again." (Several told me their parents "lied" to them about remarrying.)

Remember that you can't control anyone's else's actions or reactions. Although this point has been made in other chapters of this book, it bears repeating here. Especially if you're "a fixer" by nature, this tendency will undoubtedly reemerge when the family is under stress. I frequently hear parents say, "If only my ex would . . ." or "If my ex were a different kind of father/mother . . ." or "If she/he had married a different kind of person . . ."

Give it up! You can't moderate other people's behavior any more than you can stop the flow. Change—and reaction to change—are normal. Know the limits of your own power. You don't control economic realities that force a move; you can't stop your ex from behaving a certain way, marrying someone you don't like, or having another child; and you can't choose how your kids will react to any of it. Often, all a parent can do—the best a parent can do—is let the child or adult go through the process, experience the feeling . . . and get out of the line of fire!

Remember, too, that sometimes other people's responses to a particular circumstance or turn of events may not be as *bad* as you had imagined. Michelle Varnet, who recently became involved with another man—her first serious relationship since her divorce ten years ago—expected that Etienne would be quite upset. "I was sure his reaction would be terrible, but it hasn't been." Michelle realizes that, at fourteen, Etienne was actually "relieved" by the presence of another man.

Christopher Derby was a bit anxious when he "came out" to his ex-wife, Myrna, and their three children two years after the divorce. He, too, was pleasantly surprised. "The kids took it well. They love and respect Hank; he's become kind of a third parent. Myrna's reaction was mainly relief, because she was able to say and feel that the marriage's ending wasn't her fault," says Chris. "Now we hold most of the family celebrations at our house—even Myrna's birthday—because Hank's such a great cook!"

Broaden your viewpoint.   Seeing problems through eyes other than your own will give you a better grasp on any situation. So before you condemn your co-parent's new partner for being "unreasonable," consider that she or he walked into *your* family apart, with *your* kids, perhaps even into *your* house. Helen Rogand recalls an incident with Laura, her ex-husband's wife, that exemplifies this principle. "She called to tell me my oldest son had gone into their bedroom and went through their stuff. Then she blurted out, 'He gets it from *you!*' " What made the difference—and averted an all-out war—was Helen's response. Instead of getting angry at Laura for being so accusatory, Helen put herself in her place and realized how "invaded" the woman must have felt. "Unfortunately, the kids go there and treat it like it's here where we're much looser about things like that. I immediately apologized. I also told my son that what he did was wrong. She appreciated that."

Likewise, you're in a committed relationship and your co-parent is single, be sympathetic to how that must feel. "During the first year of our separation, my ex frequently included his girlfriend in outings with our daughter and," admits Marsha Resido, "this threatened and alarmed me, especially when it was obvious that the girlfriend was trying to woo our daughter, so to speak." Marsha suggests, "People should read sensitivity manuals during such times!"

Rekindle your support network.   Once you're "over" the initial trauma of your divorce, a natural inclination may be to pull inward, go about your own business, and live a fairly isolated life. Overcome the feeling that divorced parents often have that others have "heard enough." Asking for help when you need it is a sign of psychological strength, not weakness. Make phone calls to trusted friends or family members, good listeners who also might offer an extra pair of hands or time off—a rare commodity in the life of any parent. Your kids will also benefit from having relatives and adult friends around; sometimes, they open up more easily to someone who's not in the thick of the family drama. Grandparents—as long as they don't take sides—are especially wonderful when it comes to doling out unconditional love (see "We Are Family," pages 292–296).

Others struggling with similar problems are also a vital resource when you feel overtaxed. For one thing, they can remind you that you're not the only one who has ever had to relocate or break the news to kids that their stepmother is pregnant! A peer support group (see Resources, p. 000) can help you to realize that it's possible to live through the situation.

If you have a good co-parenting relationship, list your ex as part of your support system. Co-parents endow each other with the gift of private time, because there are predictable days and nights when you know that the kids will be safe and sound in the other parent's care. And for many parents, the rewards go further. "My ex-wife is one of my best friends," says a long-divorced father. I can certainly relate to that kind of connection. After all, when I am concerned about the kids, Mark is the logical person to talk with. I've also gone to him over the years when I have questions about my mortgage or other financial issues, areas in which he's quite knowledgeable. And since I relocated to Massachusetts a few years ago, on several occasions he even provided weekend lodging on my trips into Manhattan.

Focus on what you've done right and do more of it! Too often, we highlight the mistakes and ignore our successes. Ease up; applaud yourself (and your co-parent) for your achievements, heroic or mundane. Presumably, you've already had experience with your co-parent trying to resolve conflicts or getting kids to talk about what's bothering them. Review the past, and look at how far you've already come.

Family Meetings: Talking, Planning—and Remembering to Have Fun!

Naturally, what works in one family won't necessarily work well in another. One of the best ways to find out what's good for your brood and to include a new partner in the family is through regular meetings—a forum in which everyone gets a chance to come up with and vote on family procedures and practices. "If you're going to unite Russia and the U.S. you have to talk about how you're going to coexist," says parent educator Betty Lou Bettner, whose excellent primer on family meetings, *Raising Kids Who Can,* written with colleague Amy Lew, is an invaluable one-stop resource.

Family meetings can be used to discuss the news of the week, talk about the good things that happened, the nice things people did for one another and, most important, to confront challenges. They give the kids a chance to get in on family negotiation and help determine how roles are defined.

Whenever you develop procedures, assign chores, or make family plans, consider your co-parent. For really important issues, you might want to invite him or her to participate in family meetings. Establish a clear understanding between the two houses that daily schedules may have to be flexible at times and that it's important to have a consensus about important matters like family vacations, rather than making unilateral pronouncements ("I'm taking the kids to my new wife's condo in Florida this Christmas").

By giving everyone a voice, family meetings can also help head off arguments. A child who feels that a parent isn't spending enough separate time with her or that chores are divided unfairly can bring up these issues in a safe, welcoming environment. And by airing such problems, creative, workable solutions can be devised.

I remember my kids complaining about Mark's second wife leaving them notes that enumerated their chores for that week—a common remarriage scenario. "We would have been less resentful about doing things if *Dad* had at least written the notes," insists Jennifer. I hasten to add that the tension also would have been eased if the kids had felt included in the process and had some input. (Likewise, if Mark's wife hadn't felt so impotent in the parenting arena, she probably would not have been so overbearing with the kids.)

Children are less apt to feel that they have no control over their own lives—a frequent complaint of kids I interviewed—when they have a role in the decision-making process. Through family meetings, they can learn to express grievances without blaming others and to problem-solve. The parents are still in charge and still setting limits, but children who take part in creating house rules and establishing procedures that help the family function more smoothly will cooperate with greater understanding, compassion, and enthusiasm. And they are often less resistant to change as well.

Done right, family meetings can be democracy in action. Attendance should be strictly voluntary, but those who don't participate should be bound by whatever consensus is reached by the rest of the family. If you've never held a family meeting, to introduce the idea, Linda Seaver, a child and family therapist in Bedford, New York, suggests the same line that her mother used over thirty years ago in her stepfamily to launch their family meetings: "We're all going to sit around the dining table and review what's working and not working." Seaver explains, "It's better than saying 'good' and 'bad' or 'right' and 'wrong,' which are judgmental terms."

Expect some balking from teens who will probably think the whole idea is "dumb." Give them time; suggest that they "eavesdrop" on the first few meetings. One mother, whose teenage hold-out sat on the stairs outside the living room where the meeting was held, comments, "He didn't trust at first that he'd be listened to, but when he realized that we all had a chance to have our ideas heard, he became one of the biggest contributors."

Family meetings can also be used to brainstorm vacation ideas and other "fun" activities that enable you to play together as a family—backyard barbecues and picnics, building snowmen, visiting a museum, beach, or park. Time and energy can be spread incredibly thin in today's fast-paced world, and too often, busy families forget that the best antidote for stress is "down" time.

It's imperative to make time for your relationships, to be with kids and, if there's a new partner in your life, to nurture your couple relationship, too. Avoid the trap of having to choose between adult time and time for the kids; set aside both, even if it's just a ten- or fifteen-minute break.

Can You Ride the Waves of Change?

A book or a counselor can only alert you to typical problems, propose certain suggestions that have worked for other families, and help you gauge your progress. *You* are the expert when it comes to your family and your child. And in the end, *you* have to take the action—*you* have to ride the waves.

Most parents admit that they had no idea how hard it would be to get back into the social swing after divorce, shepherd children back and forth between two homes, deal with a co-parent on a regular basis, *and* manage all the normal ups and downs of family life. You don't find out until you're there!

The greatest stumbling block is high (read "unrealistic") expectations. You want your children to love the new day-care center. You want your former spouse to be happy because you're happy. You want your new partner to adore being a stepparent. Give them time and hope for the best, but be practical; there's no such thing as a magic "fix."

Gregory Macnamara (see illustration, page 262) admits that the entire process of divorce and especially remarriage has been "very stressful." He observes, "Alice kept thinking a lot of this would change. In the beginning, she would say, 'The relationship with the kids will be better when we get engaged.' Then it became, '. . . when we get married' and then, '. . . when we have a child of our own.' " As Greg wisely points out, nothing magically "cures" a complex situation; often, it only becomes more complicated!

Don't expect magic, miracles, or "instant" anything! Gary Shannon says, "Gloria and I cooperate tremendously, but it's not always conflict free. We have had to work through several 'bumps in the road.' " In the four-year period following their divorce, Gary moved, Gloria remarried a man with three kids, and Gary remarried. How could there *not* be a few "bumps" in their road?

Life after divorce is anything but carefree, but it can present wonderful opportunities, richly rewarding experiences, and improved relationships. Parents who successfully ride out the changes often talk about how much they've "grown" from their postdivorce trials. "At first, you tend to see your life as *over*. Everything you envisioned for yourself and the family seems out of the question," observes Steve Posner, who says he "finally stopped looking backwards" when he committed to a new relationship. Steve feels that as he matured from the experience of divorce, remarriage, and a new baby, he also became a better father to Brian. "There have been tensions. Brian would come and I'd have less time for my wife. But we'd talk about it, and we've been able to work it out."

The best role model for a child is a parent who tolerates change. Don't dismiss kids' gripes or, worse, offer soothing platitudes ("In time you'll get used to this"). Instead, let them know that adults need time to adjust, too. And validate for them that it's also hard for you at times—to accept differences, to adjust to new regimens, to put yourself in another person's place, to have to react to someone else's needs and timetable, to solve problems. This will give them the insight to understand that change is a process and the permission to go through it in their own way and at their own speed.

If you regard each postdivorce "wave" as a challenge, it may not prevent you from going under every now and then, but it will give you a different sense of purpose. Adults and children of divorce who fare best in the aftermath of the experience develop a sense of responsibility and independence which, in part, is borne of their burden. It takes sacrifice on the adults' part, and it *is* difficult, but there are gains, too. You and your kids *can* profit from the ordeals of postdivorce life. If you don't dread new or difficult situations, they won't. As you become better able to tap inner and outer resources and to learn to gather support when you need it, so will they. And as you become more adept at problem solving and going with the flow, they will, too.

— *11* —

'TIL DEATH DO YOU PART

Key #10: Know That Co-Parenting Is Forever

Rewriting the Rules

When I initially entertained the idea of writing about co-parenting, I believed that Mark and I were in the homestretch. Our children were becoming more independent: one was in college; the other was also living away from home, at boarding school. We had fewer and fewer reasons to communicate. Our ties would probably weaken as the kids got older. It was a perfect time to write about what I had learned, because we were living our own final chapter. Or so I thought.

Six years later, I realize how wrong I was. Mark and I still talk to each other fairly regularly. Besides sharing impressions of the kids' progress, we coordinate birthday gifts (only once did we buy Jeremy the same CD), discuss the holidays (assuming the kids are even around), review their vacation plans (which, nowadays, seem to exclude both of us!). By the time this book is published, we will have been co-parents for as long as we were spouses. And much to my surprise, we have gotten closer in some respects— not married close, *co-parent close!*

We have certainly gotten better at making plans and engineering joint events—a sentiment echoed in many co-parenting stories. According to my survey, 77 percent of co-parents can "always" or "almost always" attend a joint celebration; half can plan one together. What these respondents have learned and accepted is that through their kids, they are still, and always will be, *related.* Although a minority bristle at the statement "I believe that as long as we're both still alive, my ex and I will always be kin—connected through our children," 67 percent responded "always" and 15 percent "almost always."

Co-parenting *is* forever. If you're just beginning the process, that may feel like a dreadful notion, but the sooner that you accept this vital key to successful co-parenting, the happier your children will be. Celebrations, school and camp events, holidays, vacations, and interactions with your respective extended families will be recurring tests of your maturity and consideration for your kids' feelings. Rise to the occasion, and everyone around you will follow your lead.

Attending her ex-mother-in-law's funeral, Vicki Lansky, whose children are now in their early twenties, told her daughter she was proud to be a role model for future generations: "You have a lot of cousins here," she observed, looking around the room at her ex-husband's extended family, "and some day some of them might get divorced. I hope that my being here shows them that a different kind of postdivorce relationship is possible."

"Easier said than done," you say. *"You don't know my ex's family. And you can't imagine how difficult my ex's new spouse is."* Perhaps you've even had to wrestle with questions like these:

- Who sits at the head of the table at a joint celebration when both parents have remarried?
- Is one co-parent obliged to save seats for the other at a school play, graduation, or similar event?
- Should you allow your child to participate in the other parent's wedding ceremony?
- If you're paying for a child's party, do you have to include your ex in the planning?
- Is it wrong to have a live-in lover act as a co-host at your child's birthday party?
- Whom do you invite to your daughter's Sweet Sixteen Party— your new in-laws, who hardly know her, or your ex-in-laws?
- Should your new spouse be included in the family portrait?
- Who should participate in a candle-lighting ceremony at a Bar Mitzvah or similar rituals on other occasions?
- How do you handle your aging parents—your kids' grandpar-

ents—who tell you they're going to be lonely over the holidays, because you're "letting" the kids go to your co-parent's house?

- Who walks the bride down the aisle at your child's wedding? Who pays for the reception?
- If a parent divorces a second time, should the ex—your children's stepparent—still be invited to family celebrations?
- Is it okay to take your own kids on a vacation—without your new spouse and stepkids?

Such dilemmas routinely come up in families apart—but there are no routine answers. There is no such thing as "proper," so don't bother to consult Emily Post or Miss Manners! This chapter, which offers broad guidelines and examples of how some parents have handled these and other difficult situations, can help. Another good resource is *Whose Kid Is This Anyway and Over 400 Other Questions for Divorcing, Dating, and Remarried Families* (see "Resources," page 321). Still, no one can anticipate every situation that will come up. You have to determine what's "right" for *your* family. The bottom line is that your children shouldn't feel torn or deprived.

No matter what the occasion, find out how your children feel well in advance of any event. Although they might not say what you want to hear or act thrilled about a particular occasion—for instance, going to a new partner's parents' house for Christmas dinner—give them time to adjust; try to listen to their complaints, fears, and suggestions. You don't have to arrange everything according to their demands, but don't force children to participate in ways that make them uneasy, just because you want the "look" of family togetherness.

When a milestone event or the holidays are on the horizon, remember that cooperation, advance planning, and thinking out the ramifications of a guest list can help avoid celebration anxieties. If you're still quite angry at your co-parent, it's probably wise to minimize the joint celebrations. You're likely to pull at your child, who will be painfully aware of the competition. So don't push your own limits too far. As Sandy McGee wisely observes, "The animosity felt by us toward each other is not so easily hidden in proper behavior and decorum. Julia is amazingly intuitive, and she knows." Sandy has a point. Because she and her ex are still on shaky ground with each other, she can't "fake it" around her six-year-old; chances are, neither can you.

However, being flexible, open-minded, and creative might also help you figure out suitable compromises. Instead of planning an intimate birthday dinner where you're all trapped at one table and forced to make eye contact, plan a buffet and invite lots of people on *both* sides of the family. If circumstances force all of you to be at a dinner together, sit at a round table so that there isn't any "head." If there are new partners in the picture, in place of one family portrait, have several versions taken.

Recognize that these situations can be difficult for your co-parent, too, and that being generous—financially *and* emotionally—usually feels better in the long run. For instance, instead of not inviting him or her because you think it conflicts with your plans, might you relocate to neutral ground instead of having the party at home? Or if you're paying for a catered celebration and your ex-wife feels left out of the planning, would it kill you to assign a portion of the arrangements to her, subject to your approval—like the flowers? If your co-parent lives farther away than you do—or is chronically late—isn't the more hospitable choice to save seats for him?

Some parents worry that *too much* togetherness at school events, birthdays, and on the holidays will encourage children's reconciliation fantasies. Certainly, that's possible, but most experts think the benefits of cooperation far outweigh the damage of closeness. As family therapist Janine Roberts sees it, "Kids have fantasies of their parents getting back together even when the parents are unfriendly!"

The sad truth is that an otherwise-joyous event can become a nightmare for a child of divorce when parents can't cooperate. I was tremendously disheartened at Jennifer's graduation to see kids whose parents sat on opposite sides of the auditorium. Those poor kids had to greet two separate sets of families after the ceremonies—unlike Jennifer who was able to run into the waiting arms of both her proud parents, grandparents (Mark's parents), and brother. Throughout the weekend, other graduates whose parents were divorced had to juggle their own schedule of parties and brunches with their parents' different and conflicting schedules. After meeting Jennifer's entourage, one girl admitted to me, "This weekend has been a drag. I'm so afraid my parents will start fighting if they get too close." Some *celebration*!

One important note: Milestone events aren't necessarily happy occasions. Grandparents die, parents die, and—saddest of all—children die. Funeral directors these days often have an added burden when they guide families through these kinds of transitions: dealing with the complexity of divorced and married families. And who is considered part of *the family*? Where will everyone sit? What if the exes are uncomfortable being in the same room? "The same thing happens there as at weddings," explains Emily Visher. "People are in a very heightened emotional state. They're so raw that they can hurt each other very easily." Her advice is to "respect that there are other people hurting, too."

In all situations if parents don't take responsibility for writing their own rules of etiquette, these difficult moments often fall smack in children's laps. Kids—no matter how old they are—deserve to have their parents shoulder their own burden, so do whatever you can to make life easier for them, especially during such family times.

Children's Milestones: Caring Enough to *Do* the Very Best

For years, Hallmark has targeted greeting cards to "people who care enough to send the very best." When it comes to any rite of passage or celebration that marks a significant transition in a child's life, co-parents have to care enough about their kids to *do* the very best. That doesn't necessarily mean including both parents at all times. In fact, some co-parents prefer to celebrate birthdays separately. Nancy Blake and Todd Dresdin, who disagree on most things, "play it by ear," says

Nancy—they go according to whose weekend the birthday falls on. Orin Delaney's birthday is in the summer, and he has always been at camp—away from both parents, which, his mother, Sally Washington, remarks, has made it "easier," because neither parent has ever had to plan or host Orin's birthday parties.

Says Cara Rasmussen, "All of us—David's wife, Neil's new sisters, my boyfriend, his son, and I—always try to attend ball games and cub scout events. We'll sit together and chat. But we don't typically attend milestone functions together. We plan birthdays 'together' in the sense that we don't want our separate events to overlap, duplicate, or conflict."

However, many parents who fall somewhere between "civil" and "very friendly" on the parenting continuum celebrate kids' birthdays together. Typically, they alternate houses from one year to the next, or they hold the party in whichever home is more suitable or easier for everyone to get to. "I've often used Bob's home for Katie's birthday parties," says Cora Portinos. Several women comment that having joint events is no problem—as long as *they* do more of the planning! Some are fine with this; others find it an annual source of irritation.

Whether you celebrate together or plan separate events, your child's age should be a primary consideration. Plan small parties for younger children—one or two guests per year of the child's age make the hubbub more manageable. Also weigh your child's party personality, based on past experience. Some kids shine at family celebrations; others dread them. Some kids love it when the whole clan gets together, while others prefer more intimate gatherings.

With school-age kids, many co-parents opt for joint parties on neutral ground. Mark and I hosted countless parties in the school gym; other parents take kids to an inexpensive restaurant or amusement center. Work out the details with your co-parent beforehand—who's going to order the cake, bring paper plates and other supplies, pick up the ice cream. Decide what games you'll play and who will be the facilitator. You don't want to find yourselves stepping on each other's toes or glaring at each other for doing things "wrong." Sometimes older kids *look for* signs of friction between their divorced parents; and, believe it or not, their friends notice, too.

Don't be surprised if your preteen or teen doesn't want to be with *either* of you on her birthday. To some kids, separate dinners feel more sophisticated—more special. But it depends on how long you've been divorced, what kind of relationship each of you has with him, and how *he* wants to celebrate. Don't feel slighted if your eleven-year-old son wants Dad to take him to a hockey game with a group of his buddies or if your preteen daughter wants to have an all-girls pajama party at Mom's.

Some occasions simply can't be divided—confirmations, Bar and Bat Mitzvahs, graduations, weddings, christenings, camp visiting days, recitals, plays. Parents can, and sometimes do, have separate receptions, but, from the kids' standpoint, it's often nerve-wracking *and* anticlimactic when parents don't consolidate their celebrations.

When co-parents are thrown together in these time-limited situations, it behooves them to exercise maturity and restraint. Marsha Resido, who has been separated since 1979, when her daughter, Sharon, was nine, notes that over the years, she and her ex have jointly attended many events and often taken Sharon out to dinner together. "The only tough time I have experienced in this regard was her graduation, where my ex's girlfriend was included. But even there we carried it off—for our daughter's sake."

Because families apart often expand during the postdivorce years, everyone worries whether there will be enough space—and tickets—to accommodate all interested parties. At one commencement ceremony in Los Angeles, family members were asked to stand as each graduate was given a diploma. "Nine adults stood up!" laughs Jessica Rubell, who is now twenty-eight and one of the producers of a play about stepfamily life; it was her youngest brother's high-school graduation. "My father and his girlfriend, my mother and her current husband—our second stepfather—my stepbrother from her first marriage, who is now in his twenties, my ex-stepfather, and my mother's father and his wife—our stepgrandmother." Jessica admits that "a lot of family drama" preceded that day!

Holidays and Vacations: Whose Year Is This Anyway?

Speaking of drama, the holidays can offer suspense, tragedy, comedy, and even mystery (Who's Daddy going to show up with this year?). Holidays can be rough on any family because they bring up expectations of what a family is *supposed* to be like. Some co-parents build holiday schedules into their initial agreements and stick with them in the long run; more often, holidays and vacations are renegotiated as parents' lives incorporate new people and kids get older.

A few co-parents celebrate holidays together, but because of personal and family differences, most adopt some kind of revolving plan. They alternate on a yearly basis (you get Thanksgiving this year; I do next year), trade holidays (I get Christmas; you get Easter), or divide a holiday into portions (I get the night before; you get the day of). None are perfect or ideal solutions. Several kids complain that split celebrations always feel "interrupted" or "cut short" when they have to pack up and prepare to go elsewhere. And parents feel deprived. "I've yet to spend a Christmas Day with Kim," laments Barbara Palumbo, who chose Christmas Eve because "my family makes a big deal of it. We've alternated Thanksgiving, but we always had trouble remembering whose year it was."

Oddly enough, religious differences, which can wreak havoc in a marriage, often obviate this Solomon's choice in divorce because the holidays naturally divide themselves. Harold Silverman gets Channukah and other Jewish holidays, and he's quite happy to give up Christmas and Easter to his ex-wife, Martina Davis, because he doesn't celebrate them!

Splitting holidays also seems less problematic if the parents divorced when the children were fairly young; there isn't a long history of celebrating together, and the kids often feel the way Dawn Carver does: "This is my life; this is how we do the holidays; we've always done it this way." Duane Gorman adds, "Having two Christmases isn't so bad—I always get two presents!"

Although holiday celebrations can be painful reminders of the family that never was—every meal, every tradition, every ritual can evoke visions of the past—they can also present an opportunity for healing. Christine Meese, a single mother divorced for eight years, refused to acknowledge her ex-husband at first. Four years after the separation when she began dating, her then six-year-old son—a "normally accepting and easygoing" kid—began to act immature. "I realized how much he needed a father." Christine marks a recent Christmas Eve as a major turning point.

"This year, we celebrated at my home with my family (brother, wife, kids), my father, my ex-husband, his girlfriend, their daughter, my ex-father-in-law and his fiancée! I have grown up during these years. I realize there's no comfort in hatred. I even wrote to my ex's girlfriend thanking her for being so understanding."

Because holidays and vacation times are potentially so stressful, *don't make holiday plans at the last minute.* It may feel ridiculous to call the other parent and your ex-mother-in-law in August to tell them you want to take the kids to visit their other grandmother in Minnesota—even though it's your ex's "turn"—but at least that will give them time to react, to make plans of their own, or to offer a countersuggestion; and it will give both of you time to prepare the kids.

Once you have plans, stick to prearranged pickup and drop-off times, and avoid last-minute changes or cancellations except in the most dire circumstances. Never ask the children where they want to go, although with older children you certainly should take their wishes into consideration.

When co-parents respect their children's needs and lower their expectations of what a holiday "should" be like, children can have twice as much fun, twice as many adults who love them, and, of course, twice the number of presents. But their parents often have to work harder to make it all happen. Deborah Nachum acknowledges, "Between marriages, I definitely spent more time and energy including them in every bit of preparation and just being with the kids. The funny thing is, by making the holidays so kid centered, I created all sorts of new rituals, and it was better for all of us."

If you're just getting divorced, and this is your first holiday season, tune in to how your children feel—even though it will probably magnify your own feelings of loss. The changes are hard on kids: the absence of one parent, the anxiety of meeting new adults who are suddenly related, having to share the spotlight with other children. Let your child know it's okay to miss the other parent and to talk about it. Admit that you also feel a little strange this year—as if something's missing or different. Encourage your kids to call the other parent and to wish the other family well. Even though *you* don't want to be reminded that they exist, your child does.

Maintain the tried-and-true traditions, but also create new rituals for holidays and special occasions that symbolize your new family form. After her second divorce, Deborah Nachum stopped having a sit-down Christmas Eve dinner as the family had done in the past. Instead, she set out a buffet of finger foods for her children, then three, four, thirteen, and fourteen. "We called it 'Wrapping Night.' Everyone was all over the house eating and wrapping presents. The little ones could at least smoosh tissue paper together. They also memorized *'Twas the Night Before Christmas* that year, which began a new tradition."

Whatever you do, don't ignore the holidays because you feel it's easier. Family therapist Fredda Herz Brown, who counsels many young clients whose parents divorced when they were younger, says, "These grown children now say to their parents, 'When you two got divorced, it was as if we no longer had any holidays. We were never allowed to really celebrate.' They're angry about it," says Brown. "It was bad enough that the family changed, but to have no sense of the holidays made the situation worse."

Dealing with New Partners: "Not over My Dead Body!"

If one or both of you remarries, you have to take new partners into consideration when making plans for milestone events or holidays. These new players in the family drama *are* related to your kids, even when there's no official marriage to mark it. Admittedly, it may be tough. Just when you've gotten to the point of accepting that your co-parent has gotten seriously involved with another man or woman, you realize you also have to share special family moments with that person! Never issue blanket proclamations, like "I won't be in the same house with that woman/guy, no matter what!" What matters most is your child's relationship to him or her. You may have to count to ten and smile.

Kids need permission to get on with their lives, and their lives apart from you may include people you're less than enthusiastic about welcoming into the family. "My son had an awards ceremony at school, and he invited his father's girlfriend, because his father couldn't come," says Cathy Groveman, a newly divorced mother whose husband left her for another woman; their son is eleven. "He told me, 'She's like my stepmother,' " and I had to swallow hard. I don't have to love this woman, but I do have to understand how my son feels. I've tried not to channel the anger toward my husband at him."

Cathy is wise. A child can feel very close to your co-parent's new partner, whether you like the person or not. She can get very attached, especially when someone has been in her life for several years. For example, it may be your son's choice to have his father's girlfriend or wife light a candle at his Bar Mitzvah; respect his wishes.

You don't have to camouflage your feelings entirely. It's okay to say to a child, "She is your father's friend, not my friend. But it's okay for you to like her," as Helen Rogand did when she was still bitter about the end of her marriage and her oldest son asked why Helen didn't like Laura, then Mitch's girlfriend. "You could see the relief on his face when I answered—it gave him permission to feel at ease with his dad." Also bear in mind that what does or doesn't seem manageable this year may change two years down the road. Helen Rogand, whose parents and extended family live far away, now thinks of Mitch's wife as part of "our new extended family."

Certainly, remarriage almost always makes holidays and special occasions more strained at first, but time can help alleviate the tension. In the best of situations, everyone needs to give a little and be patient—and to remember that as the waves of change wash over the family, you'll sometimes need to fight to keep your heads above water (see chapter 10).

"The first two years after our divorce, we did Matthew's birthday together," notes Gary Shannon. "Then, in 1991, I was engaged, and Gloria was dating her future husband." The following year, Gloria and her new husband made a birthday party for Matthew in their home and invited her family and friends. "With all those people, my presence in 'her castle' was too much," Gary recalls. "I was greatly disappointed—it felt like we regressed." However, he explained to his ex-wife how upset he was about being excluded from Matthew's birthday party and asked if she would be willing to "compromise" by agreeing to have Matt's seventh birthday party at a Chuckie-Cheese restaurant—a neutral environment.

Gloria's knee-jerk reaction was to get angry at her ex-husband's suggestion. She thought it was another example of unnecessary extravagance, which had plagued her earlier in their co-parenting relationship. But she adds, "When I realized where he was coming from, I heard it differently. Also, Gary pointed out that two years ago we did a party at Papa Gino's and that worked out fine. It wasn't my first choice, but . . . so what?!"

Interestingly, even though these ex-spouses have different conceptions of what's "right" for their family apart, as co-parents, they are able to do what's best for their son. "I know he's into everyone being together, and sometimes my ideas are different than his," says Gloria, "but I certainly can understand why he'd want to be at his son's birthday party, and I know that it's important for my son to have him there."

When a party is held on one parent's "territory"—at her house, with her family—recognize that the other parent might feel outnumbered; inviting the new partner, a few members of his family, or a good buddy can help balance the scale and diffuse everyone's anxiety. But then, you might wonder, Where does one draw the line? Should new partners' children, parents, sisters and brothers, and their kids be included too?

There are no hard-and-fast rules. Some believe that whoever hosts and pays for a gathering determines who's invited. Cathy Grovemen comments, "I have a friend who paid for her son's Bar Mitzvah, just so she could control the guest list. I'll tell you one thing, my ex had better give me half the money if he wants *her* to be invited!" But it's rarely that simple! What happens, for example, if a function is held in the other parent's home and you share the cost?

It's best to weigh closeness, cost, and courtesy. Try to gauge how your children feel about the "players" who will be involved—parents, stepparents, step-siblings, grandparents, step-grandparents. If the climate is not tense between the two (or more!) families, and it's simply a matter of adding a few extra bodies to an at-home gathering, it may be a good idea to be inclusive. With catered affairs, the expense might be daunting, but if members of your co-parent's family are very close to your kids, you may want to extend the courtesy of inviting them anyway. The emotional "cost" of *not* inviting them might outweigh the dollars-and-cents factor.

Decisions often have nothing to do with money; sometimes you just have to be "generous" in spirit. When it comes to once-in-a-lifetime occasions, always try to consider the long-run implications of your actions. Years after the fact, Sherry Vann Farrell admits that if she had it to do over again, she would have allowed her daughters, then six and ten, to attend their father's wedding, which occurred shortly after the divorce. "Helen and Gordon wanted the girls to come, and I said no. I said I didn't think the girls were ready for it—they were feeling a lot of pain," recalls Sherry. "Looking back, I realize I didn't let them go because *I* was PO'd!"

Ironically, the girls participated in *her* wedding to Charles a year later. "It was a good way to start our marriage, for them and us, and that's what made me realize what I had done to Helen and Gordon. I remember thinking, 'I didn't give this to them.' "

(A bizarre but interesting postscript: Probably because in other ways she gave her daughters "permission" to love their new stepmother, Sherry's daughters, Karen and Nancy, who are now in their twenties, forged a tight bond with their stepmother. But now history seems to be repeating itself; Gordon is leaving Helen for another woman. "My daughters are very upset," reports Sherry, and they're determined to remain in contact with her, even though she's no longer in their father's life!")

Be sensitive to your new partner's needs, too. If you have formed a parenting coalition across households, you're less likely to have problems of any kind, including event planning. But if the relationship is fairly new, and the new partner is miffed by the amount of time you spend planning a joint occasion with your ex, find out what's behind the resistance and, if possible, try to include him or her in the planning. It might also be a good idea to have conferences with the other parent when you're at work, or at least out of earshot.

Suppose your co-parent is out of this picture, and you want to host a solo party—say for your daughter and a gaggle of her pubescent girlfriends. Your new partner may be less than enthusiastic. Some formerly childless stepparents simply aren't accustomed to any children underfoot, to say nothing of groups of them. Besides, their idea of a "special occasion" might be very different—less costly, fewer people—from yours. Don't be narrow-minded; when you understand all parties' needs, it's often just a matter of being creative about the planning. Perhaps your new partner would rather make other plans for the day, or you could have the party elsewhere.

Fathers, in particular, should take care to avoid the trap of putting a new wife in charge. It may undercut your co-parent; besides, when it comes to celebrations for *your* kids, you ought to be more than a bill payer. If your new wife doesn't have the time or want to get involved in elaborate arrangements, do them yourself, share the burden with your co-parent, ask a relative to pitch in, or, if your pocket allows, hire someone.

Holidays and special moments can be enhanced when there's more love to go around—but sometimes your children's and your new partner's needs will conflict. Also, the comings and goings of kids to different branches of their family forest during the holiday season can be hard on everyone. If both you and your new spouse have kids, especially if your brood isn't in residence as often, it's only natural to want to spend extra time with them, plan a weekend outing or a trip during one of their school breaks. Don't be defensive; simply help your partner see that this is your way of making special time for your kids—without feeling torn.

Given a chance to feel that they are part of a parenting coalition, which gives them a voice in the decision-making process, significant others—yours or your co-parent's—can become allies in planning and come up with pretty creative solutions in the bargain. When Helen Rogand was having trouble dealing with the logistics of her own wedding, Laura arranged to have Helen's parents, brother, and sister stay in the condominium development where she and Mitch lived, and they—stepmom and ex-husband—baby-sat for Helen's sister's kids while the adults went to the wedding! "It was a message that it was okay for me to get on with my life. That kind of support for one another has meant more than anything else."

We Are Family . . .

Divorce changes the rules and challenges the family status quo, and holidays and special occasions really drive this point home to the extended family. As mentioned in chapter 6, Fredda Herz Brown's father was shocked the first Passover after her divorce because she sat at the head of the table and conducted their seder, a role traditionally played by men in the family. "But after my divorce, I needed to make *myself* the head of the household."

Some members of your extended family will also think you're downright peculiar for wanting to celebrate a child's special occasion with the other parent or for inviting an ex to a wedding or your own birthday party—and yet many of us do it. Last year, for example, Mark invited me to his fiftieth birthday party; I'm sure I'll do the same next year if I have a party to celebrate mine. Gail Connors says she and her ex, Carl, "have had some very weird celebrations over the years." At one of Carl's birthday parties, she recalls, "all of his ex-wives were there, his current girlfriend, and one of his children from a prior marriage!"

The best way to deflect accusations and criticism is to be

secure in your new identity and to know why you're co-parenting in the first place. Instead of being defensive and reactive, just listen and appreciate the fact that your family may not understand your newfangled vision of "family." The point is, *you* know that you're doing what's best for your family. Although it seems odd to your relatives, let them know that you expect them to be considerate.

"I am friends with my ex-wife," notes Bill Paterson. "I invited her, her husband, and my ex-in-laws to my wedding. I felt comfortable; I think Loretta felt comfortable. However, it was unexpected to many friends and relatives who didn't feel the same way. But my close relatives—sisters, mother—accepted and supported the arrangement."

Loretta agrees. "It always works fine for us, since we attend hockey games, gymnastic meets, recitals, and conferences together—all four of us—and when our son graduates in a few years we will have a joint celebration. But this is usually more uncomfortable for friends and relations because they *expect* a strained relationship. When my husband and I attended my ex's wedding, along with my father and mother, my children were delighted to have us there. It was really important for them."

Fran Gordon also stood her ground, inviting her ex-husband into her home for their daughter's bridal shower, and a few months later, to the wedding, even though her family "wanted to kill him. They can't understand why I want to be friends." Fran is enraged by her family's response; she realizes that they're angry because her ex walked out on her ("They all loved him when we were married!"), but she says, *"They* can't understand? *I've* accepted it, and I'm working hard so that my children don't feel torn. My family can at least be socially polite for their sake."

There is no "right" or "wrong" way to deal with families. Tony Palumbo, recalling Kim's sixth-grade graduation, says, "It was close to the time of the divorce. Both families were there, and that didn't work out at all. There was a lot of tension." With Kim's high-school graduation on the horizon, Tony was having second thoughts about a repeat performance. "Barbara and I can handle it, but I don't know about the other people involved." As it turned out, rather than taking the chance and perhaps tainting the day for Kim by embarrassing or upsetting her, the Palumbos opted for separate parties.

Whether a celebration is held at one of your houses or on neutral turf, make it clear to both sides that you've called a truce. Let everyone know the ground rules: no competition, no subtle back stabbing, nothing that will make your children uneasy. In the long run, if family members realize that it's for the children, most will come around. "Our relationship definitely makes some people in my family uncomfortable," says Eleanor Gimble. "Stan has been coming to my house for Christmas dinner every year, and my parents have *had* to be with him. Once we got over a rough start, they've grown to accept it."

Things can get sticky when your family *prefers* your ex over your new partner, which sometimes happens when divorce *per se* is unacceptable in the family culture or when the family, for whatever reason, was very attached to your first spouse. "My parents continued their contact with Gabe long after the divorce," says Sally Washington, echoing a theme I heard in other parents' stories. "They were not pleased with the breakup—no one in our family ever got divorced—and they didn't like Terry very much." Then again, *you* could be the one your ex's family prefers over his or her new partner. "My ex-mother-in-law was on my side right from the beginning!" exclaims Janis Moley.

Do whatever you can to quell family dissention on either side. Naturally, it's easier to maintain ties with in-laws if you had a good relationship *before* the divorce, as Janis did. "Our relationship has changed a little since my ex remarried, but they were always good grandparents," she says. "I still call them 'Mom' and 'Dad,' I send Christmas cards, and I never say anything bad about them or their son."

Your parents and your co-parent's parents—your children's grandparents—as well as other extended family members can be invaluable resources to your family apart. Divorce researcher Judith Wallerstein has found that loving grandparents can "counteract children's sense that all relationships are unhappy and transient." She stresses that grandparents are as important to teenagers and young adults as to younger children. Family therapist Marla Isaacs agrees; she holds up the example of a woman who called her ex-in-laws almost immediately after she and her husband had decided to separate, letting them know, "I'm divorcing your son—I'm not divorcing you."

Frank R. Furstenberg, Jr., who with fellow sociologist Andrew J. Cherlin conducted the National Survey of Grandparents in 1984, found that in divorce situations, grandparents are usually pulled closer into the family sphere, although over time the "custodial grandparent"—the one whose child retains custody—was more likely to stay involved. One would hope that unlike that survey's sample, which consisted mostly of sole-custody families, when divorced parents co-parent, *both* sets of grandparents stay involved, even if it does take a little more effort.

Based on my survey, this seems to be true. These co-parents instinctively sense the importance of maintaining ties with grandparents. An impressive 81 percent "always" agreed to the statement "It's important for children to maintain contact with their grandparents—no matter what I think of them or of my ex," and 13 percent marked "almost always." Of the 6 percent who comprised the rest and answered "usually," a few explained that the one mitigating factor in not promoting grandparent/child relations was past physical or sexual abuse—situations that make the evening news but, according to other researchers' findings and the parents in my survey, are clearly in the minority.

Certainly, if grandparents are incompetent or abusive, there's good reason to keep kids away. But if you simply don't like your ex's family, don't assume that your child won't either. Sadly, some divorcing parents don't realize that when they cut their ex-in-laws out of the picture, it's their children who are deprived of a bountiful source of unconditional love and a priceless relationship that connects kids to their roots.

Looking back on their childhood, teens and young adults often regard lost grandparents as another symbol of how life flew out of their control when their parents' marriage ended. Some are angry and resentful. They may try to rekindle these forgotten connections, but they can never regain the years.

"I didn't see my dad's family from the time I was four until my early twenties," says a young woman whose parents remained enemies throughout most of her childhood. "By then, my grandparents had moved to Florida, and it was hard to have a relationship. I think they loved me, but they didn't know me. My mother was very selfish to keep me away from them."

For your child's sake, try to be open and flexible when it comes to the ex-family; make concessions for age or illness. If an aging grandparent is traveling a considerable distance, even though it's your "turn," give a little. You may regret later what you didn't heal when you had the chance.

Norman Chilton recalls his ex-wife, Paula, asking for the kids on an unscheduled Sunday, for a family New Year's party. "Her dad had just been released from the hospital. Since the kids had missed seeing their grandfather during the previous week, I agreed. So Paula picked them up and took them to the celebration." Later, that evening, when the kids were tucked into their beds at Norman's house, he got a call saying that Paula's father had suffered another stroke and died. "I was glad I agreed to let them go!"

Say It with Gifts

Birthdays, graduations, holidays, and other special occasions usually mean presents, which can shine a harsh light on co-parents' different values and financial circumstances—and can turn children into mercenaries. "We used to compete," admits one dad, "and the kids played us for who'd give them the best presents, the best vacations."

Regrettably, almost all kids these days are prone to the "gimmees." It's not easy for *any* parent to combat the effects of our kid-targeted consumer society. And if their parents aren't careful, children of divorce can be even more susceptible than their peers. Parents who can afford luxuries have to resist the temptation to "buy" a child's loyalty, love, or forgiveness; and those who have less to spend shouldn't feel guilty for not being able to buy as much.

Children understand more about economic circumstances than we credit them for. Generally, when one parent is less able to give an expensive gift, kids understand. More importantly, it does a child good to hear "no" every now and then. They don't have to own everything that's advertised on TV, everything that "all the other kids" have. Some parents split the cost of expensive presents, like computers and musical instruments. It's also a good policy to check with the other parent about what he or she plans to give the kids for their birthdays and for the holidays, thereby avoiding duplication *and* competition.

Gifts need not broadcast unintentional messages or promote competition. A gift can symbolize love and sacrifice; and gift giving can be an opportunity to pass on these values to your children. Around the holidays, many single parents give baked goods or handmade items as presents, instead of buying them, and use newspaper for wrapping, which is less expensive than store-bought paper *and* ecologically responsible. And they encourage their children to do the same. Further, by making children save money and work for things they want, you're building their self-esteem and teaching them a valuable lesson about delayed gratification.

Let members of your family know that you and your co-parent have decided neither to overindulge the kids nor to one-up each other with lavish gifts, and that you expect them to be equally considerate. They should be particularly sensitive about gift giving if your new partner has children. Your parents don't necessarily have to treat grandchildren and stepgrandchildren the same way—although many compassionate grandparents do—but they can at least try to understand stepchildren's feelings when they walk in the door laden with presents for their biological grandchildren.

If a grandparent wants to buy a child an exceptionally expensive present or one that requires parents' involvement (for example, a guitar often leads to music lessons), stress that both parents should be consulted. My ex-mother-in-law told Jeremy that her high-school graduation gift to him would be a generous contribution toward his first used car. I was extremely grateful that she talked to me first and readily agreed to my proviso: she warned him that unless his grades were worthy of the privilege, she wouldn't make good on her promise.

The I-Don't-Have-the-Kids Blues

One common reason co-parents fight over "having" the kids for special occasions and holidays has nothing to do with the children: *they* feel deprived. My first "no-kids" Thanksgiving, I remember going to my brother's house. As was the custom in our family in years past, in addition to his wife and their two kids, the guest list included his wife's entire extended family (mother, aunt, sister, sister's spouse, their kids), my father, my sister, brother-in-law, and their four kids, and my nieces' and nephews' respective spouses or dates. Over twenty people were there! I was restless and uncomfortable all afternoon; I kept flitting from one unsatisfying conversation to another. When I left, fortunately to meet friends, I vowed I'd never do it again. Seeing all those "complete" families was just too painful. Thereafter, for most of the next several "off" years, I made plans to be out of town, or to celebrate Thanksgiving with friends.

Other parents had similar epiphanies the first year they found themselves alone on a child's birthday, a holiday, or any meaningful day that evoked family memories. Knowing that her first Father's Day as a single mom might bring a torrent of memories, Vicki Lansky invited all the single and divorcing mothers she knew to a brunch that led to the founding of a support group (see pp. 62–64); fifteen years later, they still celebrate together! Misery loves company—and it's certainly better than feeling lonely, cheated, and a bit sorry for yourself.

It's really hard on children to come home to a parent who looks sad and dejected; they get the message that it's not a good idea to celebrate without you. Therefore, it's important to find your own comfort zone. For some parents, being alone is fine. Others find solace in the bosom of their families or within a circle of close friends. And some need to change the scene entirely—to celebrate in a different place, with different people. If you're not sure what's best for you, try them all; talk to other single parents and find out how they handle the I-Don't-Have-the-Kids Blues.

It also helps to change your thinking. Don Warren, divorced

for four years, celebrates Thanksgiving on the Saturday after the official day. He's convinced that his eight-year-old daughter, who has been doing this since she was four, thinks nothing of having two Thanksgivings; and, for him, the holiday is not depressing—in his mind, Saturday *is* Thanksgiving Day with his daughter.

Jason Stern, who usually has no problem planning holidays with his ex-wife because he only celebrates the Jewish holidays, had to observe Passover a week early one year. "It turned out that Easter and Passover fell on the same weekend. Who says a holiday or a birthday has to be celebrated on the same day exactly? I thought to myself, *No one in America is having a seder tonight.* It was a little weird, but it still felt like a celebration. After all, what is *a family?* You can have four people who don't like each other, sitting around having a miserable time on the right day!"

Happily Ever After . . . Or as Close as Anyone Gets

"Your kids are soooo lucky," a beautiful, blond, blue-eyed young woman, a good friend of Jennifer's, told me at Jen's twenty-first birthday party, which I co-hosted with Mark at his apartment; by that time—six years after our legal divorce, ten since our separation—we had mastered the art of joint party-giving. "My parents got divorced around the same time as you guys, and they *still* can't be in the same room together. I wish they could take lessons from the two of you."

I knew what she meant; my own parents, who divorced when I got married, couldn't spend an evening in each other's presence, no less co-host parties or commencement festivities, as Mark and I have done for our kids. Far from a final chapter, we still have many holiday seasons to coordinate and new milestones—the kids' and ours—to celebrate. Someday, we'll probably even walk down the aisle again—as co-parents of the bride or groom. The saga continues.

Some co-parents have far less contact than Mark and I, while a rare few are even more intimately involved in each other's postdivorce lives. Most have simply achieved a workable truce that enables them to coordinate special occasions. Wherever you and your ex-spouse fall on the continuum, it's wise to remember the advice Charles Farrell gives to other parents: "You are going to be the parents of these children forever. It doesn't stop at eighteen."

Like it or not, you and your ex-spouse will also be connected forever—or 'til death do you part. For your children's and some-day your grandchildren's sake, make the best of it.

— 12 —

BE STILL, THE VOICES IN MY HEAD

A Personal Postscript

Throughout the writing process, I have heard voices in my head: those of my children, of other parents, and of social observers who decry divorce and the demise of the American family. I could not close this book without answering each of them.

My children say, "Yeah, Ma . . . *right!*" as they look over my shoulder, reading portions of this book filled with advice. *"You and Dad* didn't always do that!" And they're right. Sadly, I have learned almost as much from what Mark and I didn't do as from what we did. Looking back, I know we could have listened a little better and been more responsive to Jennifer and Jeremy's needs, less focused on our own.

The divorced parents in my head remark, "Easy for you to say, Blau. Your ex-husband was willing to cooperate" or "You two had resources—you could afford a family therapist, afford two households" or "Your family didn't treat you like a social pariah." All are true to some extent. But there are degrees of postdivorce difficulty—difficulty that, I believe, can be mitigated through the efforts of one parent who can tip the balance and set the healing process in motion. This belief is based not only on my own and other parents' experience but on that of counselors who work with divorced families and researchers who study them. Granted, the recommendations in this book are difficult; cooperative co-parenting is not for the selfish or the immature. And, I admit, the advice is simpler to dispense than to follow. Wisdom is never easily applied.

Of all, the voices of social observers have been the loudest and most unsettling. Divorce, which continues to be a major social (and personal) reality, has become central in the family-values debate, and the backlash is palpable. I got my first taste of it last year, when *Our Turn: The Good News About Women and Divorce,* a book I co-authored with researchers Christopher Hayes and Deborah Anderson, was published. Producers of various TV morning news programs, while serving incest and serial murder as suitable breakfast fare, said they wouldn't "touch" the subject of midlife women who are growing and thriving in the aftermath of divorce. And one reviewer, judging the book by its cover, charged that the subtitle implied a cavalier attitude about divorce: "It's like saying 'The Good News About Alcoholism!' "

We gave in to the backlash, subtitling the paperback *How Women Triumph in the Face of Divorce,* but the critics missed the point. There *is* good news about alcoholism: because of public awareness, mushrooming peer support, and a rash of literature that inspires alcoholics to dare to imagine life sober, people are recovering in record numbers. The same is true of divorce. There *is* good news, not only about women but also about children. In both cases, however, "recovery" requires a great deal of effort and a willingness to rethink old ways of doing things.

Just as early efforts to "reform" alcoholics were met with skepticism, co-parenting—a new way of looking at family life—is an easy target. Sheltering kids from the fallout and cooperating with an ex-spouse *are* difficult, but research confirms that about half of the parents who divorce can; and education will increase their numbers. Clinical psychologist Marla Isaacs, co-author of *The Difficult Divorce,* maintains, "People have a capacity to manage divorce much better. With guidance, most can. Parents don't really want to damage their kids."

Social critics who express moral outrage about divorce can find plenty of reports and figures that support their grim prognosis. They accuse divorcing parents of being self-centered and unrealistic about relationships and marriage. They say that whereas divorce may be good for the parents, it is rarely good for their children; statistically, children of divorce are prone to poor academic performance and psychological problems. And, the critics note, as adults, these grown-up children bear witness to the pain of growing up in conflict-ridden households, of having to take care of their parents, of being afraid to commit to work and to relationships.

However, the bleak profile certainly doesn't fit *all* children of divorce, especially children whose parents have cooperated with each other and acted responsibly. Furthermore, divorce may be a convenient scapegoat for society's ills, but it's not *why* so many children today are in trouble. One reason divorce happens in the first place is that people know very little about being partners— communicating, sharing space, problem solving. And one reason children suffer is that their parents—divorced or not—know very little about being parents. Until we start giving people lessons in relating and in parenting, some families will flourish, some will flounder, and more than a few are bound to fail.

Divorce is emotionally wrenching, incredibly disruptive, and it has lasting impact. But divorce is a fact of life—and a far better alternative than condemning children to live with warring parents who stay married. Besides, parents rarely "jump" into divorce; they stand on the precipice for years, looking behind them and wondering where they "went wrong," looking ahead and wondering how they and their children could possibly survive.

Most important, the debate about divorce takes the focus off the real issue, which is not family values, but family support. Families have precious little institutionalized or moral support in this country, and many are fighting against disheartening odds. It makes no sense to blame parents who divorce or to feel sorry for their kids. These families need help.

Therefore, I would hope that family-court services throughout the country and advocacy groups, like the Children's Rights Council, are successful in their continuing efforts to educate parents and to inspire laws that support shared parenting over sole custody and mediation as a humane alternative to adversarial divorce. I would hope that enlightened legislatures will also enact laws that mandate education and counseling services—for *all* families. I would hope that schools will routinely offer peer-support groups, similar to the successful Banana Splits program for children whose families are undergoing profound change (see

page 328), which has been replicated in school systems throughout the U.S.

I wrote this book in spite of the "voices" in my head, and I
would hope that divorcing parents don't listen to them, either—
that they take to heart the creative suggestions of other successful
co-parents and that they aspire to a better future for their children
than the critics would have them believe is possible. I certainly do
not advocate divorce, but when a marriage must end, I am
convinced that the next best alternative is a healthy "family
apart." In the final analysis, cooperative co-parenting is the only
way to guarantee children their "right" to two parents.

Appendix I

Families Apart Questionnaire:
Sharing Parenting after Divorce

[PLEASE NOTE: Any information provided is confidential. Unless specifically agreed upon *in writing,* real names will *not* be used, and, if necessary, identifying details will be changed to ensure anonymity. Use extra sheets of paper if necessary. Label each response—for example, "I-A."]

Name _____   Home Telephone _____

Address _____   Work Telephone _____

_____   Best time & place to contact you?

What year did you get married?   _____

_____   Name & age of child(ren), includ-

What year did you separate?   ing date of birth: _____

_____   _____

What year did you get divorced? List in chronological order with oldest child first

_____   _____

_____   _____

SECTION I: THE DIVORCE—AND BEYOND

A. Who initiated the divorce:__husband?__wife?__mutual decision? Please explain below:

Explain: _____

_____

B. On the following continua, please note your postdivorce relationship with your ex at each point in time:

	EXTREMELY HOSTILE	HOSTILE	MODERATELY ANGRY	CIVIL BUT COLD	FRIENDLY	VERY FRIENDLY
During the first year	____	____	____	____	____	____
During the second year	____	____	____	____	____	____

	EXTREMELY HOSTILE	HOSTILE	MODERATELY ANGRY	CIVIL BUT COLD	FRIENDLY	VERY FRIENDLY
Between two and four years	___	___	___	___	___	___
After five years	___	___	___	___	___	___

C. To what do you attribute the change in your relationship over the years? Check whichever apply and explain below:

___the passage of time
___the need to co-parent
___the children getting older
___child(ren) leaving home
___a particular incident or crisis
___realizing my ex was "good" with and for the children
___personal growth
___individual therapy
___family therapy
___influence of clergy
___influence of the media
___pressure from my own parents
___influence of other postdivorced couples
___a new love interest
___my remarriage
___my ex's remarriage

___education regarding the effects of divorce on children
___change in my financial status
___change in my ex's financial status
___change in the children's life
___change in my ex's circumstances/attitude
___started job/launched a career
___different job/career
___involvement in outside activity (e.g., sports, volunteer work)
___making new friends
___membership in a support group
other _____
_____

Explain the above selections and make any additional comments here or on an extra sheet of paper.

_____
_____
_____

SECTION II: CUSTODY AND PARENTING TIME

A. What is your *legal* custody arrangement?___joint___sole custody mother___sole custody father

B. How does that work out in *actual parenting time?* Describe "visitation" or living arrangements below.

_____

_____

_____

_____

C. How have the schedule and living arrangements changed as the children got older? Was it because *their* needs, *your* needs, or *your spouse's* needs changed? Please explain:

_____

_____

_____

_____

_____

D. What issues, events, or situations cause(d) problems when you and your ex share parenting responsibilities?

___who pays for what
___pickup/drop-off time
___different standards (e.g., cleanliness, dress)
___discipline
___curfew
___stepparent or live-in lover
___school performance
___last-minute changes in schedule

___putting children's needs first
___making decisions about school
___buying necessities for kids
___buying gifts for kids
___vacation time
___wanting more flexibility
___wanting more structure
___relationships with in-laws (grandparents)

___attendance at school
functions (conferences,
plays, games)
___religious difference
___different ideas about health
___things that bothered you
when you were married
___your ex's dating habits

___your ex's personal habits
(e.g., drinking, cursing)
___activities in which your ex
involves the children
___crisis management (e.g.,
the child has a problem)
___division of parenting time
___which is primary residence

Please explain the above selections in greater detail. Mention whether the difficulty still exists—and include any problem areas *not* cited above. Again, use extra paper if you need additional writing space:

_____
_____
_____
_____
_____

SECTION III: WORKING AS A CO-PARENT WITH YOUR EX

For each of the following statements: (1) Rate yourself by indicating where you fall: "never," "rarely," etc. (2) On the lines provided, explain or make more detailed comments about your rating. (3) Describe how your situation has *changed* over time since you were first divorced. Use an additional piece of paper, if necessary, to add whatever thoughts come to mind as you're completing Section III. (Remember to label your comments—"III-A," "III-B," etc.)

	NEVER	RARELY	SOMETIMES	USUALLY	ALMOST ALWAYS	ALWAYS
A. Even when my ex and I disagree on a personal level, I am able to put aside our differences to deal with the children.	___	___	___	___	___	___

	NEVER	RARELY	SOMETIMES	USUALLY	ALMOST ALWAYS	ALWAYS
B. Although my physical and mental health are vital parts of my ability to be a parent, my children's needs come first.						

	NEVER	RARELY	SOMETIMES	USUALLY	ALMOST ALWAYS	ALWAYS
C. I respect my ex as a parent.						

	NEVER	RARELY	SOMETIMES	USUALLY	ALMOST ALWAYS	ALWAYS
D. When it comes to "milestone" events, like birthdays and graduations, my ex and I can attend a joint celebration.						

	NEVER	RARELY	SOMETIMES	USUALLY	ALMOST ALWAYS	ALWAYS
We can *plan* a joint celebration.						

IF POSSIBLE, CITE A SPECIFIC EXAMPLE OF SUCH AN EVENT.

	NEVER	RARELY	SOMETIMES	USUALLY	ALMOST ALWAYS	ALWAYS
E. If I don't agree with my ex's standards or approach to child rearing, I can accept that we're different.						

EXPLAIN YOUR DIFFERENCES.

	NEVER	RARELY	SOMETIMES	USUALLY	ALMOST ALWAYS	ALWAYS
F. I communicate with my ex about what happens when our child(ren) is (are) with me.						

	NEVER	RARELY	SOMETIMES	USUALLY	ALMOST ALWAYS	ALWAYS
G. I am able to step out of "traditional" gender roles when necessary—e.g., a mother fixes a bike; a father cooks dinner.						

	NEVER	RARELY	SOMETIMES	USUALLY	ALMOST ALWAYS	ALWAYS
H. I restrain myself from talking badly about my ex in front of the children.						

	NEVER	RARELY	SOMETIMES	USUALLY	ALMOST ALWAYS	ALWAYS
J. If I have something to communicate to my ex, even if it's about *the children,* I don't ask them to convey the message.						

	NEVER	RARELY	SOMETIMES	USUALLY	ALMOST ALWAYS	ALWAYS
K. I respect the power of change in our family life, and I try to antici-pate the effect of big changes (re-marriage) or tran-sitions (going to a new school).	___	___	___	___	___	___

	NEVER	RARELY	SOMETIMES	USUALLY	ALMOST ALWAYS	ALWAYS
L. No matter what *I* think of my ex, I know it's important that he/she is in my child-(ren)'s life.	___	___	___	___	___	___

	NEVER	RARELY	SOMETIMES	USUALLY	ALMOST ALWAYS	ALWAYS
M. I believe that as long as we're both still alive, my ex and I will al-ways be "kin"—connected through our children.	___	___	___	___	___	___

	NEVER	RARELY	SOMETIMES	USUALLY	ALMOST ALWAYS	ALWAYS
N. I think it's important for children to maintain contact with their grandparents—no matter what I think of them or of my ex.	⎯⎯	⎯⎯	⎯⎯	⎯⎯	⎯⎯	⎯⎯

THIS QUESTIONNAIRE WILL BE USED AS A GUIDELINE FOR FOLLOW-UP INTERVIEWS. THANK YOU FOR TAKING THE TIME TO FILL IT OUT. —MB

Appendix II

Sample Parenting Agreement

The following Parenting Agreement appears in *Mom's House, Dad's House,* by Isolina Ricci, Ph.D. In the pages that precede it, Ricci notes that her composite couple, Carole and James McKay, have prepared for their initial meeting by following the Guidelines for Negotiations with the Other Parent and using the other extremely helpful guidelines offered in her book. In offering the McKay's agreement to her readers, Ricci notes, "The McKay's agreement is unusually long because it contains many of the standardized forms and terminology of the two-home approach. But it can be used as a guide for your own words of a technical nature—provisions for tax exemption, head of household assignment, and the out-of-state clause. You should consult an attorney and accountant for the best course for you and then see that these provisions are incorporated."

Parenting Agreement

We, Carole McKay and James McKay, the parents of Jesse and Carolee McKay, enter into this agreement in order to better meet our parental responsibilities and to safeguard our children's future development. We both recognize that they wish to love and respect both of us, regardless of our marital status or our place of residence, and that their welfare can best be served by our mutual cooperation as partners in parenting and by each of us providing a home in which they are loved and to which they belong: their mother's house and father's house. We also jointly recognize that court proceedings regarding children and custody and visitation matters can be detrimental to children, and we therefore have decided to resolve these questions ourselves, using this Parenting Agreement.* Finally, we have chosen to avoid the traditional terminology surrounding divorce and children by using terms that more accurately describe the reorganization of our former family to new, one-parent families. Accordingly, we wish to instruct our respective attorneys, if necessary, to inform any courts involved in our dissolution that our desires are as follows regarding the custody and upbringing of our children.

1. Terminology: In order to reaffirm our commitment to our two-status, we choose to use the terms "live with mother" and "live with father" in describing our arrangement, rather than the more traditional one-home, one-visitor terminology of "custody and visitation."

2. Responsibility for Jesse and Carolee: Jesse and Carolee will be our joint responsibility.† Both of us recognize that each of our contributions toward our children's welfare is real and genuine, and we agree to cooperate with one another on establishing mutually acceptable guidelines and standards for development, education, and health. We agree further to discuss all major issues jointly and that day-to-day decisions for the children will be the responsibility of the parent in residence. Each of us will have equal access to all health and school records and unlimited phone contact with our children. Jesse and Carolee will live with their father every other Friday beginning at 6:00 P.M. through the following Monday at school time. The remainder of the time they will live with their mother. During the summer vacation they will

---

*This last sentence is used by just a few parents. Further, it might displease the judge asked to approve it.

†Notice the word "custody" is omitted entirely. Your attorney may want to put it in, however. If this happens, be sure you understand the ramifications of the type of "custody" he or she adds.

live with their father the entire months of July and August. This schedule will continue throughout this year, unless their normal development seems impaired by this arrangement, in which case we will review and reassess the arrangement. Changes in scheduled times at either home will require immediate substitution of times of equal length and will be subject to our mutual approval. If an acceptable substitute is not found, the parent unable to be home with the children will hire a sitter or make arrangements with friends or relatives to care for the children during the period of his or her responsibility.

3. Contributions: Each parent will contribute time and energies on a daily basis toward the children's day-to-day care when they live with him or her. In addition, the father will contribute $225 per child (child support) toward the expense incurred in the mother's residence on or before the fifteenth of each month. During the summer months when the children live with the father, the contribution will be reduced to $200.*

The mother agrees to give the father a written, simplified accounting of this contribution three times a year (every four months), on the first of January, May, and August.

4. Medical and Dental: It is agreed that the mother will carry and pay all the cost of the children's medical health insurance. The father agrees to pay 75 percent of all medical costs over and beyond that covered by insurance. Dental costs will be paid by the mother.

We also agree that transportation to medical appointments will be the responsibility of the parent in residence.

We agree that although the parent in residence has final responsibility in making day-to-day medical decisions, the other parent is to be involved in all major discussions and decisions, and consulted and advised about illnesses or accidents.

5. Education and Child Care: Both parents agree that Jesse and Carolee will remain in their present schools, and child-care

*Some people add a cost of living clause here.

arrangements will remain the same for this year. Tuition costs will be the responsibility of the father; child-care costs, the responsibility of the mother. We agree to attend teacher conferences on a rotating basis, to be active in school events as our schedules allow, and that we both will have full access to information and records regarding our children's progress.

6. Holidays: We both agree that the Thanksgiving holiday, beginning with the day before and ending the following Monday morning at school time, will be this year with the mother and next year with the father.

We further agree that for this year Jesse and Carolee will live with their father the first week of Christmas vacation through the twenty-seventh of December, when the children will then be with their mother. Next year the situation will be reversed and the children will spend the Christmas period first with their mother. Other holidays, Memorial Day, school holidays, and Easter vacation will be negotiated between the parents.

7. Children's Activities: Summer activities will be the responsibility of the father and will also be undertaken at his discretion and expense. School-year activities are anticipated to be ballet and guitar for Carolee and Pony League Softball for Jesse. We agree to the continuance of these activities and will share the responsibilities for transportation, costs, and communications in the following manner: Jesse's Pony League activities will be supervised by his father, and all costs incurred will be met by him. Carolee's ballet and guitar lessons will be the responsibility of the mother, and all costs will be met by her. It is not anticipated that the ballet lessons will continue past June of this year. The father agrees to transporting Carolee during his times with her so that she can have her guitar lessons on some Saturdays.

8. Respect for One Another's Parenting Style and Authority:
We agree to honor one another's parenting style, privacy, and authority. We will not interfere in the parenting style of the other parent nor will we make plans or arrangements that would impinge upon the other parent's authority or times with the children

without the expressed agreement of the other parent. Furthermore, we agree to encourage our children to discuss their grievances directly with the parent in question. It is our intent to encourage a direct child-parent bond.

9. Agreement Time Period and Renegotiations for New Agreement:

We both agree that this Parenting Agreement is to be in effect a minimum of two years and is automatically renewable if no revisions are sought. If revisions are sought after two years, we agree that this agreement will be considered binding until a new agreement is reached. If unusual circumstances arise before the end of the two-year period, all or part of this agreement will be negotiated, either privately or with the aid of a third party, given thirty days' notice before either of us seeks modification through the courts. We further agree that, should any serious dispute arise between us relating to our children's education, health, or other aspect of their welfare, before either of us seeks modification through the courts, we will first seek the services of an objective third party, such as a trained counselor or arbitrator.

_____   _____
Date   Signature

_____   _____
Date   Signature

_____   _____
Date   Witness*

Wording Your Agreement

Parents have used the sample Parenting Agreement paragraphs and vocabulary in several ways. Some use the examples just as they are and simply insert their own decisions in their own words.

*A witness is probably not necessary, but it does add a more formal tone to the procedure.

Others redesign paragraphs, still others build a total agreement from scratch. Many parents find the idea of a Parenting Agreement a good chance to write down their own joint philosophy on their commitment to their children, as well as their decisions.

I suggest that you consider your own Parenting Agreement in the same way that you might any other public document or ceremony, such as a ritual of confirmation, graduation exercise, or a wedding ceremony. This agreement is your chance to bring some kind of formal validation to your beliefs. It's an excellent opportunity to show yourself and your children that you and the other parent are working it out and that you have a plan for the children. Like writing the script for your own wedding ceremony, writing your own Parenting Agreement has important symbolic as well as realistic value to your peace of mind and to that of your children.*

*Reprinted with the permission of Macmillan Publishing Company from *Mom's House, Dad's House: Making Shared Custody Work,* by Isolina Ricci. Copyright © 1980 by Isolina Ricci.

Appendix III

Resources

Recommended Reading for Adults

Divorce: General/Legal/Financial Issues

Adler, Robert E. *Sharing the Children: How to Resolve Custody Problems and Get on with Your Life.* Chevy Chase, M.D.: Adler & Adler, Pubs., Inc., 1988.

Belli, Melvin, and Mel Krantzler, Ph.D., with Christopher S. Taylor. *Divorcing: The Complete Guide for Men and Women.* New York: St. Martin's Press, 1988.

Briles, Judith. *The Dollars and Sense of Divorce: The Financial Guide for Women.* New York: Master Media Limited, 1988.

Herman, Stephen P., M.D. *Parent vs. Parent: How You and Your Child Can Survive the Custody Battle.* New York: Pantheon, 1990.

Margulies, Sam, Ph.D., J.D. *Getting Divorced Without Ruining Your Life: A Reasoned Practical Guide to the Legal, Emotional, and Financial Ins and Outs of Negotiating a Divorce Settlement.* New York: Fireside/Simon & Schuster, 1992.

McKay, Matthew, Ph.D., Peter D. Rogers, Ph.D., Joan Blades, J.D., and Richard Gosse, M.A. *The Divorce Book.* Oakland, Calif.: New Harbinger Publications, 1984.

Ricci, Isolina. *Mom's House, Dad's House: Making Shared Custody Work.* New York: Macmillan, 1980.

Wallerstein, Judith S., and Sandra Blakeslee. *Second Chances: Men, Women, and Children a Decade after Divorce, Who Wins, Who Loses and Why.* New York: Ticknor & Fields, 1990.

Warshak, Richard A., Ph.D. *The Custody Revolution: The Father Factor and the Motherhood Mystique.* New York: Poseidon Press, 1992.

Adults' Emotional Recovery

Adler, Allan J., M.D., and Christine Archambault. *Divorce Recovery: Healing the Hurt Through Self-Help and Professional Support.* Washington, D.C.: PIA Press, 1990.

Beattie, Melody. *The Language of Letting Go.* New York: HarperCollins, 1990.

Colgrove, Melba, Ph.D., Harold H. Bloomfield, M.D., and Peter McWilliams. *How to Survive the Loss of a Love.* New York: Bantam, 1981.

Fisher, Bruce. *Rebuilding: When Your Relationship Ends.* San Luis Obispo, Calif.: Impact Publishers, 1982.

Hayes, Christopher L., Ph.D., Deborah Anderson, and Melinda Blau. *Our Turn: The Good News about Women and Divorce.* New York: Pocket Books, 1992.

Lerner, Harriet Goldhor, Ph.D. *The Dance of Intimacy: A Woman's Guide to Courageous Acts of Change in Key Relationships.* New York: Harper & Row, 1989.

Mason, Marilyn J., Ph.D. *Making Our Lives Our Own: A Woman's Guide to the Six Challenges of Personal Change.* San Francisco, Calif.: Harper San Francisco, 1991.

Napolitane, C. *Living and Loving after Divorce.* New York: Signet, 1977.

Passick, Robert, Ph.D. *Awakening from the Deep Sleep: A Powerful Guide for Courageous Men.* San Francisco, Calif.: Harper San Francisco, 1992.

Viorst, Judith. *Necessary Losses: The Loves, Illusions, Dependencies and Impossible Expectations That All of Us Have to Give Up in Order to Grow.* New York: Ballantine, 1986.

Weiss, Robert S. *Marital Separation: Coping with the End of a Marriage and the Transition to Being Single Again.* New York: Basic Books, 1975.

Anger, Conflict Management, and Negotiation

Hendrix, Harville, Ph.D. *Getting the Love You Want: A Guide for Couples.* New York: Henry Holt and Company, 1988.

———. *Keeping the Love You Find: A Guide for Singles.* New York: Pocket Books, 1992.

Kline, Kris, and Stephen Pew, Ph.D. *For the Sake of the Children: How to Share Your Children with Your Ex-Spouse in Spite of Your Anger.* Rocklin, Calif.: Prima Publishing, 1992.

Lerner, Harriet Goldhor, Ph.D. *The Dance of Anger: A Woman's Guide to*

Changing the Patterns of Intimate Relationships. New York: Harper & Row Perennial, 1986.

Weeks, Dudley, Ph.D. *The Eight Essential Steps to Conflict Resolution: Preserving Relationships at Work, at Home, and in the Community*. Los Angeles, Calif.: Tarcher, 1992.

Weiner-Davis, Michelle. *Divorce Busting*. New York: Summit, 1992.

Gender Issues

Ehrensaft, Diane. *Parenting Together: Men and Women Sharing the Care of Their Children*. New York: Free Press, 1987.

Kimball, Gayle, Ph.D. *50–50 Parenting: Sharing Family Rewards and Responsibilities*. Lexington, Mass.: Lexington Books, 1988.

Riessman, Catherine Kohler. *Divorce Talk: Women and Men Make Sense of Personal Relationships*. New Brunswick, N.J.: Rutgers University Press, 1990.

Tannen, Deborah. *You Just Don't Understand: Men and Women in Conversation*. New York: Morrow, 1990.

Tavris, Carol. *The Mismeasure of Woman: Why Women Are Not the Better Sex, the Inferior Sex, or the Opposite Sex*. New York: Simon & Schuster, 1992.

Parenting

Berman, Claire. *Adult Children of Divorce Speak Out: About Growing Up With—and Moving Beyond—Parental Divorce*. New York: Simon and Schuster, 1991.

Bettner, Betty Lou, Ph.D., and Amy Lew, Ph.D. *Raising Kids Who Can: Using Family Meetings to Nurture Responsible, Cooperative, Caring, and Happy Children*. New York: Harper Perennial, 1989.

Bienenfield, Florence, Ph.D. *Helping Your Child Succeed after Divorce*. Alameda, CA: Hunter House, 1987.

Cohen, Miriam Galper. *The Joint Custody Handbook*. Philadelphia: Running Press, 1991.

———. *Long-Distance Parenting: A Guide for Divorced Parents*. New York: New American Library, 1989.

DeMarea, Barbara. *Reshaping Your Family Structure: Stamp Out Divorce Wars: A Workbook Designed to Help Divorcing Couples*. Shawnee Mission, Kans.: DeMarea Books, 1989.

DeSisto, Michael. *Decoding Your Teenager: How to Understand Each Other During the Turbulent Years.* New York: Morrow, 1991.

Dinkmeyer, Don, and Gary D. McKay. *The Parent's Handbook,* rev. ed. Circle Pines, Minn.: American Guidance Service, 1989 (see also STEP, under Parenting Education, below).

————. *Parenting Teenagers.* rev. ed. Circle Pines, Minn.: American Guidance Service, 1990 (see also STEPteen, under Parenting Education, below).

————. *Parenting Young Children.* Circle Pines, Minn.: American Guidance Service, 1989 (see also Early Childhood STEP, under Parenting Education, below).

Edelman, Marian Wright. *The Measure of Our Success: A Letter to My Children and Yours.* Boston: Beacon, 1992.

Francke, Linda Bird. *Growing Up Divorced.* New York: Simon & Schuster, 1983.

Gardner, Richard A. *The Parents' Book about Divorce,* second edition. Cresskill, NJ: Creative Therapeutics, 1991.

Gordon, Thomas. *PET: Parent Effectiveness Training.* New York: Penguin, 1970.

Grief, G. S., and M. S. Pabst. *Mothers Without Custody.* Boston: D.C. Heath, 1988.

Grollman, Earl A., and Gerri L. Sweder. *Teaching Your Child to Be Home Alone.* New York: Lexington Books, 1992.

Kalter, Neil. *Growing Up with Divorce: Helping Your Child Avoid Immediate and Later Emotional Problems.* New York: Free Press, 1990.

Khavari, Khalil A., Ph.D., and Sue Wiliston Khavari, M.A. *Creating a Successful Family.* Chatham, NY: One World Publications, 1989.

Lansky, Vicki. *Divorce Book for Parents: Helping Your Children Cope with Divorce and Its Aftermath.* New York: Signet, 1991.

Levy, David L., ed. *The Best Parent Is Both Parents: A Guide to Shared Parenting in the 21st Century.* Norfolk, Va.: Hampton Roads Publishing Company, 1993.

Lynch-Fraser, Diane. *Life's Little Miseries: Helping Your Child with the Disasters of Everyday Life.* New York: Lexington Books, 1992.

Ricci, Isolina. *Mom's House, Dad's House: Making Shared Custody Work.* New York: Macmillan, 1980.

Sabo, Marcella M., Ed.S., L.M.F.T., Rosana Gershman, and Geraldine Lee Wasman, J.D., F.M. *Whose Kid Is It Anyway? And 400 Other Questions for Divorcing, Dating, and Remarried Families.* Astoria, Oreg.: Next Step Publications, 1989.

Schaefer, Nathan, M.D. *Families Are Forever.* Saratoga, Calif.: R & E Publications, 1985.

Stinnet, Nick, and John DeFrain. *Secrets of Successful Families.* Boston: Little Brown, 1985.

Taffel, Ron, with Melinda Blau. *Parenting by Heart: How to Be in Charge, Stay Connected, and Instill Your Values When It Feels Like You've Got Only 15 Minutes a Day.* Reading, Mass.: Addison Wesley, 1991.

Teyber, Edward. *Helping Children Cope with Divorce.* New York: Lexington Books, 1992.

Walker, Glynnis. *Solomon's Children: Exploding the Myths of Divorce.* New York: Arbor House, 1986.

Ware, Ciji. *Sharing Parenthood after Divorce: An Enlightened Custody Guide for Mothers, Fathers, and Kids.* New York: Viking, 1982.

Remarriage and Stepfamily Life

Berman, Claire. *Making It as a Stepparent: New Roles, New Rules.* New York: Harper & Row Perennial, 1986.

Bernstein, Anne C., Ph.D. *Yours Mine and Ours: How Families Change When Remarried Parents Have a Child Together.* New York: Scribner's, 1989.

Bloomfield, Harold, M.D. *Making Peace in Your Stepfamily: Surviving and Thriving as Parents and Stepparents.* New York: Hyperion, 1993.

Dinkmeyer, Don, Gary D. McKay, and Joyce L. McKay. *New Beginnings: Skills for Single Parents and Stepfamily Parents.* Champaign, IL: Research Press, 1987.

Ephron, Delia. *Funny Sauce: Us, the Ex, the Ex's New Mate, the New Mate's Ex, and the Kids.* New York: Viking Penguin, 1986.

Various authors. *Stepping Ahead: A Program for Successful Stepfamily Living.* Lincoln, Nebr.: Stepfamilies Press, 1988. Available from the Stepfamily Association of America, $9.95 plus $3 for shipping and handling (see below).

Visher, Emily and John. *How to Win as a Stepfamily.* New York: Dembner Books, 1982.

Books for Children

The following descriptive information is taken from bibliographies supplied by Beech Acres' Aring Institute, the Children's Rights Council, and the Children's Divorce Center, in Woodbridge, Connecticut. Suggested age levels are approximate; review books yourself to see if the reading level and content are appropriate for your child.

Preschoolers and School-Agers

Berman, Claire. *What Am I Doing in a Stepfamily?* New York: Carol Publishing Group, 1982. A starting point for parents to talk with their children about stepfamilies. For children five through ten. Beautifully illustrated.

Boegehold, Betty. *Daddy Doesn't Live Here Anymore.* Racine, Wis.: Golden Books/Western Publishing Company, 1985. Casey, a young girl whose parents divorce, is forced to accept the reality of her dad's leaving home. She tries several schemes to change the situation and is comforted by both of her parents and assured that everything will be fine; appealing and plentiful illustrations.

Boyd, Lizi. *The Not So Wicked Stepmother.* New York: Puffin Books, 1987. For kids three to eight, pictures with text. According to *School Library Journal,* "This is a choice bit of reading."

———. *Sam Is My Half Brother.* New York: Viking 1990. Takes off where her previous book left off, following the birth of a new baby.

Brown, Laurene Krasny, and Marc Brown. *Dinosaurs Divorce.* Boston: Little Brown, 1986. An excellent book presenting specific issues about divorce and remarriage with directness, humor, and imagination. Cartoon-style story form to help children four through twelve understand divorce words and what they mean, why parents divorce, how children feel, having two homes.

Christiansen, C. V. *My Mother's House, My Father's House.* New York: Atheneum, 1989. A little girl in a dual-residence situation compares life in each parent's home and, in the end decides that one day she'll have her own house; wonderfully illustrated and an honest message about how kids feel.

Fassler, David, M.D., Michele Lash, M.Ed., and Sally Ives, Ph.D. *Changing Families.* Burlington, Vt.: Waterfront Books, 1988.

———. *The Divorce Workbook.* Burlington, Vt.: Waterfront Books, 1985. Both of the above are workbook-style books for parents and children to use together, explaining separation, divorce, and remarriage; space is provided for drawings and coloring.

Gerstein, Mordecai. *The Story of May.* New York: HarperCollins, 1993. Although not about divorce *per se,* this beautifully illustrated story about May and December, two months of the year who can't get along and therefore must separate, has a wonderful underlying message for co-parenting families.

Lebowitz, Marcia. *I Think Divorce Stinks*. Woodbridge, Conn.: CDC Press, 1989. Cartoon-style story form that helps children recognize that it is appropriate to have negative feelings about divorce and to express those feelings.

Sinberg, Janet. *Divorce Is a Grown-up Problem*. New York: Avon, 1978. The text stresses the feelings of a young child whose parents get divorced. Both parents are present and supportive in the story, and the simple drawings are appealing.

————. *Now I Have a Stepparent and It's Kind of Confusing*. New York: Avon Books, 1979. A picture book for young children in a blended family.

School-Agers and Preteens

Blume, Judy. *It's Not the End of the World*. New York: Bradbury Press, 1972. Karen, in sixth grade, tries to understand her parents' divorce; her goal is to bring them back together again.

Brogan, J., and W. Maiden. *The Kid's Guide to Divorce*. New York: Fawcett, 1986. An easy, conversational workbook that discusses the practical issues that affect children. Offers a questionnaire so kids can compare their answers with others who have taken it.

Byars, B. *The Animal, the Vegetable, and John D. Jones*. New York: Delacorte, 1982. Two teenage sisters visit Dad for vacation and discover Dad's girlfriend and her son will be joining them.

Cleary, Beverly. *Dear Mr. Henshaw*. New York: Morrow, 1983. An award-winning book about a ten-year-old boy who writes letters to an unmet hero describing how he misses his father.

Danziger, Paula. *The Divorce Express*. New York: Delacorte, 1982. A fourteen-year-old girl lives in a joint-custody situation. Problems arise when her mom plans to marry.

Goldman, Katie. *In the Wings*. New York: Dial, 1982. A young girl goes through stages of fantasy, denial, sadness, and finally acceptance of her parents' divorce.

Kagy-Taylor, Kathy, and Donna Marmer. *All About Change*. Cincinnati: Beech Acres, 1990. Helpful for parent or professional to discuss the global concept of change. Raises awareness about healthy expression of feelings and ways to cope with change. Geared to second and third graders.

Klein, Norma. *Taking Sides*. New York, Pantheon, 1974. Twelve-year-old Nell adjusts to living with her father and five-year-old brother; father is portrayed as a nurturing parent.

Krementz, Jill. *How It Feels When Parents Divorce.* New York: Knopf, 1984. A sensitive view of the experiences of children, mostly adolescents.

LeShan, Eda. *What's Going to Happen to Me? When Parents Separate or Divorce.* New York: Macmillan, 1986. Many questions about divorce are answered in simple language. Which parent will you live with? Will your parents remarry? Will they still be friends? Parents should review answers to see if they fit their needs and situation.

Park, Barbara. *Don't Make Me Smile.* New York: Knopf, 1981. A young boy feels life will never be the same again after parents divorce; people try to cheer him up to no avail. He goes for professional counseling.

Stinson, Katherine. *Mom and Dad Don't Live Together Anymore.* New York: Annick Press, 1985. A simple text with effective illustrations portraying the feelings of a young girl.

Note: Additional reading lists, including books for professionals, parents, and children, are available from organizations noted with an asterisk (*) below.

Organizations and Support Groups

Counseling

American Association of Marriage and Family Therapists
1100 17 Street N.W. 10th floor
Washington, D.C.
800/374-2638

Membership includes a variety of mental-health professionals (among them, psychologists, psychiatrists, social workers) who specialize in the family; they will send a list of clinical members in the zip-code area you specify, along with *The Consumer's Guide to Marriage and Family Therapy.*

American Psychological Association
750 First Street, NE
Washington, DC 20002-42422
202/336-5500

This national organization leaves referrals up to its state associations but will give you the name and number of your state's referral service. When you call the local office, ask for a licensed psychologist who deals with divorce issues; and be specific about your other needs, including gender preference, if you have one.

Aring Institute at Beech Acres*
6881 Beechmont Avenue
Cincinnati, OH 45230
513/231-6630

Information, counseling, and peer support for parents and children. Write for their divorce bibliography or visit them if you live in the area.

Family Service America
11700 W. Lake Park Drive
Milwaukee, WI 53224
800/221-2681

The largest network of accredited community-based family counseling and support services in North America, this organization has 280 member agencies in the U.S. and Canada. Call for free referral to local family service agency in your community or for free information.

National Association of Social Workers
750 First Street, NE (Suite 700)
Washington, DC 20002
202/408-8600

Has national referral service which will provide names of licensed social workers in your area, who specialize in mediation and/or family issues.

Stepfamily Foundation, Inc.
333 West End Avenue
New York, NY 10023
212/877-3244

Send a SASE (with 58 cents postage) for free packet of information; also provides in-person and telephone counseling throughout the country.

General Information & Support

(Organizations that offer reading lists or catalogs are followed by asterisks). In addition to the following groups, local Y's, churches and synagogues, and community centers often have divorce seminars, children's programs, social groups for singles, and other networking opportunities.

Banana Splits

A voluntary low-cost, peer-support group for children who need to process family change brought about by the death of a parent, divorce, or remarriage. Contact your local shool district or community facilities to find out if it's offered, or help set up a group in your area. Write for course manual: Interaction Publishers, P. O. Box 997, Lakeside, CA 92040, 800/359-0961.

Children's Rights Council (CRC)*
(formerly National Council for Children's Rights)
220 "Eye" Street NE
Washington, DC 20002-4362
CRC Hotline: 800/787/KIDS or Office: 202/547/6227

Child-advocacy group interested in divorce and custody reform and "assuring a child's access to both parents." Write or call for further information about membership ($35, annually), where local chapters exist (twenty-three states), publications, cassettes, catalog, services, local support groups, or "if you're panicky and just don't know where to go."

The Divorced Parent's X-change
P. O. Box 1127
Athens, OH 45701-1127
Fax: 614/594-4504

Geared toward educating and informing divorced, separated, and stepparents; the $24 annual membership fee includes a subscription to the monthly newsletter, referrals, information about parenting and legal issues, and networking potential—such as "pen friend," whose situation is close to your own. Send S.A.S.E. for sample newsletter.

Joint Custody Association
10606 Wilkins Avenue
Los Angeles, CA 90024
310/475-5352

A nonprofit organization founded by James Cook, the unoffial grandfather of California joint-custody legislation, who continues to advocate for joint custody in other states. For $40 ("which barely covers the cost of copying"), Cook will send you a seven-hundred-page packet containing a wealth of information about joint custody. Good if you're just beginning or in the midst of the legal process or if you want to lobby for better laws in your own state.

Mothers Without Custody
P. O. Box 27418
Houston, TX 77227-7418
800/457-6962

> Has chapters in more than twenty states at present, offering support for mothers living without children; has newsletter; send business-sized SASE (with 58 cents postage) for more information or leave your number and they'll call back collect.

National Organization of Single Mothers
P. O. Box 68
Midland, NC 28107
704/888-KIDS

> Clearinghouse for a network of support groups; $15 annual membership includes support group information and subscription to bimonthly news journal, *SingleMOTHER*. For a free copy of *SingleMOTHER,* send a SASE (with 58 cents postage) or call their twenty-four-hour hotline.

National Organization for Women (NOW)
1000 16th Street NW
Washington, DC
202/331-0066

> Can make referrals for general information about women's issues, including divorce.

Parents Without Partners
8807 Colesville Road
Silver Spring, MD
800/637-7974

> Six hundred chapters in the U.S. and Canada; $14 national membership, includes subscription to *The Single Parent* magazine; local chapters' dues vary.

Rainbows for All God's Children
111 Tower Road
Schaumburg, IL 60173
708/310-1880

> Peer support groups for all-aged children of divorce (four through college) and single parents, led by trained group facilitators; located in forty-eight states. Call for further information and name of registered director in your area.

Stepfamilies Association of America (SAA)*
215 Centennial Mall South (Suite 212)
Lincoln, NE 68508
402/477-STEP

National support group for stepfamilies, publishes *Stepfamilies* quarterly bulletin; annual dues, $35. For "General Information Packet," which lists local chapters, send your request and $3 for postage and handling.

Mediation and Legal Advice

Academy of Family Mediators
1500 S. Highway 100
(Suite 355)
Golden Valley, MN 55416
612/525-8670
> Call or write for information regarding mediators and mediation services.

American Arbitration Association
> Call your local regional office (there are thirty-six throughout the U.S.) for further information regarding their Family Arbitration/Mediation services.

American Bar Association
> Most state bar associations have referral services; attorneys who sign up agree to charge $15 for the first half-hour consultation. Their "Tel-law" hotline also provides basic explanation of divorce and custody laws.

Association of Family and Conciliation Courts
329 West Wilson Street
Madison, WI 53703
608/251-4001
> Makes referrals of mediators, counselors, judges, and evaluators who are members.

NOW Legal Defense Fund
99 Hudson Street
New York, NY 10013
> Will answer written requests only for legal resource kits, "Divorce and Separation," "Child Custody," and "Child Support"; send check or money order, $5 each.

Parenting Education

A variety of parenting classes and support groups are offered throughout the country by local school districts, community centers, health centers, churches and synagogues, adult education programs, counseling centers, civic groups, psychologists, and social workers. Unfortunately, no single resource list exists, so you have to call your local school district or other possible providers to find out if any of the following programs are offered in your area.

NEW BEGINNINGS: Skills for Single and Stepfamily Parents
> Eight-session program; order materials from Research Press, 2612 North Mattis Ave., Champaign, IL 61821.

PET (Parent Effectiveness Training)
> Based on the book by Thomas Gordon; call for class information: 800/628-1197.

STEP (Systematic Training for Effective Parenting)
> Nine-session program for parents of school-agers that uses *The Parent's Handbook*.

Early Childhood STEP
> Seven-session program for parents of children under six that uses *Parenting Young Children*.

STEP/teen
> Ten-session program for parents of preteens and teens that uses *Parenting Teenagers*. Materials for all STEP programs can be ordered from American Guidance Service, Publishers' Building, Circle Pines, MN 55014-1796.

Survival Skills for Healthy Families
> Twelve-hour course, available in different locales. For information about instructors in your area, contact: Family Wellness Associates, P.O. Box 7869, Santa Cruz, CA 95061-7869. 408/426-5588.

Career Information and Networking

In addition to the following organizations, local Y's and women's centers often have workshops and seminars for women returning to the workforce or entering it for the first time.

American Business Women's Association (ABWA)
9100 Ward Parkway
P. O. Box 8728
Kansas City, MO 64114
816/361-6621
> Has 1,900 chapters; membership, which is $45 the first year, $27

thereafter, includes various services, networking, business training, spring conference, and subscription to *Women in Business*

Displaced Homemakers Network
1625 K Street, NW (Suite 300)
Washington, DC 20006
202/467-6346

Represents about 1,200 programs around the country that serve
women in transition; call for information about DHN or for
resources in your area.

National Association for Female Executives (NAFE)
127 West 24 Street (4th floor)
NY, NY 10011
1-800-927-6233

240,000 members, 250 local chapters, providing networking
resources and educational and career seminars; $29 annual fee
includes subscription to the bimonthly *Executive Female.*

Women's Information Network
National Capitol Station
P.O. Box 76081
Washington, DC 20013-6081
202/467-5992

Dedicated to the "advancement and empowerment of all
women"; $20 fee for the first year, $25 for renewal, includes
access to job listings, résumé services, educational and mentor-
ing programs, and monthly newsletter *(The Winning Slate).*

Bibliography

Administrative Office of the Courts, California Statewide Office. "Mediation and Joint Custody in the News." *Family Court Services News,* August, 1991.

Ahrons, Constance R., and Roy H. Rodgers. *Divorced Families: Meeting the Challenges of Divorce and Remarriage.* New York: Norton, 1989.

Ahrons, Constance R. "Parenting in the Binuclear Family: Relationships between Biological and Stepparents." In *Remarriage & Stepparenting: Current Research & Theory,* edited by K. Pasley and M. Ihinger-Tolman. New York: Guilford Press, 1987.

————. "After the Breakup," *The Family Therapy Networker,* November/December 1989.

————. "21st-Century Families: Meeting the Challenges of Change." *Family Therapy News,* October 1992.

————. "Families and Divorce: Choices, Challenges, and Changes." Plenary address at the annual meeting of the American Association for Marriage and Family Therapy, 7 October 1990.

Allen, Jo Ann, and Sylvia Gordon. "Creating a Framework for Change." In *Men in Therapy,* edited by Richard L. Meth and Robert S. Passick. New York: Guilford Press, 1990.

Beavers, W. Robert, and Robert B. Hampson. *Successful Families: Assessment and Intervention.* New York: Norton, 1990.

Berman, Claire. *Adult Children of Divorce Speak Out.* New York: Simon & Schuster, 1991.

Beuhler, Cheryl T., and Belinda Trotter. "Non Residential and Residential Parents' Perceptions of the Former Spouse Relationship and Children's Social Competence Following Marital Separation: Theory and Programmed Intervention." *Family Relations Journal,* 39, 395–404 (1990).

Blau, Melinda. "Divorce Family Style," *New York,* 8 October 1990.
———. "In It Together," *New York,* 4 September 1989.
Brody, Jane E. "Children of Divorce: Steps to Help Can Hurt." *New York Times,* 23 July 1991.
Brotsky, Muriel, Susan Steinman, and Steven Zemmelman. "Joint Custody Through Mediation: A Longitudinal Assessment of the Children." In *Joint Custody & Shared Parenting,* edited by Jay Folberg. New York: Guilford Press, 1991.
Brown, Fredda Herz, ed. *Reweaving the Family Tapestry: A Multigenerational Approach to Families.* New York: Norton, 1991.
Cain, Barbara S. "Older Children and Divorce: The Price They Pay." *New York Times Magazine,* 18 February 1990.
Carter, Betty, and Monica McGoldrick, eds. *The Changing Family Life Cycle: A Framework for Family Therapy.* Boston: Allyn and Bacon, 1989.
Cherlin, Andrew J., and Frank R. Furstenberg, Jr. *The New American Grandparent: A Place in the Family, A Life Apart.* New York: Basic Books: 1986.
Children's Rights Council. *Joint Custody and Related Dissertations: A Guide for Advocates.* Report compiled by staff (1990).
Clark, Gloria. "Parenting Through the Worst of Times." *INSTEP* 3, No. 3 (Fall 1989).
Cohen, Miriam Galper. *The Joint Custody Handbook.* Philadelphia: Running Press, 1991.
———. *Long-Distance Parenting: A Guide for Divorced Parents.* New York: New American Library, 1989.
Coleman, Marilyn, and Lawrence H. Ganong. "The Cultural Stereotyping of Stepfamilies." In *Remarriage & Stepparenting: Current Research & Theory,* edited by K. Pasley and M. Ihinger-Tolman. New York: Guilford Press, 1987.
Coontz, Stephanie. *The Way We Never Were: American Families and the Nostalgia Trip.* New York: Basic Books, 1992.
Cowan, Carolyn Pape, and Philip A. Cowan. *When Partners Become Parents: The Big Life Change for Couples.* New York: Basic Books, 1992.
DeMarea, Barbara. *Reshaping Your Family Structure: Stamp Out Divorce Wars: A Workbook Designed to Help Divorcing Couples.* Shawnee Mission, Kans.: DeMarea Books, 1989.
Dinkmeyer, Don, and Gary D. McKay. *The Parent's Handbook.* Circle Pines, Minn.: American Guidance Service, 1989.
Doub, George, M.Div., M.F.C.C., and Virginia Morgan Scott, M.S.W. "Family Wellness: An Enrichment Model for Teaching Skills That

Build Healthy Families." *Topics in Family Psychology and Counseling,* January 1992, 72–83.

Elder, Sean. "Divorce: The First Five Minutes" *California,* November 1989.

Elkin, Meyer. "Joint Custody: In the Best Interest of the Family." In *Joint Custody & Shared Parenting,* edited by Jay Folberg. New York: Guilford Press, 1991.

Epstein, Cynthia Fuchs. *Deceptive Distinctions: Sex, Gender, and the Social Order.* New Haven: Yale University Press, 1988.

Erikson, Erik H. *Identity: Youth and Crisis.* New York: Norton, 1968.

Everett, Craig A., Ph.D., and Sandra S. Volgy, Ph.D. "Mediating Child Custody Disputes: A Clinical Model." In *Handbook of Divorce Therapy,* edited by Martin Textor, Ph.D. New York: J. Aaronson, 1989.

———. "Treating Divorce in Family Therapy Practice." In *Handbook of Family Therapy,* Rev. ed., edited by A. Gurman and D. Knickern. New York: Bruner/Mazel, 1990.

———. "Family Assessment in Child Custody Disputes." *Journal of Marriage and the Family* 9, no. 4 (October 1983).

———. "Joint Custody Reconsidered: Systemic Criteria for Mediation." *Journal of Divorce* 8 (March/April 1985).

———. "Systemic Assessment Criteria." *Journal of Psychotherapy of the Family* 1, no. 3 (1985).

Family Court Services Department. "An Attorney's Guide to Family Court Services." Pamphlet from The Conciliation Court, Marriage and Family Counseling Services, Superior Court, County of Los Angeles.

———. "Cooperative Parenting Following Dissolution: Your Child Needs Both of You." Pamphlet from The Conciliation Court, Marriage and Family Counseling Services, Superior Court, County of Los Angeles.

Fay, Robert E., M.D. "Joint Custody of Infants and Toddlers." *Medical Aspects of Human Sexuality* 19, no. 8 (August 1985): 134–39.

Feldman, Larry B. "Fathers and Fathering." In *Men in Therapy,* edited by Richard L. Meth and Robert S. Passick. New York: Guilford Press, 1990.

Figley, Charles R. *Helping Traumatized Families.* San Francisco: Jossey-Bass, 1989.

Fisher, Bruce. *Relationships Are My Teachers.* Boulder, Colo.: Family Relations Learning Center, 1991.

Folberg, Jay. "Custody Overview." In *Joint Custody & Shared Parenting,* edited by Jay Folberg. New York: Guilford Press, 1991.

Furstenberg, Frank F., Jr., Kay Sherwood, and Mercer L. Sullivan. *Caring and Paying: What Fathers and Mothers Say About Child Support.* New York: Manpower Demonstration Research Corporation, 1992.

Furstenberg, Frank F., Jr., and Andrew J. Cherlin, Jr. *The New American Grandparent: A Place in the Family, A Life Apart.* New York: Basic Books, 1986.

Ganong, Lawrence H., and Marilyn Coleman. "Preparing for Remarriage: Anticipating the Issues, Seeking Solutions." *Family Relations,* January 1989.

Golden, Daniel. "Second Families, Second Thoughts: Divorced Dads and the Anxiety of Starting Over." *Boston Globe Magazine,* 20 September 1992.

Goodrich, Thelma Jean, Cheryl Rampage, Barbara Ellman, and Kris Halstead. *Feminist Family Therapy.* New York: Norton, 1988.

Gottman, John M., and Lynn Fainsilber Katz. "Effects of Marital Discord on Young Children's Peer Interaction and Health." *Developmental Psychology* 25, no. 3 (1989): 373–81.

Grebe, Sarah Childs, M.A., M.Ed. "Development Stages of Children—Implications for Custody. *Gatherings,* Fall 1988

———. "A Mediator's Perspective on Divorce, Custody, and Mediation." *Jacob's Well* 1, no. 4 (May/June 1983).

Guisinger, Shan, Philip A. Cowan, and David Shuldberg. "Changing Parent and Spouse Relations in the First Years of Remarriage of Divorced Fathers." *Journal of Marriage and the Family* 52, no. 2 (May 1989).

Hare-Mustin, Rachel T., and Jeanne Marecek, eds. *Making a Difference: Psychology and the Construction of Gender.* New Haven: Yale University Press, 1990.

Hayes, Christopher L., Ph.D., Deborah Anderson, and Melinda Blau. *Our Turn: How Women Triumph in the Face of Divorce.* New York: Pocket, 1992.

Hetherington, E. Mavis. "Family Relations Six Years After Divorce." In *Remarriage & Stepparenting: Current Research & Theory,* edited by K. Pasley and M. Ihinger-Tolman. New York: Guilford Press, 1987.

Hetherington, E. Mavis, and Adeline S. Tryon. "His and Her Divorces," *The Family Therapy Networker,* November/December 1989.

Hetherington, E. Mavis, and Frank R. Furstenberg, Jr. "Sounding the Alarm." *Readings: A Journal of Reviews and Commentary in Mental Health* 4, no. 2 (June 1989).

Hetherington, E. Mavis, Martha Cox, Ph.D., Roger Cox, Ph.D. "Long-

Term Effects of Divorce and Remarriage on the Adjustment of Children." *Journal of the American Academy of Child Psychiatry* 24, no. 5 (1985).

Hochschild, Arlie, with Ann Machung. *Second Shift: Working Parents and the Revolution at Home.* New York: Viking, 1989.

Imber-Black, Evan, Ph.D., and Janine Roberts. *Rituals for Our Times: Celebrating, Healing, and Changing Our Lives and Our Relationships.* New York: HarperCollins, 1992.

Irving, Howard H., and Michael Benjamin. "Shared and Sole-Custody Parents: A Comparative Analysis." In *Joint Custody & Shared Parenting,* edited by Jay Folberg. New York: Guilford Press, 1991.

Isaacs, Marla Beth, Braulio Montalvo, and David Abelsohn. *The Difficult Divorce: Therapy for Children and Families.* New York: Basic Books, 1986.

Isaacs, Marla Beth, and Braulio Montalvo. "The Difficult Divorce." *Family Therapy Networker,* November/December 1989.

Jacobson, Doris S. "Family Type, Visiting Patterns, and Children's Behavior in the Stepfamily: A Linked Family System." In *Remarriage & Stepparenting: Current Research & Theory,* edited by K. Pasley and M. Ihinger-Tolman. New York: Guilford Press, 1987.

Jublin, Joann S. "After Couples Divorce, Long-Distance Moves Are Often Wrenching." *Wall Street Journal,* 20 November 1992.

Kalter, Neil. *Growing Up with Divorce: Helping Your Child Avoid Immediate and Later Emotional Problems.* New York: Free Press, 1990.

Kantrowitz, Barbara. "Breaking the Divorce Cycle." *Newsweek,* 13 January 1992.

Kaslow, Florence W., Ph.D., and Lita Linzer Schwartz, Ph.D. *The Dynamics of Divorce: A Life Cycle Perspective.* New York: Bruner-Mazel, 1987.

Kelly, Joan B. "Examining Resistance to Joint Custody." In *Joint Custody & Shared Parenting,* edited by Jay Folberg. New York: Guilford Press, 1991.

————. "Parent Interaction After Divorce: Comparison of Mediated and Adversarial Divorce Process," *Behavioral Sciences and the Law.* 9, 4 (1991).

————. "Longer-Term Adjustment in Children of Divorce: Converging Findings and Implications for Practice." *Journal of Family Psychology* 2, no. 2 (December 1988): 119–40.

————. "Mediated and Adversarial Divorce Resolution Processes: An Analysis of Post Divorce Outcomes." Final Report, prepared for the Fund for Research in Dispute Resolution. December 1990.

Kimball, Gayle, Ph.D. *50-50 Parenting: Sharing Family Rewards and Responsibilities.* Lexington, Mass.: Lexington Books, 1988.

Kitson, Gay C., with William M. Holmes. *Portrait of Divorce: Adjustment to Marital Breakdown.* New York: Guilford Press, 1992.

Lansky, Vicki. *Divorce Book for Parents: Helping Your Children Cope with Divorce and Its Aftermath.* New York: Signet, 1991.

Lawson, Carol. "Requiring Classes in Divorce." *New York Times,* 23 January 1992.

Levy, David L., ed. *The Best Parent Is Both Parents: A Guide to Shared Parenting in the 21st Century.* Norfolk, Va.: Hampton Roads Publishing Company, 1993.

Los Angeles Committee to Implement California's Joint Custody Statute. "Parents Are Forever: Guidelines for Parents." Pamphlet from The Conciliation Court, Marriage and Family Counseling Services, Superior Court, County of Los Angeles.

Luepnitz, Deborah Anna. *The Family Interpreted: Feminist Theory in Clinical Practice.* New York: Basic Books, 1988.

———. "A Comparison of Maternal, Paternal, and Joint Custody: Understanding the Varieties of Post-Divorce Family Life." In *Joint Custody & Shared Parenting,* edited by Jay Folberg. New York: Guilford Press, 1991.

Maccoby, Eleanor E., and Robert Mnookin. *Dividing the Child: Social & Legal Dilemmas of Custody.* Cambridge, Mass.: Harvard University Press, 1992.

Maccoby, Eleanor E., Charlene E. Depner, and Robert Mnookin. "Co-Parenting in the Second Year After Divorce." In *Joint Custody & Shared Parenting,* edited by Jay Folberg. New York: Guilford Press, 1991.

McIsaac, Hugh. "Child Custody, The Lawyer, and Family Court Services." Family Court Services, Los Angeles Superior Court, *Procedure,* 1021–36.

———. "California Joint Custody Retrospective." In *Joint Custody & Shared Parenting,* edited by Jay Folberg. New York: Guilford Press, 1991.

McIsaac, Hugh, and Maxine Baker-Jackson. "Issues of Gender." *Family and Conciliation Courts Review* 30, no. 1 (January 1992): 9–12.

McKinnon, Rosemary, and Judith Wallerstein. "Joint Custody and the Preschool Child." In *Joint Custody & Shared Parenting,* edited by Jay Folberg. New York: Guilford Press, 1991.

Myers, Michael F. *Men and Divorce.* New York: Guilford Press, 1989.

National Council for Childrens Rights Staff. "Evaluating and Presenting

Joint Custody Research: A Guide for Joint Custody Advocates," *Speak Out for Children* (NCCR Newsletter). Fall, 1990.

Nichols, Michael. *Family Therapy: Concepts and Methods.* New York: Gardner Press, 1984.

Nunan, Shary Anne. "Joint Custody Versus Single Custody." Doctoral dissertation. The California School of Professional Psychology, Berkeley (1980). UMI Order No. 81–10142.

Otten, Alan L. "Joint Custody's Success Depends on the Parents." *Wall Street Journal,* 15 November 1991.

Pasley, Kay, and Marilyn Ihinger-Talman. "Divorce and Remarriage in the American Family: A Historical Review." In *Remarriage & Stepparenting: Current Research & Theory,* edited by Kay Pasley and Marilyn Ihinger-Tallman. New York: Guilford Press, 1987.

————. "Family Boundary Ambiguity: Perceptions of Adult Stepfamily Members." In *Remarriage & Stepparenting: Current Research & Theory,* edited by K. Pasley and M. Ihinger-Tolman. New York: Guilford Press, 1987.

Payne, Julien D., and Brenda Edwards. "Cooperative Parenting After Divorce: A Canadian Legal Perspective." In *Joint Custody & Shared Parenting,* edited by Jay Folberg. New York: Guilford Press, 1991.

Pittman, Frank S., III. "Divorce and Remarriage: Fragments and Emulsions." In *Turning Points.* New York: W. W. Norton and Company, 1987.

Ricci, Isolina. *Mom's House, Dad's House: Making Shared Custody Work.* New York: Macmillan, 1980.

Riessman, Catherine Kohler. *Divorce Talk: Women and Men Make Sense of Personal Relationships.* New Brunswick: Rutgers University Press, 1990.

Seligmann, Jean. "It's Not Like Mr. Mom." *Newsweek,* 14 December 1992.

Stacey, Judith. *Brave New Families.* New York: Basic Books, 1990.

Stone, Lawrence. "A Short History of Divorce." *The Family Therapy Networker,* November/December 1989.

Stinnet, Nick, and John deFrain. *Secrets of Strong Families.* Boston: Little Brown, 1985.

Tannen, Deborah. *You Just Don't Understand: Men and Women in Conversation.* New York: Morrow, 1990.

Taffel, Ron, with Melinda Blau. *Parenting By Heart: How to Be in Charge, Stay Connected, and Instill Your Values When it Feels Like You've Got Only 15 Minutes a Day.* Reading, MA: Addison-Wesley, 1991.

Tavris, Carol. *The Mismeasure of Woman: Why Women Are Not the Better*

    Sex, the Inferior Sex, or the Opposite Sex. New York: Simon & Schuster, 1992.

Taylor, Alison. "Shared Parenting: What It Takes to Succeed." In *Joint Custody & Shared Parenting,* edited by Jay Folberg. New York: Guilford Press, 1991.

Teyber, Edward. *Helping Children Cope With Divorce.* New York: Lexington Books, 1992.

Visher, Emily B., and John S. Visher. *How to Win as a Stepfamily.* New York: Dembner Books, 1982.

————. "Parenting Coalitions After Remarriage: Dynamics and Therapeutic Guidelines." *Family Relations,* January 1989.

Walker, Glynnis. *Solomon's Children: Exploding the Myths of Divorce.* New York: Arbor House, 1986.

Wallerstein, Judith S., and Joan Kelly. *Surviving the Breakup: How Parents and Children Cope with Divorce.* New York: Basic Books, 1980.

Wallerstein, Judith S., and Sandra Blakeslee. *Second Chances: Men, Women, and Children a Decade After Divorce, Who Wins, Who Loses and Why.* New York: Ticknor & Fields, 1990.

Wallerstein, Judith S. Letter to the Editor. *Readings: A Journal of Reviews and Commentary in Mental Health,* 4, 3 (September 1989).

Walsh, Froma. "Meeting the Challenges of 'Normal' Families." *Family Therapy News,* April 1992.

Walters, Maryann, Betty Carter, Peggy Papp, and Olga Silverstein. *The Invisible Web: Gender Patterns in Family Relationships.* New York: Guilford Press, 1988.

Ware, Ciji. *Sharing Parenthood After Divorce: An Enlightened Custody Guide for Mothers, Fathers, and Kids.* New York: Viking, 1982.

Webb, Marilyn. "The Joys and Sorrows of Joint Custody." *New York,* 5 November 1984.

Weiner-Davis, Michelle. *Divorce Busting.* New York: Summit, 1992.

Weiss, Robert S. *Marital Separation: Coping with the End of a Marriage and the Transition to Being Single Again.* New York: Basic Books, 1975.

————. Letter to the Editor. *Readings: A Journal of Reviews and Commentary in Mental Health,* 4, 3 (September 1989).

Weitzman, Lenore. *The Divorce Revolution.* New York: Free Press, 1985.

Wolchik, Sharlene A., Sanford L. Braver, and Irwin N. Sandler. "Maternal Versus Joint Custody: Children's Postseparation Experiences and Adjustment," *Journal of Clinical Child Psychology,* 14, 1 (1985), 5–10.

Index

About the Author

Melinda Blau, journalist and co-author of two other books, is currently a contributing editor for *New Woman, American Health,* and *Child* ("The New Family" column). Over the last decade, Blau has established herself as a specialist in health, psychology, and family issues. She has several *New York* magazine cover stories to her credit and has also written for numerous other publications, including the *New York Times, Parents, Self, Family Circle, McCall's* and *Family Life.*

Blau has earned numerous awards for her writing, including the 1994 American Association of Applied and Preventative Psychology Distinguished Media Award for *Families Apart.* She was named a Best in Category (magazine) winner in the 1994 American Legion Auxiliary's Heart of America competition, in which her *Child* column, "The New Family," was named Best Series. Her column also won the 1993 American Association of Marriage and Family Therapy (AAMFT) Excellence in Media Award. In 1991, she won Honorable Mention in the APA's Excellence in the Media Awards for "Adult Children: Tied to the Past" *(American Health).* And in 1989 Blau was awarded Best in Media by the National Council for Children's Rights (NCCR) for "In It Together," an article on family therapy *(New York).*

Please Keep in Touch

How did you like *Families Apart*? Do you agree with its overall message? Did you find the suggestions helpful? I'd be interested in your comments (good or bad), experiences, or words of wisdom. Also, feel free to make a copy of and fill in the *Families Apart* Questionnaire on pages 305–311.

Write to:

Melinda Blau
P. O. Box 222
Northampton, Massachusetts 01061-0222